THE OLMEC WORLD

La Venta during the excavation of 1955, showing center-line trench leading to basalt-columned tomb.

THE OLMEC WORLD

by Ignacio Bernal

translated by Doris Heyden
and Fernando Horcasitas

University of California Press
Berkeley, Los Angeles, London

to the memory of
MIGUEL COVARRUBIAS,
the last of the Olmecs

University of California Press
Berkeley and Los Angeles, California

University of California Press, Ltd.
London, England

Copyright © 1969, by
The Regents of the University of California
First Paperback Printing, 1976

El Mundo Olmeca, first published in Mexico City
by Porrúa Hermanos, 1968

ISBN: 0-520-02891-0

Library of Congress Catalog Card Number: 68-13351
Printed in the United States of America

2 3 4 5 6 7 8 9

CONTENTS

CONTENTS

ILLUSTRATIONS

FIGURES

ILLUSTRATIONS

PLATES

THE OLMEC WORLD

The jaguar is a dweller of the forests, of crags, of water; noble, princely, it is said. It is the lord, the ruler of the animals. It is cautious, wise, proud.

Fray Bernardino de Sahagún,
General History of Things of New Spain.

INTRODUCTION

This is a study of Mesoamerica—Mesoamerica as a whole. Like other great civilizations it possesses its own history, and like other successful epics it is composed of a number of episodes, a climax, and an ending. We know a great deal about the last scene, and vast chapters have been written about the earlier episodes, but a complete study of its beginnings has never appeared. Hence the present history—fraught with perils since it is an attempt to gather all important (but isolated) data into a coherent whole; dangerous since the explorer is not only drawing a map of newly discovered islands but is forced to chart unknown seas. Archaeological exploration in Mesoamerica,[1] together with other anthropological studies, is, at best, an incomplete map of a number of islands, large and small, in an uncharted ocean. At times, in fact, these isles can hardly be called islands; they seem to be no more than poorly illuminated rocks, jutting out from the depths of a murky sea—the past.

Let us trust that there will be a minimum of errors in our factual material. My sources have been basically the reports of field archaeologists.

[1] Mesoamerica is that part of the continent differentiated from other areas by a common cultural basis and a common tradition. Geographically it extends from central Mexico—from the Soto La Marina River in Tamaulipas and the Fuerte River in Sinaloa—to central Honduras and western Costa Rica. Its cultural tradition started around 2000 B.C., but as a civilized area its history only begins with the people studied in this book. See Paul Kirchhoff, Mesoamerica, *Acta Americana*, I: 92–107, 1943; an English translation appeared in *Heritage of Conquest*, edited by Sol Tax, 1952. For a recent, excellent definition, see Willey, 1966: 85–93.

Nevertheless, as Alfred Kroeber said, "No one can really examine *all* the evidence on any major problem; at least not at first hand. This puts us in a nice fix when, as so often happens, we claim to have reached valid conclusions after having examined and weighed 'all the evidence.' I would rather publish as fast as I can feel reasonably sure of my material, even at the risk of errors and uncertainties, so that it will be out where others can shoot at it. Nothing is worth much in any profession until it is published."[2]

Besides examining the evidence as I see it, understand it, or am able to grasp it, I have formed a number of hypotheses which I believe to have a fairly firm basis, though perhaps they cannot be called "valid conclusions," since that is hardly possible.

All this adds much to the peril of misinterpretation, which fortunately or unfortunately is the danger in any study that—like the present one—attempts to transform archaeology into history. In reality such danger is inevitable in any historical study. The facts are usually indisputable and unchangeable. The possible interpretations of the same facts are almost endless. This is especially so for Mesoamerica, where so much is needed to put "all the evidence" together because the immense majority of archaeological sites are yet to be explored and the languages, customs, skeletal remains, and other clues to the ancient past are still to be studied from an historical point of view.

It is evident that I must base my history on archaeological material, since I cannot base it on contemporary documents. But the problem is the same and therefore so are the perils. "The historian selects among the facts of the human past those which seem most important, most significant."[3] This is what I have done with the monuments, the monoliths, and the potsherds. History is not a mirror which reflects only the sum of discoveries, but their place in life, although obviously this is not the totality, especially if we consider the immense difference between the artifacts found and the enormous quantity that must have existed. Therefore I must admit that much necessarily is subjective—not in the objects, naturally, but in my selection or interpretation of them. This is, as I have said, precisely the problem of the historian. So our historical interpretation is transformed from generation to generation and from historian to historian, and the personality and dominant ideas of each era are reflected in this interpretation. It has been said that history is a dialogue between the historian and the past which he studies. We must not exaggerate this point, though, since it would lead us to believe that history is not a cultural science and, like art, does not progress on its own since its knowledge and postulates must start afresh each time. This

[2] Kroeber, quoted by Alex Krieger, 1961: 20–21.
[3] Iglesia, 1944: 157.

is not necessarily so because the knowledge gained by archaeology up to the present time is solid, increases every year, and its concrete facts become permanent. Only their interpretation must be revised continually, not only because of the appearance of new data from new explorations but because of the interpretations made by different historians.

My fundamental interest lies in the history of a civilization, not in its archaeology. I have based this study on archaeology, but not because of a professional quirk. I have done so because, except for the last few centuries of the Pre-Columbian era, that science is almost our only guide to understanding what took place in this part of the Americas where civilization flourished before the arrival of Europeans. I state that it is almost our only guide because I have also made use of the information furnished by other anthropological sciences. In reality, in referring to the earliest periods I have followed to some extent the method used by linguists when they reconstruct a dead language. When I find that some cultural element exists in several cultures which all descend from a common root or which are interrelated in some way but I do not find this trait in the ancestral culture (possibly due to insufficient exploration or because it is a non-material trait), I assume its possible presence in the ancient culture when its validity is indicated. This is dangerous, and therefore I have attempted reconstruction only with the utmost caution.

Many would prefer to limit themselves to the "scientific" facts and not to enter the quicksands of hypotheses. However, I did not wish to create only a skeleton of monuments and archaeological objects but to garb my description, if possible, in the raiment of history. Even so, this history will be almost exclusively cultural, containing few names, dates, or precise events, since by its very nature our material, with the exception of the last epoch, does not permit anything else.

The history of Western civilization is so well known and so rich that the reader is accustomed to a great factual precision, reporting the names of kings or details of battles and even describing the face of the victor. The identity of the author of a work of art is known and we know, too, how many inhabitants there were in a city at a given moment. We are familiar with the lives of great men, with the verses of poets, and with the prose of Western historians; we understand the religion and the economy, the social organization and the politics.

Little of these things will appear in this volume. The few personalities we know are barely glimpsed shadows, dates are uncertain, works of art are anonymous, and statistics misleading. We perceive only the façade of religion and society. Still more confusing, many of the cultures that formed this civilization are undefined, some of them unknown. Only a hypothesis can be made about the development of Mesoamerica. Nevertheless, this book is possible because of certain factors: in the past few decades the archaeologist's spade and other anthropological tools have produced a considerable enrichment of knowledge. At least we now understand the general sequence of the cultures and we can locate, in a more or less orderly manner, the different human groups that lived in this area over the long centuries before the Spanish conquest. So, in spite of many doubts (and this book could be revised almost every year) there is now a general line of development clearly visible to us, and many objects can speak again and tell their history.

I will try to describe the birth, development, and climax, the high and low points, and the final destruction of Mesoamerica. We are dealing, therefore, with the history of a civilization which has disappeared. On the other hand, how and when the first man settled in this area; the millennia during which he was a simple nomadic hunter or food gatherer seeking plants and small animals; the long and fascinating saga of how his main crop, maize, was discovered, and how it was domesticated; how, together with it, man became sedentary and began to construct permanent dwelling places and make clay vessels—all this is a theme which will not be dealt with in this work. These things are only a prologue to the drama of civilization whose first act began around 1100 B.C.

But between the sixteenth century B.C. and end of the twelfth century B.C. cultures were born that were the direct antecedents of civilization. I will deal with this long period very briefly and only when it is indispensable for an understanding of the pages to follow.

Perhaps this is one of the positive points of this book: by ignoring the era before 1500 B.C. (not because it lacks interest or importance but because it is another story) it will be possible for us to concentrate on the central theme, giving cohesion to the history of a civilization and dealing with it as an historical phenomenon, repeated only once in Pre-Columbian America, in the Andean area, and not often in the rest of the world.

Both anthropologists and historians agree in classifying Mesoamerica as a civilization. This is not the place to repeat their reasons. For the moment let us accept it as such. In the same manner we will have to accept the consequences of this point of view in our study and approach. The first consequence is that we will not be able to study Mesoamerica simply with the techniques of the anthropologist who studies primitive peoples but with the perspective and methodology with which scientists analyze the other civilizations of the world. Data which can be obtained from other peoples of the Americas who never achieved the same level will not be especially useful except as antecedents. Nor will it be possible to establish a valid comparison between those American cultures and Mesoamerica. It will be much more useful to compare the achievements and failures of Mesoamerica with the achievements and failures of the other great civilizations, and thus to judge the accomplishments of Mesoamerican civilization. It is not possible for me to undertake this; I leave it for the specialist in the particular field. I simply point out the need for such studies. Together with Egyptologists and Sinologists, we will not be anthropologists dedicated to primitive peoples generally; we will be Mesoamericanists.

Today the Mesoamerican indigenous groups have returned to a rather primitive type of life, though this statement cannot be applied to the Mexican nation as a whole. The modern-day rural natives are not really primitives but are neo-primitives, since they ceased living in a primitive state about 3000 years ago but returned to this condition at the beginning of the seventeenth century. The Spanish conquest destroyed the elite and left only the rural culture; in Mesoamerica, as everywhere else, the latter always lagged behind the urban. Here I only wish to point out the problem in synthetic form; therefore I may be guilty of an over-simplification.

It is evident that the urban civilization of Mesoamerica was essentially aristocratic. I am referring not only to the fact that a great majority of the artistic products and many of the customs of the nobility were obviously the result of a small elite and were created for this group, but to an aspect which is more important to the progress of civilization. The very creation of this urban civilization among the Olmecs and its continuation through other cultures seem to be the work of this elite, created by this minority, known only to it, enjoyed almost exclusively by it. We have an inkling of how a civilized aristocracy can rule over a neolithic people, with little contact between the two ways of life. It is obvious that this does not mean that there never were individuals who passed from one group to the other, but the division seems to be clearly marked on this seldom recognized basis: a civilized elite and the masses of the governed who were unable to acquire the knowledge and techniques of the higher culture.

Perhaps this is why we find a curious contradiction between great progress in some aspects and none in others. I refer principally to technology, which almost stood still in contrast with remarkable developments in art, writing, and the calendric system. It is to be suspected that the aristocracy took more interest in these aspects of culture than in the others.

Thus it is easier to understand the curious phenomenon of the total disappearance of Mesoamerican civilization within a few years after the Spanish conquest. On disappearing, the elite group carried civilization with it to the tomb and to oblivion, leaving only the masses of rural population—of a different cultural level—which at present forms the modern Indian world. That is why there exists such a contrast between the Indians we see today and those revealed by archaeological explorations. At the same time, this shows us that we must be cautious in ethnographic interpretation based on contemporaneous data (i.e., after 1600 A.D.) since these data can only reflect folk life and not that of the aristocracy. This confusion produced fundamental errors like that of Bandelier, who was unable to distinguish between these two types of culture and came to conclusions based on information obtained in the rural world.[4]

From the above it may be inferred that studies of modern Indian groups cannot help us to understand ancient Mesoamerica. Nevertheless they may be applied cautiously to ancient rural culture and some of them to urban life, since some characteristics have survived, no matter how unimportant. I have tried to use these data, limiting myself to the cases in which it seemed prudent. Perhaps I have been too subjective, but we still lack techniques sufficiently advanced to permit with certainty a comparison of modern conditions with historical ones. For the time being, studies of modern Indians are more valuable in understanding the Preclassic than the Classic in Mesoamerica.

Any civilization forms a coherent whole in the sense that the totality of a civilization is coherent. This does not signify identical traits among its branches, but it does mean continuity and similarity in not only material but spiritual traits. Unity within diversity seems to be characteristic of all civilizations. All branches of a civilization possess the same basis and parallel history. Hence I have emphasized the traits which seem to indicate unity, those which are to be found simultaneously in several areas or which over a period of time pass from one to another. I am referring to the elements common to Mesoamerica either as a whole or separately, in their essence or in their form. At times other traits come into being and apparently disappear, only to be reborn much later, basically the same although with a different style. For example, the colossal heads which the Olmecs invented are not found in the Classic period. But the great head found at El Baul, dating from the beginning of the Toltec horizon, and the Aztec head of the Moon, are similar to the Olmec and yet stylistically different. How was this idea of making great bodiless heads preserved? Does it relate to the religious idea of venerating the head of a god or a human as the source of thought and expression, or to the more military one of trophy heads? We do not know. Perhaps it is the same occult process that causes all civilizations to reinvent themes they abandoned centuries earlier and which, garbed differently, suggest the same idea. The importance of renaissance and

---

[4] Adolf Bandelier (1840–1914) published three learned and famous papers on Mexican social and political organization. He followed Morgan's idea that the Aztecs were basically similar to the Iroquois and never reached a higher level. His opinions, untenable today, exerted considerable influence in the first half of this century.

of neo-styles is not to be forgotten. All this means that many relations between different sites and periods which I shall mention later are neither direct nor contemporaneous but are those ideas that are part of Mesoamerican civilization made visible through art forms that have a direct or indirect genetic kinship.

At the beginning of the Christian era Mesoamerican civilization was apparently divided into two branches: the Maya and what we shall call the Mexican (although perhaps it would be more exact to name it Teotihuacan). It may be thought—as Toynbee did—that these were two different but coexistent civilizations. I do not believe this to be so. We are dealing with one civilization, not only because of its common basis but also because both branches have parallel history as well as innumerable points of contact. If we do not take both branches into consideration in our definition of Mesoamerica, we will have lost "the intelligible unity of historical study."[5]

I wonder if this duality is not characteristic of every civilization and if actually it is not indispensable to it, if it is not another form of internal challenge, especially when the danger of an external proletariat is not too vigorous. It would be interesting to see if this duality did not exist also in other civilizations, such as the Greek and Roman, the Latin and German.

However this may be, in Mesoamerica what takes place on a large scale is also characteristic, perhaps, of smaller phenomena. Thus we observe more than one case in which duality exists within one local culture, symbolized mainly by the existence of two principal cities, a kind of double capital. In each city there are at least two different groups of inhabitants; for example, in their time Teotihuacan and Cholula seem to have been parallel capitals, each one inhabited by different linguistic groups.

All I have said will not excuse my errors but will permit the reader to understand the problem that interests me and the reason I have followed the course that I have.

One problem in the presentation of this book has been the difficulty in condensing archaeological or other evidence. Most of this material has been published before. I could have taken it for granted that the reader was acquainted with this literature and therefore dedicated myself only to my hypotheses and conclusions. This not only would have reduced the size of the book but also would have reduced the risk of having to choose, thus eliminating much of that which I consider less important. But even to us Americans, the life of Rome is better known than that of Tenochtitlan or Cuzco; thus it was necessary to present the precise bases for my conclusions.

[5] Toynbee, 1948: I, 17.

A work of this type is usually done in collaboration. Greater depth of detail can thus be achieved, since the specialist in each area naturally knows more about it than do others. But the work runs the risk of losing unity and of becoming a collection of studies which, good as they may be, do not have a vision of the whole. When one person carries out a project of this type—as I have tried to do—he sees more of the whole picture than would various authors in collaboration, although there is the danger of losing sight of details. Another danger is that the opinions of a single author, unopposed, may make the work more subjective.

Still, I venture to risk this first volume—the others are a long way off—with the hope that it may be of some use and may spur others to do something better. The manuscript was sent to three great specialists and friends, Matthew W. Stirling, Robert F. Heizer, and Michael D. Coe, who had the infinite patience to read it through and to suggest a number of changes and additions, most of which I have introduced in the text. My deepest thanks to all three. I also wish to thank Abel Mendoza for his fine drawings and Irmgard Groth-Kimball for her excellent photographs. I was only able to complete the group of illustrations thanks to the aid of Stephen F. de Borhegyi and Lee Parsons of the Milwaukee Public Museum; Edwin Ferdon; the National Institute of Anthropology and History of Mexico; Gareth Lowe and the New World Archaeological Foundation; Alfonso Medellin Zenil and the Museum of the Veracruz University in Jalapa; and Edwin Shook and Ramon Enriquez of this Museum, together with all those whose published plates or drawings I have used to good profit. The photographs used in this book vary in quality. I am very happy about the good ones my generous friends have supplied; the poorer ones could not be remedied since they correspond to moments in the past that cannot be recaptured or to inaccessible objects difficult to rephotograph. Last but not least I want to thank John Graham, who read the manuscript and suggested many important corrections, and Grace Buzaljko, whose editing has been a godsend.

PART ONE
THE METROPOLITAN
OLMECS

At a given moment, within a well-defined area, certain village cultures, in the first chapter of the story we are about to tell, began to acquire special characteristics and took the step which was to lead them to civilization. The time was toward the middle of the second millennium before Christ, and the place was the southern part of the present-day state of Veracruz. Later, around the year 1200 B.C., Olmec civilization was to flourish there, sowing the seeds of what was to become Mesoamerican civilization. I will present only a sketch of its previous history, since it is but a prelude to civilization and therefore falls outside our theme.

Why did this sensational step take place only twice and in two regions before the arrival of Europeans on the American continent—once in Peru with the Chavin culture, the other in southern Veracruz? It is not my purpose to deal with the Peruvian problem; I only mention it in passing. But the Olmec problem is essential to our theme.

The name Olmec has been the subject of much discussion, and with good reason. It means the "Dweller in the Land of Rubber" and therefore can be applied to all those who have lived within the area. It refers to the ancient archaeological civilization and to another important group called Olmec in the historical sources, whose center some 2000 years later was in the Valley of Puebla. In order to avoid confusing the first Olmecs, the later inhabitants of the region, and the Olmecs of the historical sources, it was proposed in 1942 that the more ancient peoples should be designated the "La Venta Culture." Later Wigberto Jiménez Moreno in a lecture at the Second Round Table at the Sociedad Mexicana de Antropología at Tuxtla proposed that they be called Pre-Olmecs, and he has also used the term Tenocelome (The Jaguar-Mouth People). Even though any of these designations would clarify the confusion, custom has not accepted them and these people have continued to be called "Olmec," in quotes. As in this work the culture of La Venta or Tenocelome or "Olmec" will play a much more important role than any of its synonyms, I refer to it simply as Olmec, in spite of just criticism of the custom of applying ethnic names to cultures that are only archaeological. Furthermore, it must not be forgotten, as Drucker pointed out in 1952, that the term "La Venta" refers exclusively to one site and one period of Olmec culture.

In the same manner I will call Olmecoids the inhabitants of several sites (such as Monte Alban and Izapa) which were more or less contemporaneous and show a number of Olmec traits, though their style indicates strong differences because of fusion with local groups which were not Olmec. I will apply the term Colonial Olmec to the sites where, together with the local culture, an Olmec culture appears which did not mix with the former—especially at the beginning—but was only an adjunct. That is to say, some sites were colonized by the Olmecs but were principally inhabited by local peoples (sites in Veracruz, Tlatilco, Chalcatzingo, Guerrero).

In this book the term Post-Olmec will be applied to the inhabitants of the region who were direct or indirect heirs of the Olmecs, in places where Olmec culture was no longer predominant (Cerro de las Mesas, Upper Tres Zapotes). Finally, the term Historical Olmecs will be used for the contemporary peoples described by the Indian picture books and the later Spanish writers. In reality this term does not possess a great ethnic value, since it seems to have been applied to different peoples at various times.

Although we do not believe in simple geographic determinism, it is evident that geography did play an important role in the emergence and development of Olmec civilization. I will attempt to point out, also, other possible reasons for the appearance of this relatively recent type of human society.

Even if some of the basic elements in Mesoamerica came from outside (as is probable in the case of certain domesticated plants and other Pan-American traits), the sum total of the research carried out to the present date has suggested two areas, generally speaking, where Mesoamerican civilization could have been born. One is the Mexican plateau; the other is the tropical coast of the Gulf. Two schools of thought are prevalent, each of them sustaining the primacy of one of these regions. Both agree with Toynbee's[1] brilliant theoretical supposition: the birth of a civilization must be a response to a challenge. The challenge must be powerful enough for a village culture to be transformed into an urban one, and yet not be so strong as to kill it in its cradle or to paralyze it and thus make it an "arrested" civilization. Which of the two Mesoamerican areas presents such a challenge? Which explains the advent of civilization?

Those who maintain that the answer is to be found on the Gulf Coast stress the challenge of the jungle and the tropical environment. Civilization there could have sprung from slash and burn agriculture, with the cult of the rain god as "the vehicle of its evolution."[2] Against this theory it is argued that the jungle is merely a physical challenge which can be overcome by the cooperation of small groups, without requiring the more ample organization and social planning implied by a civilization.

The other school of thought believes that civilization was born in the semi-desert highlands as a direct answer to the challenge of the difficulties of developing agriculture in an area that sees little rain. Followers of this thought feel that it was only through an irrigation system, a "hydraulic hypothesis," that this dryness could be controlled and that an economic basis permitting an important development could be organized. Irrigation carried out not by small groups but by larger communities leads to considerable social and political cohesion and therefore may directly resolve itself in urbanism. In opposition to this theory lies the fact that it is on the coast where the first and most obvious manifestations of civilization appear.

My opinion—which of necessity I try to demonstrate in this book, without forgetting dissenting opinions—may be called intermediate. Actually I believe that the first signs of civilization are to be found on the Gulf Coast, in the area I call "Metropolitan Olmec." These first signs of civilization occur not only there but also at sites such as Monte Alban and those in the highlands of Guatemala, which are not tropical and possess an entirely different habitat, even though they may be contemporaneous with the efflorescence of the Olmecs. But why then should we not suggest that it was at Monte Alban, or better still the Valley of Oaxaca, where this civilization was born? My answer is that there are no antecedents there. On the other hand, these do exist in the Olmec area of the Gulf Coast. Of course proof may be lacking there because of lack of exploration, but at the present time we must rely exclusively upon the facts we know and attempt to reach completely theoretical conclusions based on future discoveries. Therefore I accept provisionally the hypothesis of the birth of civilization on the tropical coast.

At the same time I believe that this civilization—though in many as-

[1] Toynbee, 1948: vols. I and II.
[2] Sanders, 1963: 973–974.

pects it was the mother of those to follow—did not display certain important elements such as the true urbanism which was to appear later in the highlands, at Teotihuacan. Consequently, Teotihuacan, though it inherited many Olmec traits, created or recreated many others upon the basis of a different economy—irrigation. The latter, accompanied by a much more highly developed religion, led to sociopolitical forms which were clearly more complex. Therefore both schools of thought present aspects of the truth. At the present time our knowledge is quite fragmentary; there are many lacunae. Future exploration will fill some of these. But it is also true that innumerable data have been lost in the dust of the past. Thus hypotheses will always continue to be just that—hypotheses. We must not scoff at them, however, since without them it would not be possible to construct an edifice that would stand by itself, at least until new discoveries eliminate these hypotheses.

1

THE OLMEC AREA

The archaeological sites and monuments too large to be moved[1] which have been found up to the present time are limited by the Gulf of Mexico to the north and the first slopes of the mountains to the south; by the Papaloapan River to the west and the basin of the Blasillo–Tonalá to the east.[2] This is the Metropolitan Olmec area. Perhaps at a given moment it extended eastward as far as the basin of the Zanapa River and the Laguna del Carmen or somewhat farther, to the Grijalva River.[3] Never-

---

[1] In the course of this study I will only take into account, in reference to objects which are movable, those which proceed from excavations or which are of an unquestionable provenance, since they are the only ones that can be proved scientifically. Fortunately there exists a sufficient corps of these to permit us to recognize the Metropolitan Olmec style without the necessity of considering pieces of doubtful provenance. Furthermore, this method is our only assurance that we are dealing with the Olmecs without the necessity of including vaguely related objects under the Olmec name. Covarrubias, so well informed in this field, occasionally allowed himself to be carried away by his enthusiasm, presenting as "Olmec" objects that probably should have been classified in another manner. However, the numerous Olmec objects which are to be found in private collections or in museums but which do not proceed from excavations will be cited when necessary, since without them we would have to leave out entire areas, such as Guerrero.

[2] Even though Berlin did not devote himself to this specific region, in his travels through Tabasco he rarely found Olmec remains except a few potsherds of the white-rimmed type (Berlin, 1953, 1955). He points out, furthermore, that "on the alluvial plains of Tabasco, to the east of La Venta, sculpture was an art almost unknown in pre-Hispanic times" (Berlin, 1956: 111). According to this author, it was not until Maya influence reached Tabasco that stone objects were carved (Drucker, 1947: 7).

[3] Drucker and Contreras, 1953: 395.

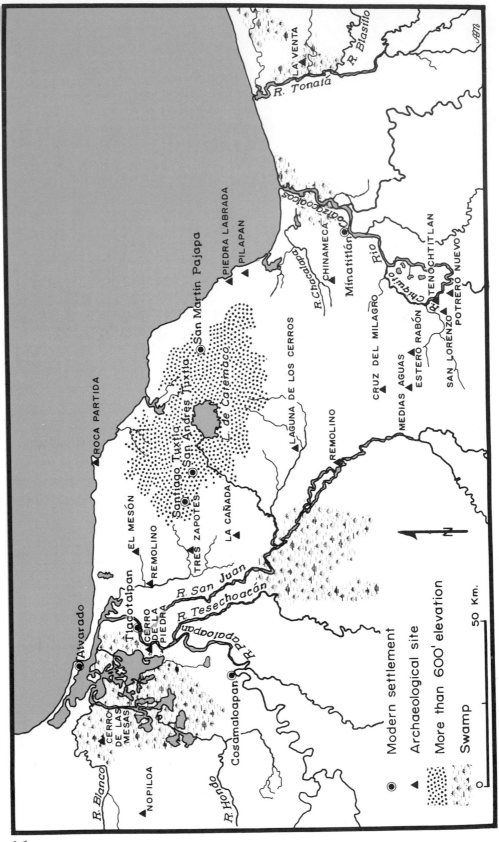

Fig. 1. Map of the metropolitan Olmec area.

theless, the greater part of Olmec history and development took place in the small area we have defined (fig. 1). The Olmec zone covered a total of about 7000 square miles. Coe[4] estimates it to be somewhat smaller, about 6200 square miles.

The area we have defined through cultural remains is clearly circumscribed by geography. To the north the ocean is a fixed boundary. To the south lie the mountains. It is true that culture can overcome geographical barriers, but the Olmecs were definitely a coastal culture, of the hot country, organized within the realm of a particular economic structure. In changing their habitat they would have had to change their ways, which is what they did later and which I will describe in the second part of this book. The Metropolitan zone never actually reached the mountains, and its southernmost sites, bordering on the cultures of Chiapas, seem to be defensive outposts rather than permanent establishments.[5]

To the west the rivers of San Juan and Papaloapan and the lakes connected by the Limón and the Cacique rivers form a region practically covered by water or at least by swamps which not only make any expansion difficult but admit of few possibilities for an indigenous economy.[6] On the east the same is true, since the enormous swamps of Tabasco make agriculture impossible without drainage of the swamps, a feat that was never achieved by the Pre-Hispanic cultures. It is only now that works of this type are being undertaken.

The area thus limited possesses a basic uniformity broken only by the mountainous mass of the Tuxtlas which rises from the plain surrounding Lake Catemaco and divides the basin of the Papaloapan from that of the Coatzacoalcos. Except for this low mountain range, which averages some 1600 feet in height, the rest of the area is not more than 300 feet above sea level. Therefore, it is all hot country, an ample tropical coastal plain formed by alluvial land containing no stone.

Since the land is flat except in the Tuxtlas and in minor spots, flooding is a peril when the great rivers of the area overflow. The principal danger zones are adjacent to the two basins of the Papaloapan and the Coatzacoalcos, which—with their tributaries—cover a vast extension of land. There are smaller basins, such as the Tonalá–Blasillo, which also played an important role in ancient history. The region possesses an enormous volume of water—the largest in Mesoamerica. "Probably nowhere else in Mesoamerica did rivers so dominate culture as here. In the *Relación de Tlacotalpan* (Medina, 1905: 2), a description is given of the destruction of crops by the Alvarado River . . . The water table is

---

[4] M. D. Coe, 1962: 86.
[5] Drucker and Contreras, 1953: 395.
[6] Drucker, 1947: 7.

very high and the two systems end in swamps and lagoons."[7]

Caso[8] has affirmed correctly that this region "could be called the Mesopotamia of the Americas, and we employ this designation deliberately in order to emphasize the fact that Mesoamerica is a civilization and not a village culture, which developed along the rivers which with their flooding renew the agricultural land and serve as easy means of communication with the interior."

From the Tuxtla Mountains descend swift, clear streams which contrast with the great sluggish and muddy rivers that flow through the flat country, their banks marked by mangroves.[9]

To the great quantity of water carried by the rivers from the mountains to the south must be added the heavy rainfall in most of the region. According to data compiled by Sanders,[10] the annual rainfall in Alvarado is 91 inches, in San Andrés Tuxtla 83 inches, and in Catemaco 74 inches. In Coatzacoalcos the rainfall is even heavier: 100 inches,[11] and in Minatitlan 122 inches. There are two rainy seasons: the most important and invariable one is from June to November; the other in January and February. Therefore, generally speaking, the agriculture of the area suffered more from excess than from scarcity of water, a unique phenomenon in Mesoamerica. Further on we will discuss this phenomenon, which had economic, religious, and other implications. The area of the Tuxtlas, with its natural drainage, is the most favorable, and it was actually there, at the foot of these mountains, that one of the early Olmec centers developed: Tres Zapotes.

> . . . it seems probable that this was the prize area of the state, especially the municipios of the Sierra Martin (that is, the Sierra of Tuxtla) where one of the major economic climaxes of the state was apparently located. The rainfall here was heavy, dependability high enough in the winter to permit good tonamil crops, and the area was elevated enough to secure better drainage. The area resembles in many ways the Petén in its geography. The Papaloapan, Coatzacoalcos basins along with Tabasco, I feel were dependent and secondary due to the excessive humidity and inundation conditions. This does not mean that the entire area of the Zona Sur was not successfully occupied, it just means that certain parts of it were more favorable for settlement and were probably cultural centers.[12]

The rest of the area, with the exception of a few humid plains and the swamps, was and is still covered with tall vegetation which in reality is an impenetrable jungle whose only open spaces are those cut by the

[7] Sanders, 1953: 38.
[8] Caso, 1965: 12.
[9] Stirling, 1943: 8.
[10] Sanders, 1953: 41.
[11] Krynine (1935: 354) gives the measurement as 115 inches.
[12] Sanders, 1953: 66.

18

rivers that form the only possible means of communication.[13] This type of vegetation, once it has been dominated by constant slashing, leaves land highly suitable for indigenous agriculture, though the clearing is not lasting. But the effort of opening virgin jungle with stone implements is considerable. This was probably the challenge that nature imposed upon the Olmecs—a challenge which was not too rigorous and which they were able to meet successfully.

Geographical studies indicate that at least from the beginning of the first millennium B.C. until the present time the habitat of the area has not changed; that is to say, it has had the same climate and bodies of water. Possibly—as the La Venta site seems to suggest—there was more water. This means that the swamp surfaces were greater, with fewer islands and other dry land surfaces.[14] The islands are, of course, hills submerged by the alluvial strata.[15]

All of the earth's "original" civilizations, or those of the "first generation," as Toynbee calls them, seem to have emerged along the course of a river or rivers. Herodotus, father of history, the first ethnologist, stated that Egypt is a gift of the Nile. The Sumerians and their successors lived in the valleys that converge where the Tigris and the Euphrates terminate; these valleys as well as those of the Indus and the Hwang Ho were witnesses to the birth of the first civilizations. Invariably we are dealing with very small areas; as Sanders observes,[16] the entire Egyptian old kingdom occupied only some 10,400 square miles. The rivers of the Old World that produced the first civilizations invariably also run through deserts which are virtually without rain, or through semiarid regions where a small amount of rainfall is concentrated within one annual season.

While I cannot elaborate on this theme, it is of the highest importance to note that, although the Olmec region possesses, like others in the Old World, not one but several great rivers, on the other hand its type of rainfall, soil, and vegetation are entirely different While the Old World civilizations had to struggle above all against the dryness of the land and therefore their great problem was irrigation, the Olmecs had to fight against the jungle and against water. Their greatest problem was the vegetation, which when not controlled suffocated all serious attempts at agriculture, as did the floods. Another great problem was the non-arable zones, the swamps which could not be drained. This contrasting situation must have had tremendous consequences; perhaps from it stems

---

[13] At the beginning of the twentieth century, González (1946: 107) found that the only means of transportation in Tabasco were the rivers. Paths were obstructed by tropical vegetation and frequently were flooded.

[14] Drucker, 1952: 4.

[15] Krynine, 1935: 354.

[16] Sanders, 1962: 36.

the lesser development of true urbanism among the Olmecs, in contrast with the more advanced urbanism in the Old World and in the highlands of Mexico, where scarcer water was the problem.

Floods within the Olmec area suggest great advantages for agriculture. For a moment they lead us to consider the classical example of Egypt. But in reality the situation is very different. The Nile runs through a valley which is limited by mountains to the east and to the west; every year, regularly, it overflows and then withdraws again to its course, leaving fertile silt. The Olmec rivers run through flat jungle land, and their flooding, except in small areas, is more harmful than profitable in a society which cannot control these avalanches of water. Thus not only the swamps but the savannas[17] are useless to a rather primitive agriculture.

The jungle was undoubtedly teeming with wild animals such as jaguars, deer, tapirs, boars, and monkeys,[18] as well as opposums, iguanas, armadillos, and wild turkeys, pheasants, partridges, and other fowl.[19] We know very little about the domestic animals of the Olmecs. The dog is known to be ancient in Mesoamerica, and the same may be said of the turkey.[20] The royal bee was probably kept for its honey.[21] Even today the Popoluca Indians who live in the ancient Olmec area practice a number of rites connected with the keeping of this insect, thus indicating its ancient origin.[22]

In the rivers, lagoons, and sea of the Olmec area there is an abundance of fish, shellfish, and turtles, together with a vast variety of aquatic fowl. Such profusion must have constituted one of the bases of nourishment, a basis which was lacking—or very scarce—in other areas. This difference is important, since the vitamins of these aquatic animals counteract the characteristic protein deficiency in a culture where the number of domestic or wild animals is not large enough to become a stable basis of diet. That the Olmecs were dependent on aquatic fauna is suggested by the importance given to manta rays in their carvings at La Venta,[23] the jade canoe from Cerro de las Mesas,[24] and the jade shells, ducks, and marine motifs,[25] as well as the stones which were probably

[17] Drucker and Contreras, 1953: 392–393.

[18] Stirling, 1943: 8.

[19] Piña Chán, 1964: 34.

[20] There is no direct proof of the use of the turkey among the Olmecs, since the bones excavated at the sites have not been preserved because of the humidity. The turkey was to appear later in representations made of clay which, though not Olmec, belong to the same area (Drucker, 1943: 113).

[21] Stirling, 1939: 203.

[22] Foster, 1942: 3.

[23] Drucker, 1961: 54.

[24] Drucker, 1955: pl. 38.

[25] Drucker, 1952: 171 and 196, or Monument 20 of La Venta (Drucker, Heizer, and Squier, 1959: 200).

weights for nets.[26] Even today, in towns like Tlacotalpan, fishing constitutes the main industry.[27]

Flora characteristic of tropical Mesoamerica had as great an influence on the economy as it had in other areas of similar climate. Naturally an abundant quantity of fruit such as guava or sapote was available,[28] as well as the rubber which gave its name to the region.

AGRICULTURE

But the basis of diet was agriculture, with the same plants that still characterize southern Mexico. The famous trilogy of corn, beans, and squash is still found in sites like Tres Zapotes.[29] We do not have definite data regarding cotton, cacao, tobacco, and other plants, but if other earlier groups planted these they must have been known to the Olmecs. Food not produced on Olmec soil could have been acquired through commerce.

The type of agriculture practiced was a result of the difficulties of a region densely covered by jungle. Thus in the Olmec zone—now and probably before—the prevalent type of agriculture is slash and burn, found in similar areas of the world.[30] It would be profitless to discuss the difficult methods adapted to different sites; I will discuss agriculture but briefly and according to its modern practice in the Olmec area.

Two crops a year may be harvested: the *milpa del año* or main crop, and the *tonamil* or winter crop. The main crop requires clearing the field, which is more difficult, of course, if the jungle is "virgin," that is, if it has not been used for a long time. Clearing is done in the month of March. In May, the driest month, all that has been cut is burned, leaving the field clean and covered with ashes. Some observers think that burning is helpful, as it kills insects harmful to the crops and deposits ashes which serve as fertilizer. Others think that burning is harmful because it eliminates many of the productive elements of the soil. June, at the beginning of the rainy season, is the best time for sowing. If only the main crop is to be sown that year, the field is weeded twice during the growing period to allow the corn to develop unhampered. If another crop is to be obtained in the winter, the field is cleaned a third time. Harvesting is

[26] Drucker, 1952: 142.

[27] Stirling, 1939: 192; Weiant, 1943: pl. 48; Drucker, 1943: 77, and so on. Some of the animals represented in the ceramics are not edible, e.g., the owl (Stirling, 1939: 191).

[28] Stirling, 1939: 197.

[29] *Ibid.*: 198.

[30] "Slash and burn" or "shifting cultivation" is the term generally used by English-speaking authors. See Conklin (1963) for an exhaustive thematic essay for the entire world.

carried out principally between mid-November and mid-December.[31]

The winter's sowing (*tonamil*) is begun in January in order to reap between May and June. Thus the soil will be prepared in time for the main crop of the year. The latter yields about a third more produce per acre and per seed than that of the tonamil.

The fact that two annual crops are possible suggests splendid abundance, but one must bear in mind that the soil becomes exhausted very rapidly, after only a few years' planting; it must be allowed to rest over a period of several years and thus return to a jungle state. Then the cycle begins again. The main fault of this system is that for every cultivated acre at least five lie fallow, meaning that in any one year it is possible to obtain economically worthwhile produce from less than twenty percent of the sum total of the land. The results of this weigh heavily upon human society. Large human groupings cannot exist, since available arable land becomes more and more distant. This means that in the long run the whole community must move.[32] As this is not possible in established societies, certain clearly defined demographic limits are imposed upon the population, or it continues to subdivide; this problem can be solved only through other means of cultivation, other natural resources, or commerce. Because of this I believe that in the Olmec era the rivers played a basic role, above all in a society without wheels for practical uses and without beasts of burden. The rivers were the great natural roads which permitted easy communication.

But another possibility may have been important: agriculture by periodic flooding. Actually many of the Olmec centers are true islands surrounded by water whose level rises and falls annually. This suggests agriculture by natural irrigation and with fertilizer produced by the silt brought by the floods, even though the latter—as we have seen—are not always favorable. Medellín has mentioned the possible existence of an agriculture by periodic flooding at sites such as Cerro de Piedra.[33] The same seems to occur in other places which are certainly Olmec; if this were the case crops larger than those suspected must have been

[31] Drucker, and Heizer, 1960: 39.

[32] It is usually thought that the farmer has always had several months a year during which he rests and that these months permit him to devote himself to other efforts which, in time, lead him to civilization. Possibly the matter is not so simple. Foster (1945: 179–180) points out that the crops occupy practically all of a man's time. "All is work," say the Popolucas of the Olmec region.

[33] Medellín, 1960: 78. Against this opinion Dr. Michael Coe writes in a letter: "Having seen many aerial photos of the Olmec area, I doubt that they could have done much with the alluvium, for almost all of it is covered with edaphic [indigenous] savannah; most farming today is of the swidden [slash and burn] type, on well-drained Miocene ridges—and this is where all the important Olmec sites are, too." This is the basic situation, and the possibility of another type of agriculture is barely suggested.

reaped. The areas which flood and then dry up again each year are now pasture land, useless for cultivation.[34]

DEMOGRAPHY AND LANGUAGE

It is impossible to determine with any precision the number of inhabitants of the Olmec area, either at its peak or at any other moment of its development or decadence. Nevertheless, it is necessary to formulate at least a hypothesis, since our concept of the Olmec culture will be affected by the number of persons who formed part of it. Obviously, the historical problems and possibilities of cultural development in a society are entirely different according to the number of inhabitants in the area.

One author, W. T. Sanders, has suggested that in 1519 the population density was 52 inhabitants per square mile, but this number is the average for the entire southern part of the state of Veracruz. This area is larger than the part of that state occupied by the Olmecs and, now as then, is sparsely inhabited, especially in the districts of Minatitlan and Cosamaloapa. Therefore, by including it, Sanders[35] reduces the average number of inhabitants per square mile for the entire area. Another study that comprehends a much smaller area, exclusively the municipality of Moloacan, is important, since it attempts to reconstruct a demographic density for the area that fed La Venta. The author of this study reaches the conclusion that the density there was about 48 inhabitants per square mile.[36] In the sixteenth century Cangas y Quiñones[37] calculated 50,000 "heads" for Coatzalcoalcos province, that is, 200,000 inhabitants in an area of about 4600 square miles, according to Sanders,[38] or an average of 43 persons per square mile. But perhaps Cangas y Quiñones included the uninhabited region to the south, as it has been in modern calculations; on the other hand, his estimate did not include that part of the state of Tabasco inhabited by the Olmecs.

Actually we do not have trustworthy data to base an estimate on, but several factors suggest that the demographic pressure on the area was quite powerful. Our main argument is the extensive colonization by the Olmecs in other regions outside their area. This colonization would not be easily explained had there not been overpopulation in relation to the food supply. If we judge by cultural remains, toward the beginning of the first millennium B.C. no other area of Mesoamerica was

[34] Drucker and Contreras, 1953: 192.
[35] Sanders, 1953: 52.
[36] Drucker, 1961: 69.
[37] Cangas y Quiñones, 1928: 176.
[38] Sanders, 1953: 51.

so densely populated. Thus it is that the centrifugal movement of the Olmecs becomes comprehensible.

Contrary to what is usually believed and contrary to the present-day situation, the hot country was not unfavorable to human development, as in Pre-Hispanic times the tropics were more healthful than today for two reasons:

(1) The absence of domestic animals, though a negative factor on one hand, eliminated the possibility of serious water contamination, which was a problem from the sixteenth century on. Thus in Olmec times the frequency of dramatic intestinal ailments was much lower than in later times.

(2) It is probable that malaria did not exist in Pre-Hispanic times, at least in its more serious forms. One must not forget that until very recently this disease was a direct cause of a very large number of deaths.[39]

Be it as it may, we can consider provisionally that the Olmec area contained some 350,000 inhabitants. For the moment I can see no way of confirming or denying this figure, even though the abundance of inhabited centers, edifices, and objects suggests a somewhat larger population.

Up to the present time it has been impossible to discover with any degree of certainty the language spoken by the Olmecs. Nevertheless, glottochronology and linguistics have contributed interesting suggestions. Morris Swadesh[40] finds that the linguistic separation between Huastec and Maya, which are related languages, occurred some 3200 years ago, that is, around 1200 B.C. Therefore it is valid to believe, as numerous authors have done, that before that date a single language, proto-Maya–Huastec, from which later Maya and Huastec were to spring, was spoken along all the Gulf Coast, at least from the Panuco River to Yucatan.[41] The present-day separation of these two tongues suggests that speakers of another language penetrated like a wedge an area which had previously been unified, between the southern boundary of Huastec and the northern boundary of Maya, in the region where today neither of the languages is spoken. The Olmec area is to be found precisely in this place, even though it does not occupy the entire extension because its northern boundary is the Papaloapan. On the other hand, to the south it is limited by lands where Maya is spoken. If we relate this fact to the possibility that the period we have called Olmec I began, according to archeological research, around 1500 B.C. there is a certain coincidence in the dating. This situation brings together beautifully the conclusions of two sciences and permits

[39] Chevalier and Huguet, 1958.
[40] Swadesh, 1953: 225.
[41] Krickeberg, 1933: 145–158.

us to postulate that those who broke the unity of proto-Maya–Huastec in the area were the carriers of the Olmec culture.[42] These may have been Jiménez Moreno's Pre-Olmecs; he suggests that in language they were related to the Maya, "even though there may have coexisted groups of other linguistic affiliations, such as the Zapotecs."[43]

THE OLMEC AS A PHYSICAL TYPE

Because of the humid climate and the acidity of the soil where Olmec burials have been found, not one skeleton has been preserved to reveal the physical type of these people.[44] We can reconstruct a type only on the basis of representations in clay, stone, or jade which the Olmecs themselves left, or (if the present-day inhabitants of the area are their direct physical descendents) by observing some of the ancient racial characteristics they might have preserved.

Covarrubias, with an artist's eye, deals with the latter possibility: ". . . there is an emphasis on a definite physical type, radically opposed to the bony and aquiline type we are accustomed to regard as Indian. However, the type occurs frequently today among the older Indian groups of southern Mexico . . . and the distribution of the living type coincides with the general distribution of the art style of La Venta."[45]

Drucker affirms that "it is not necessary to postulate some exotic racial group as the models (and presumably also the makers) of Olmec sculptures, nor is it necessary to venture that the ancient carvers invented an artistic ideal unlike themselves in its distinctive features. It seems very probable that the type represented in the carvings is an idealization of a southern Mexican physical type."[46]

Both authors refer, of course, to the type represented in most of the stone or clay figurines (which give us a clue to cultural characteristics), showing persons of low stature (brachytype) but with well-formed

[42] According to Jiménez Moreno (1942: 134, chart I) we are dealing with the Totonac Zoques, though he feels that the separation between the Huastec and the Maya occurred during the Classic period (Teotihuacan II–III), corresponding to his Proto-Olmec (*ibid*.: 145); he limits the term "Olmec" to those of the historical period. Therefore his Proto-Olmecs came too late to be carriers of the La Venta culture, since they lived after it had disappeared.

[43] *Ibid*.: 194. I do not believe that the Zapotec language was already formed, but it is possible that we are dealing with a pre-Zapotec.

[44] The burial in Trench 1 of Tres Zapotes could only be photographed before the bones disintegrated (Drucker, 1943: 16). Apparently it was a secondary interment; that is, the bones had been reburied once the flesh had disappeared. The decorated teeth found in the burial in Trench 24 probably belong to the Post-Olmec period. They correspond to Type A-2 (Romero, 1958: 51). See fig. 9.

[45] Covarrubias, 1944: 32.

[46] Drucker, 1952: 192.

bodies tending toward obesity, slanted eyes that are puffy and have the epicanthus fold, a short wide nose, mouth with thick lips and corners turned downward, a prominent jaw, and a short, heavy neck. This is essentially the type frequently associated with the tiger in Olmec representations and defined by Caso[47] and Piña Chán.[48] As Heizer has pointed out, the colossal heads perhaps best define the physical type that does not have cranial deformation (see pl. 3).

I believe that this is the "Olmec type" as well as we can reconstruct it. Nevertheless there are still other problems. Let us observe the epicanthus a moment—the most typical trait of Mongoloid faces; it clearly indicates its Asiatic provenance and does not offer any special problem. But at the same time let us remember that it has often been said that the colossal heads represent a Negroid type; this would indicate the presence of true Negroes who reached the Gulf Coast.[49] This migration is improbable though not impossible,[50] and even more improbable is the combination of the epicanthus with Negroid faces. The combination is frequently found in Olmec figures which are not men but children, and which form one of the basic themes of Olmec art. Children everywhere tend to have more rounded and chubby-cheeked faces, shorter and wider noses, and thicker lips than the adults they will be in time. The same appearance results when the human face is combined with the short, wide nose of the jaguar. Both the children and the men-jaguars represent an aesthetic ideal and not a definite race.

Another type, "fine-nosed and thin-lipped," corresponding to taller individuals, is also represented. But, as Caso has pointed out, the type has characteristics in common with the other "which permit the objects which represent these people to be placed within the same culture."[51] It seems to me that this great archaeologist is completely right, even though it is possible that the second or elongated type appeared a little later in Olmec art[52] and that it is only an idealization of the original brachy-type, which is far more frequent.

Thus can be explained Covarrubias' apparent contradiction when he affirms that there are two distinct types in the clay figurines: the jaguar-child "Mongoloid" and the bearded type with aquiline nose, exemplified by the main personage in the magnificent Stela 3 of La Venta (pl. 4). Covarrubias feels that this was a visitor.[53]

[47] Caso, 1942: 44.
[48] Piña Chán, 1964: 37.
[49] Medellín, 1960: 87 ff.
[50] Aguirre Beltrán, 1955: 13–14
[51] Caso, 1942: 44.
[52] Piña Chán, 1964: 37.
[53] Covarrubias, 1944: 31.

Juan Comas[54] is of the opinion that "the anthropomorphic representations in Olmec art may not be considered an expression of physical Olmec type, that is, of men who pertained to the Olmec culture and who spoke or speak languages of the Olmec stock. In any case it may be admitted that some of the physical traits represented do have their model in real characteristics, but not as an expression of the general type. Rather, they are exceptional cases which, precisely because of this, attracted the artist's attention." This contradictory opinion must be taken into consideration, since it is based on the study of bone remains and not on artistic impressions like that of Covarrubias. Comas, however, does not refer to the problem I study here since the scarce material he was able to utilize came from Cerro de las Mesas, a site I do not include in the Olmec area. In my opinion its inhabitants are not Olmecs, as we have defined them here, nor do they belong to the same period, but to a later one.[55]

Two other authors affirm that there is "a series of traits which, anthropologically, could be used to characterize individuals of very different ethnic origins."[56] The work of these authors deals with two principal aspects: artificial deformation of the head (which I will speak of as a cultural trait) and representations of pathological individuals. Naturally, the latter occur everywhere; what is unusual is that the Olmecs took such marked interest in them, as in dwarfs and other monsters. But this is rather within the field of social psychology and is of no help in our quest for the "normal" physical type that typified the bearers of that culture. Nor am I referring to the idealization of a physical type which occurs within all the great schools of art and produces an aesthetic ideal that no longer represents reality with exactness, though it may be based upon it. Not all the Greeks were like Apollo, nor all the Egyptians like Rameses. Later we will deal with these cultural aspects.

Summing up, it is plausible that these brachy-types, whose descendants are alive today, really represent the bearers of the Olmec culture, even though another, somewhat different group or groups—who at times appear in their art—coexisted with them. So it is that any apparent resemblance to other races is only accidental, the result of an aesthetic ideal.

It is interesting to note that both physical anthropologists and linguists suggest, in that area and period, the probable coexistence of two or more different groups. This situation may be due to geography, since the Isthmus of Tehuantepec was a bottleneck in which the groups that

[54] Comas, 1942: 69–70, and 1945.
[55] See Drucker, 1943: 141.
[56] Dávalos and Ortiz de Zárate, 1953: 95.

passed through or established themselves were forced to mix.

Nevertheless, it is important not only that, again, two branches of anthropology reach similar conclusions but that from this time on another tendency, apparently characteristic of Mesoamerica, appears. Even though this comment is premature for this book, I wish to emphasize the circumstance that the bearers of all or almost all the high cultures were made up of two or more groups which fertilized one another during their coexistence. At least Tenochtitlan, Tula, and Teotihuacan, the great highland capitals, were not inhabited by a single group, nor were the other cities, in all probability. I believe that the mixture of two traditions is one of the most potent stimuli in the development of civilization and one of its most marked characteristics: there is a sort of internationalism within Mesoamerica. With few exceptions, however, the different traditions belonged to a single family, and only time gave them different languages and styles. Originally they were similar, since all were Mesoamerican. The case is similar to western Christendom, but the development of this theme would necessitate an entire volume—a volume which unfortunately has not been written.

HISTORY OF RESEARCH IN THE REGION

To make clearer the study of Olmec culture it will be convenient to dedicate a few paragraphs to the history of its discovery; but before we approach the concrete theme I wish to point out that it follows a pattern more or less similar to that which occurred in the study of many other lost civilizations: In almost all cases certain museums or collections preserved objects from those civilizations but without any established provenance or chronology. The artifacts were grouped exclusively by vague geographic area. Curators were unable to realize that the objects represented a style that had not been classified up to that time. On the other hand, the inhabitants of these localities were usually familiar with monoliths or ruins; without paying much attention to these remains, they attribute them to the "ancient ones."

In the second stage of discovery some of the objects began to be published, usually attributed wrongly to cultures which were similar but were not the exact ones, since the latter were still unknown to scholars. It was not until the corpus of these isolated and individually insignificant publications began to grow that some archaeologist or student of art noticed that the objects were not only related among themselves but were different from those of other known cultures.

Later comes the stage at which it is suggested that in a given area there existed a culture heretofore unknown, from which the objects come. Then more or less scientific-minded travelers begin to visit the region and to publish descriptions of its buildings, monoliths, and other objects. As the next step, archaeologists decide to carry out serious excavations in the places described by travelers or by the local people. As a consequence of the excavation there appears a great wealth of information. This at last defines the new culture, even though the definition is still incomplete and its chronological position not yet understood. When I say incomplete I do not mean that its archaeological context will some day be fully known. This is impossible. I refer to the many possibilities—some in the distant future—which are open to the archaeologist. It is difficult to make full use of everything that is found in the pioneer investigation.

Then come meetings, congresses, and interpretative publications based on field data. After many discussions and contradictory opinions, a general consensus of opinions is formed. It is then that the culture becomes delimited in time and its associations with other cultures, together with its internal significance, are found. It is only then that this body of material and archaeological data becomes history—even though strictly speaking it is not documentary—which can be incorporated into the course of general history.

Olmec civilization has passed through these stages. It was totally unknown until the second half of the nineteenth century; it had not even been given a name, since the term "Olmec" was only applied to the historical Olmecs of the written sources. Some Olmec objects had reached museums. Their existence had been known at least since the eighteenth century. Such is the case of the famous small mask which belonged to the collection of the sovereigns of Bavaria and which is today—disguised as a Hindu figure—exhibited in the magnificent Residenz Museum in Munich.[57] Another example is that of a jade mask—natural size—which was taken to Europe during the sixteenth century.[58] A careful examination of written sources would probably lead us, through museum catalogs and similar publications, to data on other objects belonging to this culture. But it was in 1868 that an Olmec monolith was published for the first time by José Maria Melgar y Serrano in the *Semanario Ilustrado*. The drawing appeared again in 1869[59] and in 1871, each time published by Melgar y Serrano. The object is the colossal head at Tres Zapotes which had been discovered in 1862 (pl. 5).

Ruins in the area were referred to by other writers in 1867 and 1882. In 1883 Alfredo Chavero again published the colossal head, together

---

[57] Disselhoff, 1952.

[58] The mask was in a Hungarian collection and at the present time belongs to the museum at Dumbarton Oaks (*Handbook*, 1963: no. 31). I am grateful to Dr. Michael Coe for this information.

[59] Melgar y Serrano, 1869: 293.

with an ax-shaped stone, or celt, representing a person with jaguar features; this celt is found today in the Museum of the American Indian in New York.[60] Chavero's work is important as it possessed—and curiously continues to possess—a large group of admirers. Another celt was described in the year 1889.[61] At the beginning of our own century studies of some important Olmec pieces appeared, though they were not as yet known as Olmec. Marshall H. Saville showed his interest in objects from this culture in 1900.[62] Holmes in 1907 and 1916 studied the famous Tuxtla statuette; Batres[63] took the Stela of Alvarado to the National Museum of Mexico in 1904; other objects were studied by Seler-Sachs in 1922, who made use of her notes from the trip to the region she made with her husband in 1905; and still other objects were studied by Spinden in 1927, and by Joyce and Knox in 1931.

During this "travelers' stage" (aside from Seler, who says little about the matter[64]), *Tribes and Temples*, the book by Blom and La Farge published in 1926, is fundamental. These authors refer to hitherto unknown monuments in that area. They visited La Venta and inspected the monolith of San Martín Pajapan, as well as two other figures that had been taken to Villahermosa some years earlier.[65] In his review of this book Beyer compares the monolith of San Martín Pajapan with a celt in his collection that he calls "an Olmec idol."[66] (See pl. 25.)

Only two years later, however, in 1929, Saville[67] took a significant step forward when he christened the culture "Olmec" and stated: "I believe that, notwithstanding our lack of knowledge concerning the provenience of most of these objects, especially the votive axes, this peculiar type of mask may be safely assigned to the ancient Olmecan culture, which apparently had its center in the San Andrés Tuxtla area around Lake Catemaco, and extended down to the coast of the Gulf of Mexico in the southern part of the State of Vera Cruz."

George C. Vaillant in 1932 was the first person to designate as Olmec not isolated traits but a complex of them, thus defining a style that can be differentiated from others. With great insight he found the

---

[60] Hartt, 1867; Kerber, 1882; *México a través de los siglos*, I: 63–64. In the Madrid Exposition of 1892 commemorating the fourth centennial of the discovery of America, Paso y Troncoso exhibited a photograph of the colossal head at Tres Zapotes together with another of a "monumental carved stone . . . which is preserved there." The latter was probably one of the stelae from the same site (*ibid.*: I, 22–23).

[61] Kunz, 1889 and 1890.

[62] See also Saville, 1902.

[63] Batres, 1908: 4.

[64] Seler, 1907.

[65] Weyerstall's trip (1932) is also of importance.

[66] Beyer, 1927: 306.

[67] Saville, 1929: 285.

jaguar to be the essential element. But there is utter confusion in his identification between the historical Olmecs and the archaeological peoples, since he presents gold pieces as Olmec which we know are of a later period.[68] All that I have described is only an antecedent to scientific excavation. Real exploration in the Olmec zone began with Matthew Stirling toward the end of 1938,[69] when, after a few preliminary visits, he started excavating at Tres Zapotes and in the following years at La Venta, Cerro de las Mesas, several sites along the Chiquito River, and in general in the Olmec zone proper or in sites colonized by the Olmecs. This fundamental research showed that in the Olmec area were not only interesting objects but an entire civilization which had not been defined up to then. In 1939 even Stirling himself was still toying with the idea that he was dealing with an obscure branch of the Maya civilization.[70] The explorations undertaken by Stirling of the Smithsonian Institution with the aid, among others, of Philip Drucker and C. W. Weiant, form the solid foundations of Olmec archaeology. As soon as the archaeological evidence began to turn up, two armies faced each other: one was led by Alfonso Caso and Miguel Covarrubias, who together had studied Olmec art and who claimed that they were dealing with a very ancient civilization, in reality the most ancient in Mexico. The other camp, led by Sylvanus Morley and J. Eric Thompson, believed that the Olmecs were only a recent branch of the Maya and that it was not possible to accept the reading of Stela C from Tres Zapotes, dated either 291 B.C. or 31 B.C. according to the different correlations.

Time was to prove the Mexican school's point of view correct. In 1942 the Sociedad Mexicana de Antropología held its second Round Table at Tuxtla Gutierrez, with the specific aim of discussing the problem and defining Olmec culture and its chronological position. Its aims were fulfilled with amazing success, though this does not imply that all

[68] Some years afterward Vaillant wrote that "the simplicity of these Olmec forms" insinuates strongly that we should seek in the area of southern Veracruz rather than in the classical Maya region the origin of the temple, of polytheistic ritual, of writing, and of the calendar, developments that separate the high cultures of Middle America from those of the continents to the north and to the south (1939: 134). Even though the XXVII Congress of Americanists met in that year, the second volume of its Acts, where Vaillant's work appears, was not published until much later (1947). It is evident that Vaillant had the opportunity to revise his work, since he cites a publication which appeared in 1940. On the other hand he mentions the writings of Stirling, Drucker, and Weiant, all of which appeared in 1943, as unpublished. Vaillant, therefore, probably delivered his original manuscript to the press around 1941 and not afterwards, since he does not mention the 1942 Tuxtla Round Table. Considering the date, the paragraph quoted here is remarkable. Vaillant points out several elements associated with the tiger mask, the platyrrhine nose, and the beard (*ibid.*: 131–133).

[69] See Stirling, 1940: 1.

[70] Stirling, 1939: 183.

scientists were convinced at the time nor that important discoveries have not been made since then.

Since World War II and up to the present time, important research has been carried out and is still being done in the field by such men as Drucker, Wedel, Heizer, Squier, Contreras, Medellín, Piña Chán, and Coe. Investigation has by no means ceased and our knowledge has progressed greatly, especially in La Venta and San Lorenzo. Research has permitted us to enter the last stage in the discovery of lost civilization, that of interpretation based on the wealth of information which has been acquired. Therefore, our present field data may be converted into history. Several noteworthy works belonging to this stage are not cited here, since they will be mentioned further on; all are included in the bibliography.

It is now unquestionable that in this area there existed a style[71] which, though it belongs to the Mesoamerican world, has characteristics of its own. Nor is the antiquity of this culture to be doubted. It has been possible, also, to attempt interpretations in historical terms, no matter how many questions and problems exist. As might be expected, the most ancient civilization has been the most recently discovered.

[71] On the other hand, there are other points of view regarding the place of origin. These will be discussed later.

2

THE OLMEC SITES AND THEIR ARCHITECTURE

Up to this point I have been dealing with the Olmec world in very general terms because I believe that it is the only way of understanding it. Naturally, an archaeological expedition can hardly excavate an entire area because archaeologists desirous of carrying out a thorough exploration would have to spend an impossible number of years in the field. We have knowledge only of specific sites. Thus, field archaeologists refer to one locality or to those they have studied. They rarely see the area as a whole in its cultural, geographical sense. On the other hand, wide-ranging studies such as those by Caso and Piña Chán included not only the Olmecs but the peoples whom I call "Colonial Olmecs" and even the "Olmecoids," since it was unnecessary for these scholars to distinguish clearly between one and another. This point of view is appropriate as an attempt to see "the intelligible unity of historical study" so brilliantly expounded by Toynbee.

Nevertheless, it has seemed convenient to me to study culture in the Metropolitan zone first, with the idea of doing the same later in the sites which were influenced or inhabited by Olmecs, and finally to sum up both parts so as to obtain a view of the whole. On studying the Metropolitan Olmec area I do not wish to separate some sites from others as if they were islands, since this would make them unintelligible. It would be equally false to study only the Aztecs on the island of Tenochtitlan without seeing the territorial whole which stimulated, permitted, and explained the development of the capital city.

Therefore it is not necessary to list all the known Olmec sites since

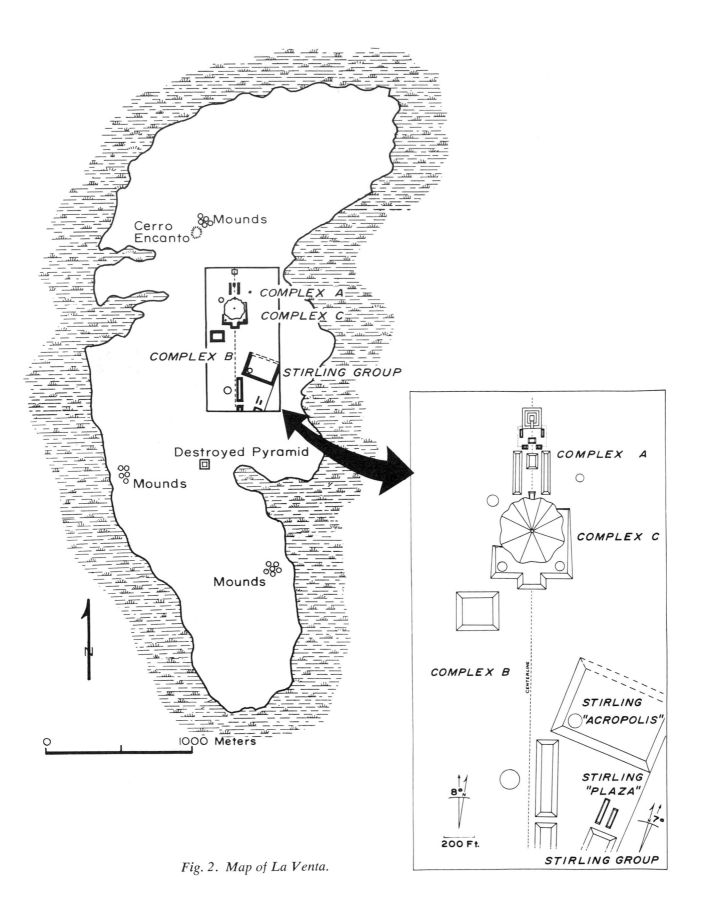

Fig. 2. Map of La Venta.

the most important, at least, appear on the map, nor is it necessary to describe in detail the main Olmec cities nor their buildings or stone sculptures. It will be necessary, however, to give a general view of the principal cities, emphasizing the aspects which (in my judgment) are relevant and which will help us to understand not only the history of the Olmecs but also later history. The maps published here are sufficient to give an idea of the distribution of these cities and their main buildings. I will make some further observations on the aspects that are impossible to represent graphically.

LA VENTA

The Tonalá River forms the boundary line between the modern states of Veracruz and Tabasco. A number of streams and sloughs that drain into the Tonalá form a region mainly covered with swamps out of which some "islands" emerge. On one of these, a little more than ten miles from the Gulf Coast, the Olmecs built their most imposing site, La Venta. Except for a few hills—one rather steep—the site is on flattish land some forty feet above the yellow swamps that surround it. Thus to the visitor the island appears as a dark green mass quite distinct from the rest of the landscape.

The total surface of the island of La Venta is two square miles[1] according to the most recent data, so it is about a third the size of the Aztec capital of Tenochtitlan-Tlatelolco. Only the central part of La Venta, containing the ceremonial edifices, has been explored.[2] It forms an irregular rectangle with the main pyramid roughly at the center and groups of mounds and monuments both to the north and south of it.

The largest structure at the La Venta site is the pyramid (Complex C on the map, Figure 2), which is built of piled-up clays. We are only now, over forty years after it was seen by Blom and La Farge, aware of its unusual features. The pyramid was shown as roughly square in a field sketch made by Drucker in 1940. In 1955 the plan on the site was drawn up by a presumably competent surveyor and took the form of a four-sided structure somewhat longer (420 feet) than wide (240 feet) with flat sides sloping up to the truncated top. In 1955 the pyramid was covered with dense forest, and the surveyor failed either to observe or, if he did, to attribute any significance to the irregularities of the outline of the base and sides of the great mound of clay. In 1967 the pyramid had been partially cleared of the vegetation cover and could be viewed

[1] Drucker and Heizer, 1960: 36.
[2] In January–February 1968, Heizer and Graham continued the exploration of the La Venta site and among other things completed the detailed topographic maps of the site.

for the first time since it was abandoned over 2000 years before. The pyramid is now seen to have been based on a nearly round plan and its sloping surface between the base and truncated top to bear a series of ridges (ten in all) which alternate with a series of valleys or depressions (ten in all). The base of each ridge extends to form a lobe, so that the plan resembles a petaled flower. The diameter of the roughly circular pyramid is 420 feet,[3] its height is 103 feet, and its mass is calculated at about 3,500,000 cubic feet.[4] The small basalt column-enclosed platforms on the southern margin of the Ceremonial Court were made of unfired red or yellow clay bricks set in red clay mortar, and the wall enclosing the Court was made of the identical construction material.[5] At least one of the pyramids, A-1, was stepped. The platforms and the pyramids or bases are solid except for those that contain a tomb. Stucco was not used for plastering walls and floors, nor was lime used in construction. The Olmecs rarely used stone in their buildings, since it was not to be found in their region; they only began to use it when their political power became great enough to have it brought from afar.

All these elements and the way they are utilized—except for the colored clay—are typical of Mesoamerica. In other words, we are now dealing with architecture which, though not of stone because of local conditions, is clearly Mesoamerican. Already present is the idea of pyramids or solid platforms whose exclusive function is that of supporting or elevating temples or dwelling places. Also present is the short *talud* or sloping wall which with time was to be enlarged,[6] but we do not yet have the *tablero* or rectangular, inset panel placed over the talud, which seems to be an invention of Teotihuacan. The attached buildings are also elements which were to become very important in Teotihuacan, though they are not typical of Monte Alban or of other sites. At La Venta the attached buildings and platforms seem to have been constructed at the same time as the pyramid,[7] which is not the case in Teotihuacan.

The La Venta ceremonial court (plaza) may have been originally a sunken patio; if so, it would be another clear antecedent of the great sunken courtyards of later times. It makes us think, especially, of Monte Alban, the great ruin in the valley of Oaxaca. On Platform E at La Venta there may have been a curb running along one side.[8] Here again

[3] Heizer and Drucker, 1968.

[4] Compare the mass of the La Venta pyramid (99,100 cubic meters) with the Pyramid of the Sun (840,000 cubic meters) and the Pyramid of the Moon (210,000 cubic meters)at Teotihuacan.

[5] Drucker, Heizer, and Squier, 1959: 18.

[6] Drucker, 1952: 77 and fig. 11.

[7] Drucker, Heizer, and Squier, 1959: 119.

[8] Drucker, 1952: 50.

we have the origin of an element that was to become extremely frequent in later times.

Stone was used occasionally in certain buildings, as can be seen in the staircases at Tres Zapotes.[9] At La Venta we have an especially remarkable example: the base of the southwest platform, which is dressed with well-cut basalt and serpentine blocks. The first row is vertical and the second forms a talud, another element which was to become typical of later constructions.[10]

The occasional use of blocks of cut stone may indicate that the Olmecs learned the practice from conquered or Olmecoid peoples who, having an ample supply of stone, used it abundantly. In places like Monte Alban and Cuicuilco—the great Preclassic ruin in the Valley of Mexico—complete architecture comes into existence. Perhaps the Olmecs copied, as far as was possible in their stoneless area, this advancement over their earth mounds. On the other hand, basalt columns seem to be found exclusively in the Metropolitan Olmec area.

The ceremonial courtyard A-1 at La Venta measures approximately 120 x 150 feet[11] and is surrounded by a palisade of basalt columns "roughly pentagonal or hexagonal in cross section, with the ends usually more or less rounded off; commonly, one surface is slightly wider, flatter, and smoother than the others. Their size varies; average diameter probably approximates 30 to 45 cm. while the length of unbroken columns ranges from 2 to 3.5 m."[12] Thus, though the columns are natural, they have been altered by the hand of man. They weigh between 1500 and 2300 pounds apiece.[13] These columns not only surrounded the ceremonial courtyard with their flat surface facing inward but also functioned as an outer wall for some of the mounds, in which case the flat surface appears on the outside,[14] thus forming a solid nucleus dressed by these columns on its exterior, as at the Southwest Platform.[15]

The famous Tomb A of La Venta is constructed totally with basalt columns placed with their flat surface inward (pl. 6). There are twelve columns along each side and five across the width; the roof consists of nine similar columns[16] supported by those on the sides. Five inclined columns, rising from the floor to the ceiling, form the door. The three last columns at the sides diminish in height in stepped fashion and

[9] Stirling, 1943: 25–26 and pl. 13–B.

[10] Drucker, Heizer, and Squier, 1959: 88 and pls. 12 and 13.

[11] Drucker (1952: 36) indicates measurements of 186 x 142 feet. This difference, however, is unimportant and is due to difficulties in measuring the palisade slope.

[12] Drucker, Heizer, and Squier, 1959: 79.

[13] Drucker, 1952: 36n.

[14] Drucker, Heizer, and Squier, 1959: 80.

[15] *Ibid.*: fig. 25 and pl. 8. This is Platform A-1-e.

[16] Drucker, 1952: 23. Though the plan shows ten columns, Heizer, in a personal communication, states that this is a draftsman's error.

close the angle between the floor and the inclined columns.[17] This type of basalt column architecture has been found in only one other place: at San Lorenzo.[18] Architecture of this kind is extremely costly and has few possibilities of development. Evidently it was not successful because it was not to be continued in Mesoamerica.

Aside from the problem of the origin and the transportation of stone and the obstacles implied, this columnar style indicates that it did not spring from a lithic tradition but emerged from wooden buildings in a zone where stone is not found.[19] Therefore the first architecture must have been based on wooden poles used for building walls and roofs, and even for reinforcing the exterior of the platforms. It is possible, therefore, that the initial periods of La Venta and Tres Zapotes and perhaps the origin of now nonexistent Olmec architecture (and therefore architecture derived from the Olmecs) was of wooden logs, but not flat boards.

Tomb A of La Venta lies in the center of Mound A-2, which was constructed especially to cover it. The tomb was never conceived as a monument placed upon the upper level of the mound nor was it possible for it to function as such,[20] but an enormous cavity was excavated in an older mound; the tomb was built within and later covered with red-orange clay.[21] Even though the mound was added to so as to cover the tomb we cannot consider that it was a direct forerunner of pyramids constructed especially to cover tombs, as was the case in later times at Palenque, Cerro de Las Mesas,[22] Cuilapan,[23] Yatachío,[24] and other sites. At La Venta we are dealing with a type of tomb dug into an already existing mound, as also occurs at Monte Alban, Holmul, and many other sites. This is the form characteristic of Mesoamerica, and it is one of the frequently discussed basic differences from the Egyptian pyramids.

At the same Mound A-2, slightly to the south but in line with it, was found a group of prostrate columns covering a burial: Tomb E.[25] Beyond this was a great stone sarcophagus with its lid (Tomb B). As in reality it is a sculpture, it will be discussed later.

[17] *Ibid.*: fig. 9.

[18] Stirling, 1955: 7.

[19] Aside from the basalt columns there are others made of granite at La Venta (Stirling, 1943: pls. 45 and 46). One of these is identical to two others found at Río Chiquito (Stirling, 1955: 7 and pl. 4). In a letter Stirling indicates that the columns at Tres Zapotes were smaller and of basalt (Stirling, 1943: pl. 15). J. Graham and R. Heizer inform me that no granite occurs at La Venta, and that Stirling may have mistakenly taken the green schist which occurs there for granite.

[20] Drucker, 1952: 26.

[21] *Ibid.*: 62.

[22] Stirling, 1941: 283.

[23] Bernal, 1958: map 2.

[24] *Excavations in the Mixteca Alta.* 1955.

[25] Drucker, 1952: 64.

The monuments of the part of La Venta which has been explored undoubtedly were placed according to rigorous planning.[26] Along the central line which forms the axis of La Venta[27] the Olmecs made great offerings and left the famous mosaic floors representing jaguar faces. These mosaics were not left visible; they were covered immediately after having been laid down, thus acquiring the quality of a ritual offering. The axis of La Venta is not a street but an imaginary line. Nevertheless, it reminds one of another central line, this time actually a street, the Street of the Dead at Teotihuacan. As in Teotihuacan, the central line at La Venta runs from north to south with a deviation of eight degrees west.[28] The axis of Monte Alban also runs from north to south, even though this may be due to the natural form of the hill there. I cannot but insist upon the extraordinary importance of this central line, because it indicates not only careful planning but also orientation and therefore astronomical knowledge and an advanced ceremonialism. These are some of the basic characteristics of Mesoamerican civilization.

At Cerro de las Mesas in our own times houses are built with their doors facing east or west, which diminishes problems brought by the strong "northers" and southern winds which affect the area.[29]

It is possible that a similar reason caused the origin of the orientations in the Olmec zone and that with the passing of time it became a fixed tradition, so fixed that the idea of orienting buildings was perpetuated in Mesoamerica until the very end, even though in later times orientation, for ritual motives, was connected with the rising and setting of the sun.

The custom of placing offerings in systematic relation to buildings, or to a central line, or to a courtyard, was to last throughout all the history of Mesoamerica. Frequently the same was true of the tombs. In this manner the archaeologist may foresee the location of a tomb in a courtyard in Monte Alban. He may know where to find the offerings associated with the buildings, not only in Monte Alban itself but in Teotihuacan or in Oaxacan sites as late as Yagul. The offerings were never placed haphazardly but followed ancient custom: along the central axis as in La Venta, at the foot of stairways, or in the corners of structures in the Classic cities of central Mexico, or in the center of courtyards in later cities. If this rigorous habit facilitates the work of the archaeologist, it also permitted the inhabitants of long ago to know where the offerings of their predecessors were located and, in case of

[26] Drucker, Heizer, and Squier, 1959: 133 and 135 *et seq.*; Drucker, 1952: fig. 14.
[27] Drucker, Heizer, and Squier, 1959: 13–15.
[28] Heizer, 1962: 310.
[29] Stirling, 1941: 303.

religious or political crises (or if the sites had been abandoned), the offerings could be removed, leaving only the hole or the stone box where they had been placed. This is what has happened almost everywhere in central Teotihuacan. At La Venta itself the famous offering of figurines (pl. 40), even though covered with several clay floors, was marked with such precision that years later the Olmecs themselves were able to open a pit of exactly the right size on the precise site in order to inspect these figurines.[30] Drucker thinks, furthermore, that a model indicating the exact site was preserved.

This rigorous planning at La Venta has permitted us to foresee the location of an offering or of a mosaic floor. The truth is that once one of a pair of offerings has been found, the discovery of its mate is inevitable.[31] One of the few exceptions probably is due to the idea that each cardinal point was associated with a color. We will deal with this later in reference to religion.

The builders of La Venta made abundant use of clays to form floors and fill for the buildings. They knew how to extract the natural clays colored without mixing the different colors. It is highly probable that the millions of cubic meters of colored clay necessary to fill the structures of groups A and C were brought onto the island from other sites.[32] This implies, together with other evidence we will see, a formidable working force.[33]

The use of these colored clays is probably unique at La Venta. After Phase I, the first architectural period of the site, the plaza was leveled; accumulated mounds of sand were removed; and low places were filled in, in order to create a flat base. Only the inclination necessary for drainage was left.[34] Each one of the next phases becomes evident through a new layer of clay of a different color which covers the floors and separates them. These changes were neither accidental nor made by chance; they were the result of careful planning. Each layer of colored clay was clean and new; this is exactly the opposite of what usually happens in Mesoamerica, where rubble of one era is used to construct the buildings of another.

The offerings of stones, celts, and jaguar mosaics are other unusually interesting elements. The great offerings of stones are unique in Mesoamerica. There are five of them at La Venta. "The characteristics of these massive offerings, on the basis of our limited sampling, seemed to be that large deep pits were dug to receive them, and the offerings

[30] Drucker, Heizer, and Squier, 1959: 154.
[31] Offering 11 may be cited as an example. Drucker, Heizer, and Squier, 1959: 177.
[32] Drucker, Heizer, and Squier, 1959: 191n.
[33] Drucker, 1952: 19. See the interesting estimations of Heizer, 1960.
[34] Drucker and Heizer, 1965.

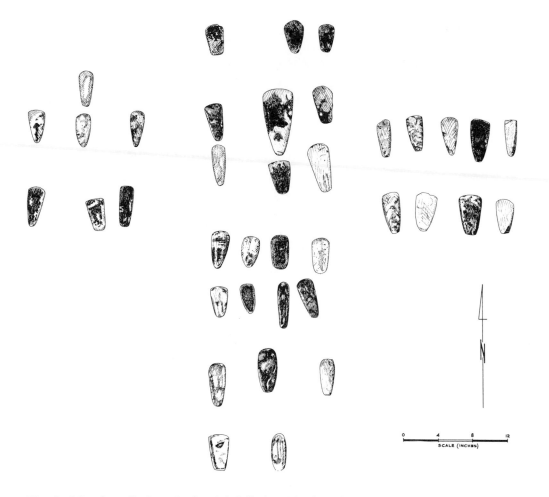

SCALE (INCHES)

Fig. 3. Massive offering of celts. (a) Offering 10. (b) Offerings 2 and 2a.

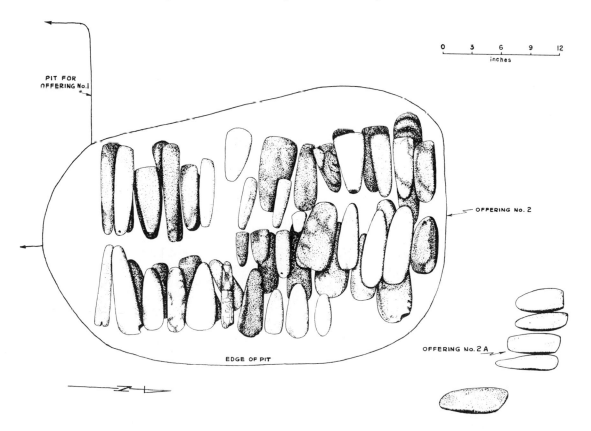

themselves consist of a very great quantity of stone."[35] They were covered with clay after having been deposited and do not seem to have served any practical function, since they were not floors nor bases for stelae or large monuments. One of them was probably carved in Phase I of La Venta and the others in the following phases. The one in Edifice A-1-C weighs some thousand tons, not including the clay.[36]

The offerings of polished celts, sometimes with incised decorations, are also exclusively part of the Olmec world (fig. 3). They contain a variable number of celts always symmetrically arranged in a cruciform design.[37] Offering 2[38] contained 258 celts, but in some other offerings only six appeared.

Some offerings of stone are associated with the mosaic floors and represent stylized jaguar faces.[39] These were also covered as soon as they were finished and therefore are true offerings and not floors constructed for practical purposes (pl. 7). Offerings, burials, and mosaics were covered with a layer of vermilion dust of cinnabar, used frequently by the Olmecs.[40] Occasionally great quantities of vermilion were used, as in Tomb D, where the layer is eight inches thick. Frequently the offerings were covered with yellow clay.[41]

Drucker speaks of burial offerings, for want of a better term, to describe deposits of objects placed in such a way as to suggest their belonging to a burial. As no traces of human bones are to be found, the reason for the deposits has remained a mystery.[42] The most interesting

[35] Drucker, Heizer, and Squier, 1959: 128 and pls. 20 and 21.

[36] *Ibid.*: 97. In the courtyard to the south of Building A at Monte Alban there was an offering of stone balls somewhat like Dutch cheeses, which corresponds to Period II. This may be founded upon an Olmec idea, and is not utilitarian.

[37] Drucker, Heizer, and Squier, 1959: fig. 51; Drucker, 1952: fig. 8.

[38] Drucker, Heizer, and Squier, 1959: 137.

[39] Drucker, 1952: 56, fig. 20, and pl. 10. Wedel found two of these mosaic floors (Drucker, 1952: figs. 20 and 24), which seem to correspond to Phase II. A third mosaic appeared in 1955; it belongs to Phase II (Drucker, Heizer, and Squier, 1959: 118 and fig. 29). They are formed of rectangular serpentine blocks placed carefully upon a base of colored clay and represent a jaguar mask. For a discussion of these masks, see Heizer, 1964.

[40] Drucker, 1952: 64 and 68.

[41] Drucker, Heizer, and Squier, 1959: 46.

[42] Drucker, Heizer, and Squier, 1959: 62 and 168; Drucker, 1952: 64, 71, 73, and fig. 22. Stirling writes me the following:

I feel sure that as a result of long years in a tropical climate the bones had completely leached away. No animal bones were found either at La Venta.

There was one exception to this, Monument 7, the tomb of stone columns. Here were traces of human long bones, some milk teeth of a child, a shark's tooth and some sting-ray tails. This preservation was probably due to the fact that the tomb had been packed with heavy red clay, which gave exceptional protection to the materials beneath. This tomb at least proves that offerings were placed with actual burials.

See Stirling, 1943a: 323–325.

deposits are in Tomb E and Tomb C, the latter being an incomplete box formed of flat stones. Its floor and roof were also made of these stones. In the interior lay the objects; it might be said that they were placed anatomically, as if they had lain upon a corpse.[43] This strange custom—if they were only offerings and not true burials—was not to be continued in Mesoamerica.

Though we know little regarding the construction techniques of the architects of La Venta, some inferences can be made. For example, when the Olmecs opened a pit to deposit a massive stone offering, they had to dig in sand, which continually sifted back into the pit. To solve this difficulty they built a retaining wall of clay, a simple and effective solution. In other cases, in excavating walls formed of basalt columns, it is found that each column had been placed in a special cavity. As is natural the columns are of different sizes, but an effort had been made to see that the upper extremities were lined up evenly. The architects, therefore, had excavated the cavity for each column according to its height; this indicates a fairly precise system of measuring.[44] This system was used in Tomb A, where it was indispensable in order to make the roof flat.[45]

To obtain a flat surface the Olmecs used upright adobe blocks fashioned like stakes, leveled by eye.[46] Before constructing an edifice they also took the precaution of removing the sand by excavating until they reached firm soil.[47] In such a rainy area the courtyards and other enclosures did not run the risk of being flooded, thanks to a functional system of open shallow drains on the earth's surface.[48] These "gutters" were later covered.

TRES ZAPOTES

The whole of Tres Zapotes is a little more than two miles in extent, along the banks of the Hueyapan, a small stream.[49] The site is on the right bank on two slightly elevated terraces (see fig. 4). The tallest buildings stand on the lowest part, at the bank of the stream, where they form a courtyard. More order is noticeable here than at La Venta, and therefore one has the feeling of a step toward planification. Stone architecture has been discovered both above and under the terraces.[50]

[43] Drucker, 1952: 67–68 and fig. 22.
[44] Drucker, Heizer, and Squier, 1959: 196.
[45] Drucker, 1952: 23.
[46] *Ibid.*: 67.
[47] Drucker, Heizer, and Squier, 1959: 20.
[48] *Ibid.*: 23.
[49] Stirling, 1943: 8; Drucker, 1943: map and fig. 2; and Weiant, 1943: map 3.
[50] Drucker, 1943: 64.

43

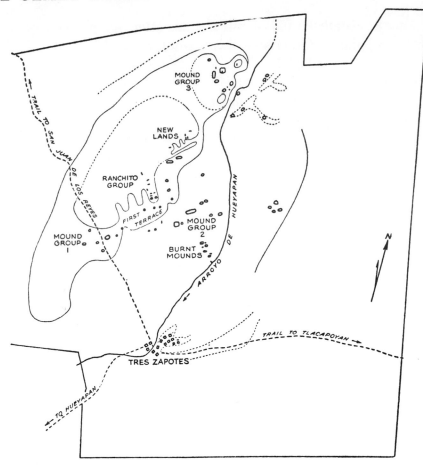

Fig. 4. Map of Tres Zapotes.

Though there is little evidence of ceramics in the mounds, the earth between the groups of mounds is covered with potsherds. This suggests inhabited areas, especially in the higher section.[51]

Tres Zapotes, perhaps due to lack of sufficient exploration, may not be evaluated from an architectural point of view. Close to fifty mounds,[52] isolated or organized in groups,[53] have been found here.

Three of the principal groups are not arranged "according to a precise geometrical plan."[54] They are placed at unequal distances, suggesting irregular courtyards. No discoveries have indicated that the builders were desirous of obtaining a fixed orientation.[55] Nevertheless, there emerged a system of grouping the mounds so that one is relatively tall and next to it stands another long and narrow one, complet-

[51] *Ibid.*: 7.
[52] Weiant, 1943: 3.
[53] Stirling, 1943: 10.
[54] Drucker, 1943: 6.
[55] Stirling, 1943: 10.

ing the group. Smaller mounds were constructed on the sides, sometimes in pairs. The two major mounds at the site are 43 feet high and 164 feet long at the base. The largest of the long, narrow mounds is 492 feet long, 63 feet wide, and 18 feet high. Except for a small platform, two small staircases, and some stone floors, the structures are made of earth because—as at La Venta—there is no stone at this site.[56]

The oldest period of Tres Zapotes, which corresponds to a time before the Olmec efflorescence—our Olmec I—is in places sealed by a layer of volcanic ash. Upon this are to be found more recent remains and the mounds of the middle period.[57]

Within a radius of ten to thirteen miles around Tres Zapotes, eight other sites are to be found. Most of these have mounds, which indicates a relatively dense population.[58]

THE RIO CHIQUITO SITES

San Lorenzo, Potrero Nuevo, and Tenochtitlan—correctly called "Río Chiquito" by Stirling to avoid confusion with the Aztec capital—had hardly been explored until Coc worked there recently. These sites are similar to La Venta in that they are islands during the rainy season and stand on similar Miocenic land. The same thing occurs, almost at the other extreme of the Olmec region[59] at the site of Cerro de Piedra.

In the dry season (January to June) of 1966 and 1967, Dr. Michael Coe of Yale University conducted large-scale excavations at San Lorenzo (Coe, 1966, 1967A, 1967B). The site occupies a level surface which has been formed by carrying up immense amounts of earth fill to cap a remnant of geologically ancient gravels. Deep and narrow gullies cut into the perimeter of this artificially capped hill and thus form a series of narrow finger-like ridges (Coc, 1966, 1967A). While unlike the alternating ridge-and-valley pattern of the La Venta pyramid, there may be some symbolic similarity between the two sites in making earth constructions with "crenellated" outlines. Coe (1967B) has found over two dozen new stone sculptures to add to the two dozen found earlier by Stirling. At the time this book goes to press, six colossal heads have been found at San Lorenzo. The sculpture of the colossal heads, altars, and animal and human figures at San Lorenzo apparently began about 1200 B.C. and came to a sudden end about 900 B.C., when most of the stone monuments were mutilated and buried, perhaps to conceal them, under

[56] Stirling, 1939: 186.
[57] Drucker, 1943: 34.
[58] Stirling, 1943: 8.
[59] Medellín, 1960: facing p. 80.

earthen mounds. Coe believes this to have been a "revolutionary act" done by the San Lorenzo people themselves.

As far as we know, this idea would not be continued in Mesoamerica. Little planning is visible at San Lorenzo although parts of it recall La Venta, on a smaller scale, as if San Lorenzo had not reached a complete development; its stone sculpture, however, is spectacular. Many of the monuments have been found aligned in a north-south direction—a typical Olmec idea. On the other hand, at Río Chiquito the mounds are important, constructed around ample quadrangular plazas. A long rectangular courtyard is bordered on its eastern and western sides by parallel mounds; to the north can be seen an edifice 60 feet high, and another limits the courtyard at the south. The whole is obviously planned and possesses a definite orientation.[60] However, there is little sculpture.[61] The difference between the two cities—one with many carved masterpieces and few buildings, and the other containing many structures and little sculpture, suggested to Stirling that the inhabitants of San Lorenzo moved to nearby Río Chiquito leaving their stone monuments in place. The cause of this change of site could have been a change in the course of a stream supplying water to a canal that at one time irrigated San Lorenzo. Its deviation might have obliged the inhabitants to follow it to a new location.

There seem to be two periods of occupation at Río Chiquito. The sculptures are from the more ancient phase,[62] and are thus contemporary with the structures at Tres Zapotes, which are from the Middle Tres Zapotes period.[63] According to Medellín's explorations, the monuments at San Lorenzo are later, but Coe on the contrary thinks they are much older, indeed probably the oldest in the Olmec area. Roughly speaking he places the monuments toward the beginning of our Olmec II. Habitation of the site goes further back into Olmec I times.

OTHER SITES

In the center of the Olmec region lies a site called Laguna de los Cerros, where some ninety-five mounds occupy almost 94 acres (fig. 5). The nucleus of the ruins is surrounded by five smaller groups of

[60] Stirling, 1955: 9. Nevertheless, other, nearby groups seem to have constructed haphazardly (Drucker and Contreras, 1953: 394). Michael Coe feels that Río Chiquito may have been planned in a form identical to that of La Venta (personal communication, November 22, 1965).

[61] Stirling, 1955: 22. Stirling also mentions a few stones that probably formed part of an aqueduct at San Lorenzo (*ibid.*: 17). Coe's recent excavations at San Lorenzo have uncovered actual drain conduits (Coe, 1967B).

[62] *Ibid.*: 7.

[63] Stirling, 1943: 11.

Fig. 5. Map of Laguna de los Cerros.

mounds; Medellín feels that these may have been ceremonial centers, though of secondary importance.[64] The site, according to the same author, is as important as Tres Zapotes, San Lorenzo, or La Venta. Some of the stone sculptures from Laguna de los Cerros are of a quality equal to that of the best pieces from La Venta and San Lorenzo.

In the southeastern part of the Olmec zone Drucker and Contreras[65] found eighty sites, most of which lie in the swamps of the coastal plain. The largest ones show a pre-established order or planning such as we have seen at places like La Venta. R. Squier has studied the pottery collected on this reconnaissance trip and has concluded that the majority of the sites do not have Olmec pottery and therefore cannot be called Olmec sites.[66] The eighty sites are of various types. Some of them seem to be

[64] Medellín, 1960: 86.
[65] Drucker and Contreras, 1953: 396.
[66] Unpublished dissertation.

simple ceremonial centers, while others show not only mounds but also the remains of dwelling places. While ceramic ware is abundant at some sites, it is extremely scarce at others. There does not seem to be a correlation, however, between the presence or absence of ceramics and the different types of ruins.[67] At the foot of the mountains, that is, at the border of the Olmec area, some places seem to have been built purely for defense, fit for habitation only in the rainy season, since they are not near any river or stream. Perhaps they were military posts, and if so they could throw light upon war among the Olmecs, a theme I will deal with later. A veritable hierarchy of sites exists, showing a complicated system of settlement patterns.[68]

The last area we will mention is the archaeological zone of El Remolino, lying to the southwest of Tuxtla on the San Juan River. This site contains more than sixty mounds which stand in good order around rectangular courtyards. Definite planning seems to exist, also, at nearby La Cañada.[69] Unfortunately, we do not know whether these two zones are Olmec.

But I do not mean to present a complete catalog of the sites that undoubtedly were inhabited by Olmecs within the region. Those we have mentioned are sufficient to assure us that the area was densely populated, perhaps more so than today.[70] To sum up, we can say that the centers were frequently patterned in accordance with a determined orientation, generally north-south. With very few exceptions buildings were of earth and adobe, which permitted little elaboration; lime was unknown, and therefore we find no stucco floors or walls. But there existed the idea of solid pyramids surmounted by a building and arranged around plazas, and at least the central part of the site was dedicated to ceremonial aims.

The fantastic number of man-hours implied by the buildings, constructions, sculptures, and other objects indicates a densely populated area. Olmec architecture is a far cry from the future triumphs of peoples who were to be their heirs, but the basic ideas that were to develop in other areas had been born.

We know little about the dwelling places of the common men, nor are there any remains of the more sumptuous adobes of the chieftains —if such edifices ever existed. It is probable that these houses were of

[67] Drucker and Contreras, 1953: 393–4.

[68] Drucker and Contreras, 1953: 395. Drucker himself affirms elsewhere that many of these sites do not correspond to the Olmec culture (Drucker, Heizer, and Squier, 1959: 300), this change of opinion being based on a study of the ceramic collections by Squier.

[69] Weyerstall, 1932: 38–40.

[70] Drucker, Heizer, and Squier, 1959: 42 or Stirling, 1943: 30.

wood with palm-thatched roofs, their walls covered with hardened mud, made with the wattle and daub system so common today. Rectangular house plans of this kind have recently been found by Coe where they are set on low mounds arranged around a "court." Similar housing plans were employed even in great cities like Monte Alban. Adobe brickwork construction is common at La Venta and is possibly an Olmec invention, since it is not usual at ancient highland sites either older than or contemporaneous to La Venta. In any case, the private life of the Olmec was undoubtedly spent within a modest framework and the chieftains did not possess the stone palaces that were to be common among the great personages of Teotihuacan or of the Maya area.

An important and long-discussed problem is that of the nature of Mesoamerican sites. Are they cities—compact or dispersed—or ceremonial centers? It is evident that beginning with the Teotihuacan period true compact cities existed, in addition to scattered or congregated hamlets of the rural population. In the lowlands and especially in the Maya world, ceremonial centers—which I would like to call dispersed cities—predominated. Many scholars, above all those who view Mesoamerica through Maya culture, have distorted the situation by claiming that there were no cities but only ceremonial centers in Mesoamerica; at the very most they concede that Teotihuacan and Tenochtitlan may have been cities. This claim seems impossible to sustain now, since it is certain that there were cities in central Mexico and in areas such as Oaxaca. Even in the tropics there are a number of sites—such as El Tajin and Cempoala in Veracruz, and Chichén Itzá or Mayapan in Yucatan—which I believe to have been cities.

By the term ceremonial center is meant a site inhabited by the leaders of society—priests or laymen—their direct dependents, and perhaps others. The remainder of the populace lived in villages which were branches of the great center and only visited the center on festive occasions in order to attend to their affairs or to carry out tasks imposed upon them by the hierarchy.

It is frequently accepted that a ceremonial center is non-urban; thus the great Maya sites of Tikal or Copan, Palenque or Uaxactun would not be considered urban. This idea, to my mind, is contradictory because I cannot envisage any civilization that is not urban and I believe that in a way the words civilization and urbanism are synonymous. Civilization, it seems, must necessarily have an urban core, although of course many of its members lead a rural life and may only indirectly be related to that civilization. Urbanism, like anything else, is found in varying degrees. The Olmec world was certainly less urban than Teotihuacan or Tenochtitlan; these cities in turn were less urban than London is.

Coe[71] has pointed out that urbanism does not necessarily accompany civilization because there do exist non-urban civilizations. Perhaps the whole matter rests on semantics, since the dispersed city is similar to the ceremonial center and its dependent villages. Still, I find a fundamental difference. We are now dealing with a civilized, urban—though dispersed—pattern. The dispersed city presupposes the existence of specialized groups, class division, elaborate religion, a great monumental art, and many of the other requisites of civilization. Of course all these—like civilization itself—exist at different levels according to the epoch and the place where they develop.

So, since Maya sites undoubtedly pertain to a civilized world, I would propose—if it is definitely proven that they are not compact cities—to call them dispersed cities. Only through ingrained habit have I, even here, continued the tradition of referring to them as ceremonial centers. The importance of the distinction lies in the fact that ceremonial centers are found among noncivilized groups, as is clear today in some areas, for instance Chiapas, where regular ceremonial centers exist but the pattern of civilized life has disappeared. I of course agree that ceremonial centers also existed in Mesoamerica, just as a rural life existed.

In what situation should we place the Olmec sites? Heizer favors the idea of La Venta as a ceremonial center. He thinks that the inhabitants associated with this place lived in an area of some 358 square miles between the Tonalá and Coatzacoalcos rivers. These inhabitants would have numbered some 18,000 persons if Sanders's demographic correlation is to be accepted.[72]

I also believe that the agriculture of La Venta itself could have sustained, in view of the small size of the island, only an insignificant population, at the very most 150 persons, that is to say, about thirty families.[73] However, we are not primarily concerned with the number of people who lived on this desolate island, though it was perhaps the most important center of the Olmec culture. What we are interested in is the number of inhabitants who formed Olmec civilization in its entirety, and how many dwelt in the metropolitan area of a city like La Venta.

La Venta may have been a religious center, a place of pilgrimages and princely burials such as the islands of Jaina, off the coast of Campeche, and Sacrificios, in the bay of Veracruz, were later. It is known that certain isolated places, especially islands, were frequently chosen as sanctuaries.

There is one concrete argument in favor of the theory emphasizing

[71] M. D. Coe, 1962: 82.
[72] Heizer, 1962: 311; Drucker, 1961. These authors arrive at similar conclusions and contribute new data.
[73] Drucker and Heizer, 1960: 43.

ceremonial centers: little ceramic ware exists at Olmec sites.[74] This suggests a small population with few homes where this ware could have been used and broken and then thrown into the rubbish heap. This scarcity is in strong contrast with the extraordinary abundance of potsherds in the archaeological zones of the highlands or of Oaxaca.

Nor do there seem to be many zones of habitation at the Olmec sites that have been studied, although some suggest a heavy population.[75] Perhaps all these doubts exist because neither the refuse heaps nor the dwelling areas have been explored. They are difficult to find and to study correctly; on the other hand, ceramic ware is easily destroyed in this type of climate. Some sites seem to have been densely inhabited even though they were of lesser ritual prestige. I realize that perhaps some Olmec sites remained in an intermediary stage between the true city such as Teotihuacan and the simple ceremonial center. Caso has suggested that the true situation must be found in a combination of both possibilities. The most recent investigations at San Lorenzo and La Venta (of 1966–1968) should provide us with information on the living patterns of the people who built these sites.

Nevertheless, in an attempt to understand the problem better, let us observe the situation of the modern Indians of Mexico in this respect, that is, that of the groups which have continued to thrive after the disappearance of their civilizations due to the Spanish conquest and who lived at sites which were not influenced by Spanish urbanization but which did lose their native Indian planning. In a manner of speaking, these modern people live a life similar to that of the Preclassic; they are in an inferior cultural state because they have lost their civilization. On the other hand the Olmecs were passing from this inferior stage to civilization. In both cases, therefore, we have a mixture of two cultural situations. In the modern it is due to survivals; in the ancient it was because of new traits that were being developed. Thus the urban situation of the indigenous people of today can throw light on the urban situation of the Olmecs of the past. Naturally we should not carry this parallel too far.

In the folk culture of today slash and burn cultivation does not permit the existence of compact villages, since a large number of families could not be supported by the lands at hand and the people would have to journey farther and farther to fell trees and open new fields to cultivation. It is at this point that

the pattern of a *ranchería*, a small cluster of huts, is established. Two or three families live there near their cornfields. But all of them recognize their political and re-

---

[74] Sanders, 1953: 71.
[75] Drucker, 1943: 8. We are not sure that many of these sites belong to the Olmec period.

ligious adherence to a ceremonial center where the church, the *mayordomo*'s house, the center of civil government, and the school stand. We call this organization *a dispersed village,* and we feel that it is the result of the same factors that operated in the pre-Hispanic epoch, which formed a certain type of urban organization very typical of Mexico.[76]

The political and religious centers of ancient times were nourished by wards which were later to be called *barrios* and which still exist today as such in our indigenous communities and are not integral parts of a city as they are in Europe but small settlements where are found the authorities, the local place of worship, and a division of labor which permits specialization in production . . . In its structure each barrio reproduces the organization of the ceremonial and political center . . . and at times is an ethnic division, representing a clan or *calpulli* whose provenance is to be found outside. . . . We suggest that this urban organization be called a *dispersed city,* since its manner of functioning is that of a city—a very large one—because it embraces within its limits the tilled fields, such as are found today in our modern villages. The lots and the houses with their yards are disseminated throughout the entire village. Each house resembles more a small farm than an urban home . . . Here we find it difficult to distinguish between the city and the country. . . .[77]

Now if we observe the large areas occupied by many of the Olmec centers and their distribution in groups of buildings, we can surmise that the houses with their lands were situated between the different groups. Therefore is it quite possible that this may have been in reality the Olmec type of urban organization, of settlement pattern. Thus we are confronted with a type that lies between the small, almost Neolithic village from which these groups emerged and the true city which we find at Teotihuacan and later at Mayapan.

Actually, La Venta, together with other large sites, suggests a long period of habitation and a considerable force of manual labor directed by specialists who were highly competent in their profession. The immense stones brought from afar and from different places necessitated a complex organization. These stones were probably brought by rafts or by canoes bridged across with a decking of logs. But also necessary were "a considerable number of laborers to fell the trees, to fabricate and carry the balsa rafts, and conduct them back to the port via the coast or the river."[78]

As Stirling has suggested, some stones destined for La Venta were perhaps transported by water along the coast as far as the mouth of the Tonalá River and were then pulled to the island. It is probable that in ancient times an arm of the river touched the northern end of the island.

[76] Caso, 1965: 33–34.
[77] *Ibid.*: 34–35.
[78] Drucker and Heizer, 1960: 44, and Heizer (personal communication) suggest in a most logical way that a series of canoes bridged over by logs would have been simpler to make and maneuver than rafts made of logs.

Even today one can travel inland by canoe to Tonalá, which is ten land miles upriver from La Venta.[79]

But the problem that the Olmecs faced was not only that of transporting the monoliths in order to convert them into splendid sculpture;[80] it was also necessary to "maintain the center alive, to mine great quantities of serpentine, to transport the stones to the site and to dress them into the surfaced blocks for use in the jaguar mosaic 'masks' and the pavementlike massive offerings . . . to carry in the carefully selected colored clay fills and surfacing materials,"[81] besides digging the immense pits and building the numerous structures. The archaeologists who excavated La Venta wrote: "Each of the successive surfacings of the . . . floors involved the efforts of a number of persons as will be readily apparent if we compute the cubic mass of a . . . sand flooring one-half inch thick distributed over the surface area of the Court. We have made such a computation, which, though admittedly approximate, amounts to 885 cubic feet."[82]

These great programs of construction, preservation, and reconstruction were carried out in periods of intense activity, during which the laborers had to remain near, if not at, the actual site. All the evidence—and the list could be prolonged—indicates that there must have been a sufficiently large human concentration at Olmec cities, even though the inhabitants may have been scattered in nearby settlements.

In order to carry out their great construction projects, the leaders must have found it necessary to count on numerous specialized workers, besides the manual laborers, since the latter could have accomplished nothing unless they were directed by a corps of specialists, engineers who knew how to cut the rock, extract stones, transport them, set them up, and complete the excavations while trying to prevent the sand from covering the stones. Furthermore, it is evident that there were lapidaries —of great virtuosity—to work the jade, and first-rate artists to carve the stone monuments. These specialists must have been directly under the orders of the chieftains; they probably lived within the city or in nearby wards.

Even the most common laborer can hardly have dwelt very far away if he was obliged to collaborate in all these activities and at the same time attend his agricultural work. All this implies a sedentary population, as Stirling has suggested,[83] referring to Tres Zapotes. If we admit,

[79] Stirling, 1943: 50.

[80] Aside from the offering that weighs a thousand tons there is another that weighs 500. Stela 3 was calculated at 50 short tons (Drucker and Heizer, 1960: 43–44), but a later and more precise computation reduces its weight to 26 metric tons or 27 short tons (Heizer 1967: 28).

[81] Drucker, Heizer, and Squier, 1959: 269.

[82] *Ibid.*: 33, n. 3.

[83] Stirling, 1943: 8.

therefore, that the population was quite numerous—as it must have been —and was confined to a relatively restricted area, we reach the same conclusion proposed by Caso about the "dispersed city." The embryo of the future Mesoamerican metropolis is to be found here.

The Maya world preserved—with some exceptions—this type of dispersed city, no matter how big it may have become in later times in great urban areas such as Tikal. In this the Maya culture was a direct heir of the Olmec patterns. On the other hand, in the highlands, with the emergence of Teotihuacan, a further step was taken, producing compact cities where the houses were limited only by streets and not by cultivated fields. Naturally some spaces remained open, the way later Mexican cities were dotted with orchards until recent times. It is only modern population pressure that has eliminated this type of organization from a metropolis such as Mexico City. In a later volume, when I deal with the culture of Teotihuacan, I will return to this point and will compare its progress according to the criteria of Childe (1950) in reference to urban civilization.

At the beginning of this work I mentioned the possibility that an urban civilization could have emerged from slash and burn farming. In the Olmec area I see two factors in favor of the emergence of a primeval civilization. In the first place it is possible, as has been said, that aside from slash and burn farming, flood agriculture could have existed. This could have, as is still the case today along the Tonalá and Coatzacoalcos rivers, utilized the river banks where periodic floods were not too violent. If it seems evident that the Olmec sites cannot be considered formal cities like Teotihuacan, at the same time it is feasible that with its dispersed city pattern the Olmec community may have produced the same results. On the other hand not only agriculture—and it must be remembered that this is the most important economic element—but also other economic factors such as commerce, and even motives of an entirely different character such as religion, were capable of creating a given civilization.

In short, I feel that the Metropolitan Olmecs were the initiators of a civilization in which urbanism was at the base of the dispersed city, and that the peoples of the central plateau transformed this civilization into one based on compact cities.

In Mesoamerica, as everywhere else, a vast proportion of the inhabitants continued to live in completely rural hamlets or small communities, which in one way or another were subordinate to the urban center. Actually this situation occurs even today throughout the world except for small areas which have been intensely industrialized.

But before going on to the social and political organization of the Olmecs, let us consider other aspects of their culture.

3

THE ARTS OF SCULPTURE
AND CERAMICS

SCULPTURE

Olmec sculpture can be dealt with separately, since it has little connection with architecture. Except where the great monoliths are associated with buildings, they do not form an integral part of the structures.
This is the opposite of what was to take place later among the Maya,
Teotihuacanos, and their heirs, whose sculpture was inseparable from
architecture. This unity came about because in the later civilizations
architecture was of stone and not of earth, as it was among the Olmecs.

If something of the Olmecs has endured that allows us to speak of a
civilization, it is their extraordinary sculpture, which in many aspects
has not been surpassed by any other Mesoamerican people. In order to
study this sculpture more profoundly we must first consider the great
monoliths and then the small sculptures, not forgetting that both types
represent the same style, for they are products of the same culture.

A good number of monoliths have survived. Undoubtedly they were
carved in the Olmec area, not only because they were found there but
also because their tremendous weight eliminates the probability that
they were transported after carving. At the same time their style is
proof that they were not created by a later people.

I do not intend to catalog these pieces but only to discuss them as
groups or to illustrate some point relative to the Olmec culture; detailed
descriptions have already been given in various publications.[1] On the

[1] Above all in Stirling, 1943; Stirling, 1955; Drucker, 1952; Drucker, Heizer, and
Squier, 1959; Medellín, 1960.

other hand, I will deal with the aesthetic aspects mainly in relation to their cultural implications.

THE COLOSSAL HEADS

Twelve colossal human heads, sculptures in stone, have been discovered so far (see pls. 8–11). Four are from La Venta, two from Tres Zapotes, and six from San Lorenzo.[2] Perhaps there is another, unfinished, in San Lorenzo.[3] The heads found at the latter site were moved in ancient times, some having been thrown into a ravine, but of course they never left San Lorenzo. Therefore with one possible exception we cannot determine their original positions.[4] Of the heads at the other two sites, four face north[5] and one (Monument 1 at La Venta) stands at the foot of the flat platform of the great pyramid which faces south. Since the colossal heads were placed with relationship to nearby architecture, they had to face the same direction as the main orientation of the constructions. This special case does not disprove the probability that they were meant to face north, as were the mosaics with jaguar masks.[6]

The significance of these enormous sculptures, whose height is anywhere from 4.70 to 9.85 feet, has long been discussed. They always existed as heads alone and never possessed bodies. These heads, which some have described as Negroid because of their broad features, wear a sort of helmet. I do not believe them to be portraits since they are almost alike and especially because the portrait—except among the Maya—seems not to have been characteristic of Mesoamerican art, which does not seek the reality of nature but an interpretation of it. The heads might represent chieftains or warriors in a general sense. I

[2] "The head at Santiago Tuxtla definitely came from Tres Zapotes. When we first saw it many years ago, we obtained the story of its removal and later on a return visit to Tres Zapotes, the people there showed us the spot from which it was taken at the foot of a hill almost 2 miles S.E. of the other Tres Zapotes head." (Letter from Stirling, July 19, 1965. See Heizer, Smith, and Williams, 1965.) Clewlow, Cowan, O'Connell, and Benemann (1967: 30–32) show that this head actually comes from a different site which has been called, provisionally, Nestepe.

[3] Stirling, 1955: 17.

[4] *Ibid.*: 9–13. Stirling notifies me in a letter of February, 1956: "The only exception is Head 2, which lay face upward. If it was only cast there and not moved in some other form, when erect it should have faced north." Coe (1967B) has suggested another interpretation for the placement of the San Lorenzo colossal heads. He believes that they lie in their original position and that the seven to eight meters of earth over them is an artificial fill laid down to cover the surface and the sculptures.

[5] Drucker, 1952: 9; Stirling, 1943: 17.

[6] In Drucker, 1952: 57 and 74, and Drucker, Heizer, and Squier, 1959: 93 and 227, the heads of the jaguar mosaics face north. In the latter work the one in fig. 29 however, appears in the opposite direction. However, Drucker and Heizer (1965) changed their original opinion on the direction in which the mosaic jaguar mask faces are oriented and are in agreement with the interpretation of M. Coe (1965) and Coe and Stuckenrath (1964).

56

doubt that they are gods, even though their fixed orientation suggests ritual connections.

It is Charles Wicke's opinion that they are monuments raised to honor dead chieftains; in part he bases his opinions on the conclusions of Proskouriakoff (1960) and Kelley (1962) regarding the Piedras Negras monuments and the glyphs of Quiriguá, respectively, in Guatemala. Wicke has enlarged upon a work initiated by George Kubler[7] in an attempt to place the heads in a chronological order. If Wicke's idea is correct, the twelve heads (plus those which have not yet been discovered and those which have disappeared) would cover a period of at least 240 years and therefore would have been carved during many generations. I find it difficult to accept this theory because, as Kubler has stated, it is probable, considering their similarity, that at least some of the heads were the work of the same family during two or three generations. Furthermore, each one of the Olmec cities has its own slight differences of style.[8] Nevertheless, the chronological sequence proposed by Wicke is extremely interesting and seems to be correct, even though the time span may have been shorter and the heads may not represent dead chieftains. (A still more recently published analysis of the twelve heads concludes that all were carved within a relatively brief period of time [Clewlow, Cowan, O'Connell, and Benemann, 1967].) This was the dilemma that troubled Covarrubias when he wished to set up a chronology based on stylistic series, which can be so variable and where personal invention plays such an important role. All of this shows again the tragedy for science when monoliths are moved from their original places without taking note of all the existing information.

At Laguna de los Cerros two smaller heads were found, one of them only about 30 inches high (pl. 12). They wear remarkable jaguar masks which distinguish them from the others. However, the faces under the masks, as far as can be seen, indicate that they are representations of a physical type similar to that of the colossal heads.[9]

[7] Kubler, 1962: 67. In a personal communication Michael Coe writes: "I would seriate the heads differently from Wicke or Kubler. The sequence would begin with the La Venta heads, which show close resemblances to the jade and pottery figurine style; then the San Lorenzo heads; and finally the Tres Zapotes ones, which are extremely portrait-like and lack the pseudo-drilling at the corners of the mouths." Clewlow, Cowan, O'Connell, and Benemann (1967) have published the most detailed description of the colossal heads and are of the opinion that they cannot be seriated meaningfully.

[8] Heizer (personal communication) feels that several generations were needed in order to carve such a large number of known heads, plus those which presumably exist but have not as yet been unearthed. For further argument see Clewlow, Cowan, O'Connell, and Benemann, 1967.

[9] Medellín, 1960: 86. It is probable that the colossal heads and many of the other sculptures were painted. A spot of purple color is visible on one of the heads

ALTARS AND STELAE

Almost as impressive as the heads are the altars; two were found at San Lorenzo,[10] another at Laguna de los Cerros,[11] and seven at La Venta[12] (pls. 13 and 14). It is curious that none exists at Tres Zapotes. The altars are in the form of great monolithic rectangles frequently adorned with figures or scenes on the carved sides in both low and high relief. A favorite theme is that of a personage seated in a niche with a child in his arms. For example, on Altar 5 at La Venta[13] this theme appears several times. It is not easy to interpret: we do not seem to be dealing with the worldwide motif of mother and child, since the larger figure always looks masculine. In some of the scenes the children appear to be dead but in others they seem to be playing, talking, or arguing in the arms of the men who carry them. Could these altars have possessed a religious implication or perhaps a dynastic meaning, showing the importance of the child as heir to the throne or something similar as it did many centuries later in the Bonampak mural? Actually, in the magnificent Maya murals of about the ninth century A.D. at Bonampak (pl. 13d), we have what is practically a reproduction of the scene on Altar 3 at La Venta.[14]

The altar from Potrero Nuevo near San Lorenzo is very different,[15] since it is supported by two atlantean figures carved in high relief on the front of the base (pl. 15). This is the oldest Mesoamerican example of the theme of atlantes holding up altars or ceilings—later to be found abundantly. Here the atlantes are attached to the background; they are not sculptures in the round as they are later among the Toltecs at Chichén Itzá and Tula. This Olmec invention was to be long-lasting.

Though the colossal heads and altars are easily separated into groups, the same cannot be said of the carved stelae, slabs or which are extremely different one from the other, even though each is a stone, more or less flat and smooth, and shows motifs sculptured in low relief on its main surface. Even though the stela trait is present in Olmec culture we do not find in these stones the rigor—we might almost say the mass fabrication—which was later to be typical of Maya art.

---

from San Lorenzo (Stirling, 1955: 20). Actually, ancient sculpture was customarily painted in vivid colors, such as the atlantes of Tula, the Toltec capital. This use of color, so contrary to modern aesthetic patterns, seems to be characteristic of all civilizations.

[10] *Ibid.*: pls. 21 and 22.
[11] Medellín, 1960: pl. 19.
[12] Stirling, 1943: 52–56; Drucker, 1952: 182.
[13] *Ibid.*: 77.
[14] *Ibid.*: fig. 51.
[15] Stirling, 1955: pl. 23.

The Olmec stelae are of different heights, varying from less than three feet, such as Monument 19 at La Venta (if this may be considered a stela), to 17.4 feet, such as Stela A at Tres Zapotes, the largest and only stela carved in volcanic breccia, a rock consisting of sharp fragments embedded in a fine matrix. Most of the rest are basalt. Five stelae were found at Tres Zapotes, eight at La Venta, and one each at San Lorenzo, Cerro de la Piedra, El Mesón, Piedra Labrada, and Roca Partida.[16]

Several stelae are plain or have been so defaced that nothing is left on them now except perhaps a jaguar mask, as on monuments 25, 26, and 27 at La Venta.[17] This is one of the basic themes also to be found, with variants, on the three stelae at Tres Zapotes known to have been decorated. Another theme is related to the jaguar mask: that of the open mouth of a feline, within which there appear human figures forming a scene, as on Stelae A and D of Tres Zapotes (pl. 16a and b). Stela 1 at La Venta shows only the figure of a standing woman who wears a sort of helmet reminiscent of those of the colossal heads. The stelae at Tres Zapotes are among the most interesting and the best carved, even though they are markedly different from each other. Each is composed of three figures; we do not know their significance, though they may have represented scenes of war. There seems to be a trophy head on Stela A, and on D a warrior holding a lance; the latter, together with another figure, possibly a standing woman, is receiving the homage of a kneeling person.

Only two other stelae show several figures (La Venta 2 and 3). These are the most famous in spite of their poor condition. The first (pl. 17) represents an imposing personage wearing an extremely tall headdress which seems to be a forerunner of those of many priests and sovereigns in the Maya stelae of later times. Stela 3 is engraved with two central figures; one seems to be a woman,[18] but the other is that of the famous individual of "Semitic" features, who is perhaps intended to be a distinguished visiting foreigner (pl. 4). On both stelae six secondary figures surround the central images; these have been interpreted as possible *chaneques* (see p. 100) and are reminiscent of the children carved on the altars. They are among the few figures that seem filled with movement, in many different positions,[19] which we will not find again until the Olmecoids of Monte Alban, and which are not common in the strictly ritual

[16] Covarrubias, 1957: 65.

[17] Drucker, Heizer, and Squier, 1959. Stirling believes that the stela originated in an open-mouthed jaguar head which became progressively stylized.

[18] Stirling, 1943: 51; Drucker, 1952: fig. 50. Nevertheless, in a more recent reconstruction it seems to wear a loincloth instead of a skirt. In this case it would be a man (Drucker, Heizer, and Squier, 1959: fig. 67 and p. 213).

[19] Drucker, 1952: 202. A detailed description and analysis of the scenes portrayed on stelae 2 and 3 from La Venta has been published by Heizer, 1967.

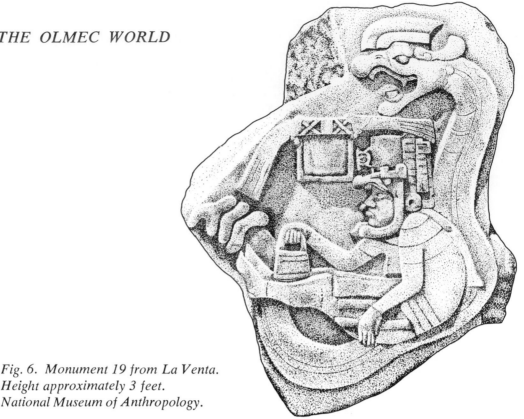

*Fig. 6. Monument 19 from La Venta.
Height approximately 3 feet.
National Museum of Anthropology.*

arts of later times. These two stelae—carved to take advantage of the
natural irregularities of the stone—were not smoothed before carving.[20]
There are other examples in which the figure was conceived obeying the
natural form of the stone, as is clear in Monument 19 from La Venta
(fig. 6). The same occurs frequently in the "danzantes," or dancing
figures, of Monte Alban.

In both the stelae and the altars it is evident that the Olmec style is a
style of sculpture, not painting[21] and is in direct contrast to Maya art,
which seems to be derived from painting. I have some doubts regarding
the second part of my last statement, since I consider a fixed sequence of
the great arts typical of Mesoamerica, and painting always appears at
the end. In some backward areas mural painting never emerged, such
as in the case of western Mexico. It is obvious that we must take into
consideration a material element essential to mural painting: the flat
coating of lime on walls which is not found among the Olmecs and very
rarely in western Mexico.

The theme of a head or a complete human figure emerging from the
jaws of an animal was to be extremely popular in late times and is to
be found even in Aztec art. Among the Olmecs the chosen animal is the
jaguar. This occasionally is found in the form of a headdress.[22] We will

[20] Stirling, 1943: 51.
[21] Drucker, 1952: 217.
[22] As in Monument 19 of La Venta (Drucker, Heizer, and Squier, 1959: 198).

Fig. 7. Monument C, Tres Zapotes. Width at base 4 feet.

discover that, from Olmec times on, the combination of man-animal is present, in which sometimes the man emerges from the animal and at other times he only uses the head of the animal as a headdress. The jaguar or eagle warriors of the Aztec world are an example of this. The personage shown on Monument 19 of La Venta could be called a "jaguar knight." This admirable relief may, in all justice, be included within the varied series of stelae. It represents a seated man wearing a jaguar helmet,[23] while behind him appears a magnificently carved rattlesnake. The snake is executed in a highly realistic manner, even though on its head appears the famous but unreal eyebrow that is typical of all serpents in Mesoamerican art. The entire stela is strongly reminiscent of the man-bird-serpent of Tula, in spite of the differences in time, style, and perhaps even theme; here, however, we are dealing with a man-jaguar-serpent.

This same theme of the man with the serpent appears on Monument 47 at San Lorenzo, on the upper part of Stela 3 at La Venta, and it has been stated that here and on Monument 19 we are seeing a feathered serpent.[24] Frankly, as I cannot distinguish feathers anywhere on this

[23] Drucker, Heizer, and Squier (1959: 199) believe that the man is bearded. I suggest that the beard could be a jaguar's tongue.

[24] Drucker, Heizer, and Squier (1959: 199) believe it to be a feathered serpent. The lines along the body of the ferocious serpent, they maintain, are more suggestive of scales or of a different color which actually is found on a reptile on the part between the back and the belly. The other small lines have scales (*ibid.*: 200 and fig. 67).

sculpture, I agree with Drucker when he states that "the feathered serpent never appears."[25] Neither do feathers appear on the other two existing serpents; the snake on Monument 1 at Potrero Nuevo is twisted around the legs of a jaguar, and the other, on Monument 3 at the same site,[26] does not resemble in any way the representations of twisted snakes which were later to become so frequent in the highlands. There is only one possible exception, and this may belong to a later period: the famous box at Tres Zapotes (Monument C)[27] (fig. 7). Here ". . . a profile head of a plumed serpent possibly is represented."[28] I feel that, although there are many curvilinear elements on the box (which suggest a late date), associated with other elements that seem to be feathers, there is no clear indication that the figure is a serpent.

The stelae of El Mesón and its counterpart (known as the stela of Alvarado, fig. 8) possibly belong to a later period.[29] Aside from the interest of the scenes (they show a standing personage in front of whom sits a bound captive), the El Mesón stela is carved of the same basalt which is typical of the monuments from Tres Zapotes. At El Mesón and at Alvarado, however, we are not dealing with natural columns only but with columns that bear inscriptions in a typical Olmec style. Engravings of heiroglyphs and numbers existed, and remains of them can still be seen.[30] Another column which is probably a stela shows a jaguar mask, an obvious antecedent of the Olmecoid of Monte Alban and the Chicanel period at Uaxactun.[31]

Unfortunately only a fragment remains of the most outstanding of all, Stela C of Tres Zapotes (pl. 18b), made of olivine basalt similar to that of La Venta;[32] this has been the cause of many chronological problems, to be discussed later. On its reverse side it carries a weeping-jaguar mask which in reality is Cocijo, the Zapotec rain god. This is very similar to

[25] Drucker, 1952: 223.

[26] Stirling, 1955: 18 and 20.

[27] Drucker, 1952: 210.

[28] Stirling, 1943: 18.

[29] The "Alvarado stela" could have come from Cerro de la Piedra, as Medellín suggests (1960: 79). Cerro de la Piedra is actually outside the Olmec area but is very close by. Batres (1905: 17), however, affirms that it was found on an estuary to the south of the Papaloapan River and from there was brought to Alvarado. The other stela at this site (Medellín, 1960: pl. 6) I consider Olmecoid because of its style and because it represents, perhaps, a ball player (Smith, 1963: 141). Regarding the El Mesón stela, see Stirling, 1943: 28–29 and pl. 16a.

[30] See Thompson, 1941: 15. On the other hand, it is not plausible that the stela of San Miguel Chapultepec at the National Museum of Mexico came from the Chapultepec in the city of Mexico. It bears a striking resemblance to Stela 5 at Cerro de las Mesas (Stirling, 1943: 3) and almost surely was brought from there. In any case, neither of the two belongs to the Olmec style but to another which is a distant heir.

[31] Drucker, 1952: fig. 54.

[32] Williams and Heizer, 1965: 16.

Fig. 8. Stela from Alvarado or Cerro de la Piedra. Height 12 feet, 3 inches. National Museum of Anthropology of Mexico.

early masks at Monte Alban (pl. 18d), according to observations made by Caso.[33] It is true that this corroborates the early date of the inscription in the Maya Long Count. (The system is explained on p. 93.)

Stela C at Tres Zapotes was used twice in Olmec history. We are ignorant of its original position, when undoubtedly it was still intact. After it was broken it was set up again in association with a very crude altar[34] that was placed in front of it. This indicates that the new use came from the idea of combining an altar with a stela. It does not seem to be an original Olmec trait, as this is the only example in the area and corresponds to a later period, perhaps Olmec III. Still, it is the most ancient combination of the two elements that we know of, a combination which was to become characteristic of the Maya world and would also be found frequently in the Classic period of Veracruz.

[33] Stirling, 1939: 212–213.
[34] San Lorenzo 12 (Stirling, 1955: pl. 16b) could be feminine, although this is doubtful because it seems to wear a breechclout. The figure has been considered a woman because it carries a child in its arms, resting on the knees, but we have seen that frequently men are shown carrying children in their arms.

HUMAN FIGURES

We are acquainted with about twenty statues in the round representing human figures; these vary greatly in quality and belong to different periods. Unfortunately, most of them were found incomplete, so it is impossible to classify them with precision. Almost all of them represent nude men; an occasional one wears a breechclout or belt. Some wear a helmet, necklace, or breastplate[35] (pl. 19). In general they are seated, with their hands on their knees[36] (pl. 20); less frequently their hands are placed on their chests or at their sides, or each arm is in a different position, as in Monument 11 of Laguna de los Cerros[37] (pl. 21).

I have mentioned the figures that emerge from altars and carry children in their arms (cf. pl. 22). Other figures hold objects like a chest[38] (pl. 23) or a cylindrical bar, such as is shown in the splendid Monument 11 from San Lorenzo[39] (pl. 24). The bars seem to be antecedents of the famous ceremonial staffs of the Maya stelae. The magnificent human figure from the crater of the San Martín Pajapan volcano (pl. 25) originally held a bar in its hands also;[40] the headdress of this figure bears an enormous mask with the open mouth of a jaguar.[41]

Another statue, number 8 from Laguna de los Cerros, seems to have been left unfinished[42] (pl. 26). But among all these the most magnificent work, although far smaller, is the famous "wrestler" from Santa María on the banks of the Uxpanapa River,[43] one of the greatest of Olmec works of art (pl. 27). This figure is realistic, as, centuries later, were to be many others, such as the Aztec green diorite squash or the grasshopper. The wrestler's anatomy, which is a proud example of the mas-

[35] Cruz del Milagro and La Venta, Monument 23; Drucker, Heizer, and Squier, 1959: pl. 52.

[36] They may have been antecedents of the Oaxaca urns which were to be so numerous later. Among these at least one is of stone, which makes it even closer in style to the seated Olmec sculptures.

[37] Medellín, 1960: pl. 23.

[38] For example, Monument 21 of La Venta, the so-called "Grandmother," which is really a man.

[39] Stirling, 1955: pl. 16.

[40] Beyer, 1927: fig. 41.

[41] Covarrubias, 1946: fig. on p. 80. Very recently an excavation at the site uncovered the missing part of the statue. It has been taken—finally complete—to the Museum of the University of Veracruz, and a photograph is available (pl. 25c) as this book goes to press. I publish the modest original sketch and Covarrubias' excellent drawing—now only of historical interest—because this matter illustrates the difficulties of full discovery and the time involved, and is an example—even if minor —of the procedure which must be followed toward fuller archaeological understanding.

[42] Medellín, 1960: pl. 22. A very similar one comes from Morelos, perhaps from Chalcatzingo.

[43] Corona, 1962: 12.

culine muscular system, reminds us also of a possible descendant: the "scribe" of Cuilapan of the Monte Alban II period (pl. 28).

Monument 13 at La Venta, variously described as an altar[44] and as a low column, is carved in bas relief and displays a man in profile wearing a headdress, breechclout, sandals, and jewels. Four glyphs surround him (pl. 29). The glyph on the left is a foot, probably the earliest appearance of this character so typical in all the writing of the highlands and also found in Oaxaca.

If my interpretation is correct, Monuments F and G of Tres Zapotes and Monument 6 at San Lorenzo are remarkable. The first two are in the form of a stem that ends in what is possibly a human or feline head or arm which might have been the end of a balustrade, though this does not seem probable since the stem is highly polished. This polish would be pointless if the latter were meant to remain hidden from view within a building. Monument F (pl. 30) shows a slight indentation down the center of the head. Monument 6 of San Lorenzo now consists of only a head, but the break suggests that there was a body and that it may have been in a reclining position. Thus, all three monuments give evidence of a horizontal surface or flat part which could have served as a seat; in this way they might be forerunners of the jaguar thrones in the Maya area. Furthermore, the indentation on one of the monuments, together with its reclining position, indicates the possibility that we might be dealing with an ancestor—a very vague one at that—of the Chacmools of Toltec and later art, the reclining figures with flexed knees. As the monuments lie at the entrance of a temple, the indentation might have been used for offerings.[45]

The standing human figure of massive proportions from Laguna de los Cerros[46] wears a breechclout and a long cape which reaches the ground (pl. 31). Since its head is lacking, it is not possible to be sure of its style, but it seems to me that it dates from a period later than the Olmecs.[47]

Another extraordinary sculpture is the recently discovered Monument 34 at San Lorenzo. It is "a magnificent half-kneeling figure from which the head had been knocked off before its burial. Perforated disks placed at the shoulders show that it was once fitted with movable arms,

[44] Drucker, 1952: 63 and 180.

[45] Stirling, 1955: 13. A fourth monument fits into this same group: one of those which today stand in the square at Santiago Tuxtla (Anton, 1961: pl. 10). It is possible that they were in a vertical position, with the face looking up, like the monkey at La Venta Park, Villahermosa. In that case they would not, of course, be chacmools.

[46] Medellín, 1960: pls. 24 and 25.

[47] The same is not true of the head from Estero Rabón (*ibid.*: pl. 1), which seems to belong to the Olmec period and is related to the jaguar men.

a gigantic version of the jointed figurines known in later Mesoamerican contexts. A concave disk-shaped ornament decorated with a six-pointed flower or star hangs from the neck. Altogether, it is in the purest Olmec sculptural style."

Finally we have the enormous mask from Medias Aguas,[48] which is 35.5 inches high and has a somewhat feline quality (pl. 32). It is the largest mask we know of in indigenous art, and one can hardly imagine what its function might have been. It may belong to a post-Olmec epoch, but the idea of wearing masks was present in the period that I call Olmec II.[49] The magnificent sculpture of a man with a jaguar mask, gazing at the sky[50] (pl. 33), and another small jade mask also appeared at La Venta.[51] Not to be forgotten is the Tuxtla statuette of a later period (pl. 47), showing a duck mask; the face of a bird on a human figure indicates the presence of masks.[52] The figure on Altar 7 at La Venta also wears a mask, perhaps that of a duck.

Feline masks also appear at times on human figures, but not in such a marked form as the following group, which can be classified as that of men-jaguars. Representations of men with animals and of man-animals or of humanized animals, which are so evident in Olmec art, were to be highly developed in Mesoamerica. But among the Olmecs the jaguar was the essential animal; very few others appeared.[53] When one attempts to classify human Olmec figures, without realizing it one passes to jaguar figures. Human countenances gradually acquire feline features.[54] Then they become half and half, and finally they turn into jaguars.[55] This is not an evolutionary process but is the result of a typology. What is important is the intimate connection between the man and the animal in the Olmec mind and the manner in which it was reflected in their art. We will deal with the religious implications later.

Three very similar monuments seem to throw light upon the origin

[48] *Ibid.*: pls. 4 and 5.

[49] The mask from Tres Zapotes—if it really is a mask—belongs to the Middle Period of this site (Drucker, 1952: 210 and pl. 66; Drucker, Heizer, and Squier, 1959: 299). They consider these two masks to be later than Phase III of La Venta.

[50] Westheim, 1955: 4.

[51] Drucker, Heizer, and Squier, 1959: fig. 43.

[52] *Ibid.*: fig. 35b; Drucker, 1952: pl. 65.

[53] A monkey from La Venta is in the museum at Villahermosa, and perhaps there is another (*ibid.*: 179). There is a noncharacteristic serpent in Potrero Nuevo (Stirling, 1955: 20), a cetacean from La Venta (Drucker, Heizer, and Squier, 1959: pl. 50), and perhaps another cetacean found by Piña Chán and still unpublished. Monument 43 at San Lorenzo may represent a fantastic eight-legged spider (Coe, 1967, photo 6).

[54] As in Monument 10 at San Lorenzo (Stirling, 1955: pl. 15).

[55] For example, Monument 2 at Río Chiquito or Monument 7 of San Lorenzo (*ibid.*: pls. 3a and c and 17a).

of the jaguar myth: Monument 3 at Potrero Nuevo,[56] Monument 1 at Río Chiquito,[57] and Monument 20 at Laguna de los Cerros[58] (pl. 34). According to Stirling these represent the copulation of a jaguar with a woman, but Medellín points out that the upper figure is a man and suggests that they have to do with the "subjection and humiliation of the conquered by the conqueror." Unfortunately the three stones are in such a poor state of preservation that it is impossible to describe their true significance with absolute certainty. Stirling's idea is very suggestive. We are reminded of the Chichimec legend, much later in time and much farther away in space, which refers to a man and to a female dog disguised as a woman; their sons were supposed to have originated the Chichimec tribe.

Many aspects of Mesoamerican religion suggest this carnal association of humans with animals. If our excavations have disclosed the true foundations of Mesoamerica and the beginning of so many of its basic ideas among the Olmecs—and everything seems to indicate that we have—it would not be strange to find this aspect too. In Olmec representation there is no pornographic art nor phallicism, in spite of isolated traits that are found in later times and data in the chronicles which indicate—especially in Veracruz—exacerbation of the sexual instinct. Phalli appear in isolated form in both Maya sites and in the highlands, and the Codex Borbonicus, an Aztec pictorial manuscript, depicts a clearly phallic ceremony. But in general the sexual act does not seem to have been exalted in the Mesoamerican world, nor the subject represented frequently.

An art form that was to last was that of the stone boxes or representations of these.[59] Monument C of Tres Zapotes (fig. 7) is outstanding for the incised scenes on its four sides. The Aztecs revived the art of carving stone boxes with special magnificence. It is not that this art had become lost but with the Aztecs, who were notable sculptors, it found new splendor, as it had had among the Olmecs, who were also notable sculptors.

Among the Olmec boxes we must include the sarcophagus of La Venta, which has a special feeling: it represents a jaguar holding the deceased person, just as in other sculptures live persons are represented

---

[56] *Ibid.*: pls. 25 and 26a.

[57] *Ibid.*: pl. 2.

[58] Medellín, 1960: pls. 27 and 28 and p. 95.

[59] Monuments B and C of Tres Zapotes (Stirling, 1943: 17–21) and Monument 15 of San Lorenzo (Stirling, 1955: pl. 20). It is not really a box but rather a solid cube. It could be, perhaps, a symbolic box. Probably a figure was once seated on top (*ibid.*: 16). If so, it could be a forerunner of the boxes that functioned like pedestals and held urns in the later periods at Monte Alban. They remind us also of the great hollow clay cubes from Veracruz, recently acquired by the National Museum, which supported figures.

in the jaguar's jaws (pl. 35). Perhaps through one of those mysterious associations between cultures, the splendid Aztec feline in the National Museum of Anthropology is a distant heir, not converted into a sarcophagus but into a *cuauhxicalli*. Instead of containing a dead person the *cuauhxicalli* contained only the human heart, which was ritually sacrificed (pl. 36). Simple though the La Venta sarcophagus is (it also has a lid with a slight depression in the middle, but without bas reliefs),[60] it is clearly an antecedent to the sarcophagus found in the magnificent tomb under the Temple of the Inscriptions in the Classic Maya city of Palenque in Chiapas.

MATERIALS USED

STONE

The abundance of great stone monoliths is even more extraordinary when we remember that we are dealing with an area where almost no stone is found. There has been much discussion regarding the sites where the Olmecs obtained their stone and how it was transported to La Venta and to other sites where it was lacking. Heizer and Williams[61] point out that a very few of the La Venta monuments are of andesite, very similar to that found on the banks of the Teapa River; the boulders there are undoubtedly derived from the volcano of La Unión. The great majority of the large stone sculptures at San Lorenzo and La Venta are carved from stone secured in the Tuxtla mountains from the slopes of an extinct Pliocene volcano (Cerro Cintepec) just south of Lake Catemaco. The great stones were apparently dragged on wooden sledges to the banks of the Coatzacoalcos River, and either rafted upstream to San Lorenzo or downstream to the ocean, along the shore, and then up the Tonalá River to La Venta. The source of the basalt columns found in abundance at La Venta is unknown, though it almost certainly lies in the Tuxtla mountains.

Monuments at Tres Zapotes and San Lorenzo are of the same material as those commonly found at La Venta, that is, of andesite. This may have been taken from western slopes of the Tuxtla mountains. Stirling has expressed the same opinion. The boulders for monuments carved in other types of stone probably came from the Tuxtla region. None of

[60] The only other probable sarcophagus occurs in Tlalancaleca, Puebla (Noguera, 1964). Undoubtedly it indicates how the idea—like so many others—survived for 2,000 years, in spite of having rarely been used. Monument 9 of San Lorenzo is not a sarcophagus but a container representing, perhaps, a duck. The wings are very reminiscent of a Zapotec style (Stirling, 1955: 13, and Caso and Bernal, 1952: fig. 303).

[61] Heizer and Williams, 1960; also Williams and Heizer, 1965.

these variants is found at La Venta. Serpentine and other types of schists used by the Olmecs undoubtedly came from the southern Sierra Madre mountains, between Tehuantepec and Tuxtla Gutierrez. Perhaps there, too, the Olmecs found the lustrous black ilmenite from which they formed their concave mirrors. This region is about 100 miles from La Venta.

Curtis[62] thinks that the limestone for some La Venta artifacts and utensils came all the way from Chinameca, which lies some forty miles to the west, and that other stone was brought from a region about sixty miles to the south. I wish to emphasize these data since, as we will see later on, they will help us to analyze the social and political organization of the Olmecs.

A great problem arises regarding several of the striking monoliths Medellín described from Laguna de los Cerros and Pilapan. He found most of them associated with ceramics pertaining to a period later than that which we call Olmec; in this case the monoliths do not correspond to Olmec culture either.[63] Thus, many of the pieces at the two sites have not been included in this chapter, since I agree that they belong to a later period. From their style, though, it is evident that several others described by Medellín actually *are* Olmec according to my definition, and do not belong to later cultures that flourished in the same area, although the successors preserved some of the elements of the mother culture. These objects are so similar to those at La Venta that it seems reasonable to consider them contemporaneous with it or with Tres Zapotes, where "the limited archeologic evidence all points toward a relatively early period for the larger stone monument. It appears likely that all of the major stones were carved before the beginning of upper Tres Zapotes and probably belong to the Lower and Lower Middle periods."[64] Perhaps I am committing a capital crime in preferring to base my judgment on the style rather than on the stratigraphic evidence from these monuments, but many of them may well have been moved in ancient times, as they were at La Venta, San Lorenzo, and Tres Zapotes.[65]

JADE

The Olmecs were not only the first and finest sculptors of Mexico; they were also the first to work jade and indubitably were the greatest in

[62] Curtis, 1959: 284–289.
[63] Medellín, 1960: 89, 90, 92.
[64] Stirling, 1943: 31.
[65] This reminds us of the problem so brilliantly resolved by Covarrubias when, against apparent stratigraphic and calendrical evidence, he held that Olmec art was Preclassic; this does not mean, of course, that conclusions based only on style are not dangerous.

this medium. No other pre-Hispanic people were capable of producing the infinity of jade objects with the mastery of the Olmecs. Their jade carving is so splendid that it is necessary to pause here a moment to discuss this material.

"Jade is a generic term used to designate several distinct mineral species . . . The word jade was derived from the Spanish term *piedra de ijada* or 'stone of the loin' in allusion to the virtue imputed to it of relieving pains of the side or of the kidneys. From the word jade was derived the specific name jadeite . . . The Spanish term, when translated into Latin became *lapis nephriticus*, from which was derived the name *nephrite*."[66]

Stirling[67] has summed up the aspects which interest us directly:

> The jade used by the Olmecs was jadeite, basically a silicate of sodium and aluminum. The ancient Chinese jades were nephrite, a calcium manganesium silicate. It was not until the eighteenth century that the Chinese began to import jade from Burma.
>
> In general, jadeite is the superior stone. It is somewhat harder than nephrite, has more luster after polishing, and the colors tend to be brighter. Furthermore, jadeite is of much rarer occurrence.
>
> The wide variety of colors and types of jadeite used indicates that the materials must have been supplied from many different sources. . . . two types of jade appear to have been especially prized. One of these was the precious transparent emerald-green variety, known to the Chinese as imperial or gem jade. The other was a beautiful, translucent blue form, identified as diopside jadeite. This latter was unknown in China.
>
> The term imperial jade has been frequently abused, often being applied to any type of unusually bright, green jade. True imperial jade was found at La Venta for the first time in the New World, heretofore being known only from Burma. Imperial jade does not occur in large masses.

With these materials the Olmecs, especially at La Venta, may be said to have practically discovered the secret of carving jade[68] and worked it to a perfection which no other people would achieve in the history of Mesoamerica.

> . . . the Olmecs loved jade, and in the hands of their artists it was shaped to suit their ends. With apparent disregard for the difficulties involved, the tough material was mastered as though it were a plastic. This is in contrast to most later American jade products, where obvious concessions were made to the original form of the material and the finished products usually had a rigidity not present in Olmec art. In this respect Olmec jades rival the finest Chinese pieces, and the polish and surface texture has not been excelled by modern lapidaries.[69]

Scholars such as Covarrubias, Stirling, and Drucker have investigated

[66] Foshag, 1957: 45.
[67] Stirling, 1961: 52.
[68] Emmerich, 1963: 59.
[69] Stirling, 1961: 50.

the techniques the Olmecs employed in this art; unfortunately, they have not discovered the work sites where the jade objects were produced and where the chips and remains of pieces broken or left incomplete can be found.[70]

As Stirling has pointed out (1961), carving was executed with stone implements. As a first step the natural block was studied and scraped in order to ascertain its quality. Then unnecessary parts were eliminated by percussion and the protuberances were removed by sawing. This must have been done with thin slabs of stone or perhaps with ceramic fragments especially prepared for the task.[71] Traces of sawing are evident on some pieces. By means of bores[72] fragments were removed and the main features of the figure were marked out. Perforations in pendants and beads were made in the same manner. The final form of the piece was obtained by means of rubbing, and it was later carefully polished, though we are not sure of the system used for this process. Eventually the object acquired the remarkable brilliance so typical of Olmec jades. It is evident that abrasives were not used, as these always leave a mark. Brilliance was achieved, rather, by rubbing with a hard implement, another jade or perhaps bamboo.[73] Perforations on the figurines were sometimes hidden by incrustations in the eyes and in the corners of the mouth.[74]

FIGURINES AND DEFORMATIONS

Certainly jade was not the only stone from which the Olmecs carved objects and figurines, all of which existed in great abundance. Many were made of serpentine and clay, of obsidian, amber, and amethyst. The human figurines possess the same physical and stylistic features as the great monoliths and also show the two ethnic types I have described earlier. The postures vary greatly: some figures stand, some lie, some are seated, and others are contorted. The association and confusion of human and feline features is also frequent.

[70] Drucker, 1952: 172. The fact that the workshops of the stone sculptors have not been found at La Venta suggests that the monoliths were carved at another site, although this seems unlikely because of their size and the difficulty of transporting them in a finished state. In reality these ateliers, which should exist (Heizer, 1962: 315), have not yet been discovered in excavations.

[71] Drucker, 1952: 144.

[72] These have not been found, but undoubtedly they were not of the tubular type characteristic of the Maya or of Oaxaca (*ibid.*: 72).

[73] Stirling, 1961.

[74] This aesthetic need to dissimulate the holes was repeated all through Mesoamerican art. At times the incrustations, or rather the plugs, were of the same material—jade, as in Palenque. I wonder to what extent this contributed to the idea of the fine stone mosaics so characteristic of this art in later periods but which had been initiated among the Olmecs. Drucker (1952: 72) mentions one of these mosaics at La Venta.

As is natural, the aesthetic level is uneven both in objects of daily use and in great works of art. In Tomb A of La Venta, for instance, two burials of juveniles were discovered. Each burial was accompanied by two figurines, one standing, the other seated (pl. 37). One of the latter, representing a female, is perhaps the most perfect figurine bequeathed to us by Olmec culture.[75]

The deformations which the Olmecs practiced on their own bodies (whether actual or only symbolical) are more clearly visible in the figurines than in the stone monuments.

The head was deformed by binding a small board in oblique position to the forehead of the newborn child until pressure gave the still-plastic cranium the desired form. Circular deformation was carried out also, and it has been suggested that the helmets on the colossal heads or on other figurines represent molds used to produce this deformation.[76] One of the most characteristic traits is a cleft in the form of a V in the upper part of the head,[77] which at times plainly becomes a hole (pl. 38). As this appears also in the figures of jaguars it may indicate the deep indention in the top of the skull of this animal.[78] Formerly it was thought that this cleft on human figures represented the type of cranial deformation called *bilobé* which was believed to be practiced by some groups. But it has since been demonstrated that this deformation is anatomically impossible and could not have been practiced by the Olmecs or any other group.[79]

The cleft, possibly representing some real feature, was transformed into a stylistic element which lost its significance even for its makers, although they continued to represent it over a long period in celts as well as in figurines. Teotihuacan II figurines at times show this trait. On the other hand, it does not appear at Monte Alban, in spite of the fact that many Olmec vestiges, particularly the jaguar, can be seen there. Thus I believe that if the cleft actually came into existence in representing the supraorbital cavities of the jaguar, the association was lost by the time the jaguar was represented at Monte Alban, where—if this animal is identical to the Olmec beast—it does not have the V-form cleft.[80] The

---

[75] *Ibid.*: 154.

[76] Dávalos and Ortiz de Zárate, 1953: 99.

[77] *Mayas y Olmecas*, 1942: 45.

[78] Drucker, 1952: 178. Michael Coe writes in a personal letter: "This cleft has long puzzled me. I would now agree with you that it is a natural feature of the living jaguar, for on a recent visit to the Regent's Park and Washington zoos I have noted that on full-grown male jaguars there is a pronounced furrow on the top of the head, where the rather loose scalp has been almost folded over."

[79] Dávalos and Ortiz de Zárate, 1953.

[80] It is possible that the clasp of the headdress of Cocijo or the tigers on Epoch I urns from Monte Alban represent an element associated, in a certain manner, with

V cut sometimes is shown as a furrow crossing the head, as in a small sculpture found at El Tejar (pl. 39), but this site is outside the Metropolitan Olmec entity.[81] On other figurines the heads are shaved or have only a roll of hair down the center.

Perforations of the septum of the nose[82] must have been practiced, since nose plugs are represented in sculptures. Dental deformation was frequent (fig. 9). Although, as I have said, there are no skeletal Olmec remains, the existence of the practice of dental deformation can be ascertained by studying the figurines and the later burials found in the area and by comparing them with skeletons from other contemporaneous sites. The common type of mutilation is A2,[83] the serration found on figures in both El Arbolillo and Upper Tres Zapotes. For example, the famous Offering 4 of La Venta contained sixteen figurines grouped into a scene (pl. 40). Six of these, and perhaps four more, displayed mutilated teeth.[84] This group, incidentally, is strongly reminiscent of the offering of musicians at Monte Alban or of grouped figures found in western Mexico, even though the style and epoch are different.

Fig. 9. Types A2 and D4 mutilations.

A-2   D-4

Another transformation of the face, this time only stylistically, consists of the man-jaguar, and many times the child-jaguar, association. In this case human and feline features are combined; usually the mouth is the animal's and the other features are human.

I have already described the characteristics (perhaps real) of the bodies; although the latter were almost always masculine the genital organs were never carved, even though the figure was usually nude. I do not believe this to be the result of modesty; perhaps it had something to do with the curious insistence in Olmec art in representing pathological human figures. Perhaps the figures are of eunuchs. There are also

the V cleft of Olmec figurines. This element was later transformed into Glyph C of the Classic Zapotec period (Caso and Bernal, 1952: fig. 27 a, b).

[81] Cranial deformation was very common in Mesoamerica and must have been especially so in this area. As late as 1580 the *Relación de Tuxtla* mentioned this as characteristic: ". . . the mothers and the midwives squeezed the heads, and the heads became almost wide" (Medina, 1905: 51).

[82] Awls have been found which were probably used for this operation as well as for piercing ears (Drucker, 1952: 169). This custom, which began here and continued to be practiced throughout Mesoamerica, is vividly represented in the Mixtec codices.

[83] Romero, 1958: table facing p. 94.

[84] Drucker, Heizer, and Squier, 1959: 161.

figures of dwarfs (pl. 41) and hunchbacks[85] and quite realistic representations of sick persons, perhaps lepers, of cretins with thyroid deficiency, and of overweight people with glandular imbalance.[86]

In different forms and in different degrees of intensity all these aspects were to continue throughout Mesoamerica in succeeding centuries. Cranial deformation, the perforated septum, and mutilated teeth are characteristic. The representation of monsters is less frequent after the Olmec period, and yet it appears everywhere, including western Mexico, which is not typically Mesoamerican. Moctezuma himself was found surrounded by dwarfs and hunchbacks, according to the conquistadores. These unfortunates were a source of magical terror and the basis of innumerable superstitions.

Following ancient tradition the Olmecs also made clay figurines which are, unlike the stone figures, almost always feminine. Though it is true that in their simplicity they resemble (and may even be confused with) their sisters of the Preclassic period, some types undoubtedly belong to the style of the monoliths and jades, even though work in clay is so different from that in stone. The figurines are almost always modeled by hand, that is, without the use of molds. Nearly all are solid,[87] but occasionally larger figurines were produced and these are hollow. The Olmecs actually discovered the art of hollow figures, technically far more difficult to produce than the solid ones and with serious firing problems.[88] Solid figurines measuring more than a foot in height were even more difficult to produce and lacked the delicacy of the hollow ones. Some of the latter were covered with a coat of white kaolin which makes them extraordinarily attractive; this is a refinement which, like the hollow figures in general, is quite frequent among the Colonial Olmecs.

The La Venta figurines belong to some of the same types as those of Tres Zapotes, which again demonstrates a partial contemporaneity of the two sites and proves that the figurines can be called Olmec since they are

[85] Drucker (1952: 119 and pl. 51b) has suggested that these hunchbacks may be, perhaps, dancers. The famous jade figurine of a person in reclining position, unfortunately without exact provenance (Stirling, 1961: fig. 4), also reminds us of its contemporaries, the "dancers" at Monte Alban.

[86] Dávalos and Ortiz de Zárate, 1953: 101–102.

[87] Drucker, 1943: 77.

[88] Emmerich, 1963: 62. A large, hollow baby face came from La Venta (Delgado, 1965: fig. 17, left), and we are acquainted with another, like those of Morelos, bought by Seler in Tuxtla; it is probable that the piece came not far from that city (see Lehmann, 1921: 24 [no. 25] and pl. 25). It is a typical child made of white clay. which Lehmann thinks is of "Olmec style perhaps already influenced by the Spaniards" (sic). Another of these figurines comes from Tonalá (Joyce and Knox, 1931). They are also found in the valleys of Mexico and Morelos, the coast of Veracruz, and in El Salvador (Delgado, 1965), as well as in the state of Chiapas and at Teotitlan del Camino in Oaxaca (Lehmann, 1921). Many beautiful ones come from Las Bocos in the state of Puebla (Coe, 1965A).

A   B   C 5

C 9   D 1   D 2

baby face   K

Fig. 10. Different types of clay figurines.

typical of the entire area. These have been found, but in small numbers, at other sites.

The problem of the classification of Olmec clay figurines is somewhat confusing. The two classifications made by Drucker,[89] although extremely useful, are difficult to interpret. More recently new ideas, which have made the situation somewhat clearer, have appeared[90] (fig. 10).

---

[89] Drucker, 1943: 115, calls them IA, IC, and IIE. In 1952: 141 and 227 he calls them I-A-I, III-A-I and III-A-2, although he introduces a doubt (p. 227) regarding the true relationship of the Olmec type with the A of the Valley of Mexico.

[90] Drucker, Heizer, and Squier, 1959, and Piña Chán, 1964. Unfortunately Piña's valuable book was mutilated by the editor, eliminating illustrations and parts of the text.

Thanks to them one can arrive at the conclusion that in the Olmec area the most important types of figurines are those labeled A, which look more primitive;[91] D, the pretty lady type,[92] and the "baby face"; the latter sometimes turns into a baby jaguar in the jade sculptures and carved celts. Type A and the baby face type, which had been called thus by Vaillant in dealing with highland material, occur from the earliest levels at both La Venta and Tres Zapotes. Piña Chán (1964) does not indicate which types appeared in the oldest stratus, but in the second level he found baby faces. Type D appears later. I insist on the chronological position of each one of these because of the importance of making clear the area in which a cultural trait appears for the first time, and especially in this case, since it is one more argument showing that Olmec culture originated in the coastal area and not in any other, as some scholars have proposed.

DRESS AND ORNAMENT

Much of the clothing and personal adornment shown on the figurines and stone monuments is common to all the Preclassic people, inherited from the earliest origins of Mesoamerica. Other items of dress are inventions or transformations introduced by the Olmecs.

Men wore several types of breechclouts, the ends of which were rarely decorated; sometimes the breechclout is a short skirt sustained by a band with a fastening[93] but lacking the apron that appears in later cultures. Occasionally they also wore something similar to tunics or mantles (for example, in Stela 2 and in Monument 19 of La Venta [see pl. 17 and fig. 6, above]). Women wore only a skirt and a belt.[94] Sandals, as in Monument 13 of La Venta,[95] are shown rarely, though they were probably worn even in fairly remote times. It is possible that the great masses of people went about entirely naked in everyday life. However, the manner of representing dress is one of the distinguishing traits of Olmec art.

On the other hand, headdresses are extraordinarily complicated and must have been fabricated not only of cloth but also of fairly hard material such as leather, with a framework of reed. In Olmec art one can see everything from the simple turban to majestic structures which could only have been worn on ceremonial occasions. The use of enormous

[91] Weiant, 1943: 12.
[92] *Mayas y Olmecas*, 1942: 77.
[93] Piña Chán, 1964: 399 and figs. 30 and 32.
[94] Weiant, 1943: 99. Even today they do not wear blouses at home. Braids are woven with red ribbons and with flowers (Covarrubias, 1946: 43–44).
[95] Drucker, 1952: fig. 61.

headdresses was to prevail through Mesoamerican history, but the chin strap which held the headdress in place and was utilized throughout the Olmec period was to disappear gradually. In the Maya zone it occurs only in the most ancient sculptures.[96]

The appearance of true hats with brims, which is not at all typical of the New World, is extremely interesting. These hats were decorated with tassels or hanging beads, such as can be seen at Monument 14 of San Lorenzo (south side), which resemble the modern Huichol hat. Piña Chán[97] believes that the decorations represent drops of water. During Period I at Monte Alban, there are occasional representations of straw hats worn by the so-called danzantes, or dancing figures.[98] Olmec hats were perhaps made of the same material.

Not one fragment of Olmec cloth has been preserved, and we can speak of textiles only through the dress shown on the sculptures. It is to be assumed that the Olmecs cultivated and spun cotton but did not employ clay spindle whorls. These were possibly a later invention of the highlands. An exception is Upper Tres Zapotes, a post-Olmec period imbued with foreign influences.[99]

It is easy to imagine the magnificence of some of the textiles, adorned with small perforated plaques of rock crystal similar to sequins.[100] Similar plaques, of mother-of-pearl, were discovered at Monte Alban from Period II. They were cut in various forms and were probably used for the same purpose.

Adornment was much more complex than dress; during the Olmec period there existed the entire gamut of ornaments which was to last until the end of the Pre-Columbian age. There were ornaments of jade, of stone, and surely others of perishable materials (pl. 42). Noseplugs were in the form of a bead (for example, in Monuments 13 and 19 of La Venta), and tubular plugs were unknown; both simple and complex earplugs existed, made with either one or two jade beads.[101] It may be said that all this elaboration was a direct antecedent of the more complicated earplugs to be worn later, for instance, by the chieftain buried in the tomb of the Temple of the Inscriptions at Palenque. Besides bracelets and anklets, the Olmecs wore necklaces of beads in many forms and sizes, many of which were to be reproduced up to the Spanish conquest. Necklaces were sometimes composed of several strings, with

[96] Morley, 1938: vol. 4: 304.
[97] Piña Chán, 1964: 46 and fig. 43.
[98] Bernal, 1947.
[99] Drucker, 1943: 86; and Drucker, 1952: 143.
[100] Drucker, 1952: 70, 163, and pl. 58; and Drucker, Heizer, and Squier, 1959: 149.
[101] Drucker, Heizer, and Squier, 1959: 149, 162, and fig. 45; and Drucker, 1952: 161 and pl. 57.

or without pectoral pendants. The pendants vary greatly; some are abstract, and some are realistic, like the representations of split jaguar eye teeth or parts of the human body (hands, legs, fingers, or ears), the jaws of animals or tail of rays. Others, of fine stone, are in the form of an animal's head[102] similar to those to be fabricated two thousand years later in the Mixteca, the northwestern portion of Oaxaca.[103] At times the eyes of the animal heads were inlaid, as was to be done in Aztec times. Some of these ornaments are made up of twin parts.[104]

Especially remarkable are pendants composed of magnetite mirrors or of ilmenite, such as appear on the famous female figurine from Tomb A of La Venta (pl. 37a) or on Monument 23 or Altar 5 at the same site. At least eight of these mirrors have been unearthed (pl. 43). They "stand out as the most unique pieces of precision stoneworking."[105] "No verbal description can give an idea of the remarkable quality of the technical and artistic quality of the mirrors of La Venta."[106]

Frequently in Olmec sculpture there appear certain bearded personages, though their beards give the impression of being false. Perhaps they were meant to give greater dignity to the man who wore them.

Probably bodies and faces were painted according to a universal custom which was not absent in Mesoamerica, judging by the cylindrical seals which have been found and which were applied to the body with a rotary motion. They are ceramic,[107] and the motifs are geometrical. Flat seals showing figures are almost surely late and were influenced by other

---

[102] *Ibid.*: pl. 54d.

[103] Bernal, 1949: 64.

[104] Piña Chán, 1964: 26.

[105] Drucker, Heizer, and Squier, 1959: 196.

[106] Even though the dimensions and focal distances vary, probably depending upon the original block, all the mirrors are similar and therefore represent a cultural tradition and not an accident. Their polish is so extraordinary that it reaches the limit of possible perfection. This was not accomplished with the use of abrasives, for the microscope does not reveal traces that these would necessarily have left. The excellent study that I have summarized here indicates that the radius of curvature becomes progressively greater as one nears the edge of the mirror; the curve in all these examples is very similar and so perfect that it is not possible to reconstruct the technique employed to fabricate these concave mirrors. Perhaps they could serve as a camera obscura. Gullberg (1959: 280–288) does not find similarities with mirrors from other parts. Undoubtedly they show one of the most notable technical advances of the Olmecs. In a letter Dr. Heizer tells me, "At elevation of 2100 meters in the Sierra Nevada Mountains in California, where the ultraviolet intensity is much greater than at sea level, tests made with the La Venta concave mirrors showed them to be completely ineffective in generating fire. The focal length of the mirrors is so long that it is impossible to concentrate enough heat to start a fire. I believe there is no possibility that the La Venta mirrors figured in fire generation." As a hypothesis we should keep in mind that in this area in the sixteenth century mirrors were used for magical purposes in healing (Dahlgren, 1953: 147).

[107] Drucker, 1952: 142, pl. 42.

areas.[108] Among the Olmecoids many figurines with painted bodies and faces are to be found.

AXES AND CELTS

The Olmecs fashioned implements, ornaments, and numerous other objects of jade and green stone. Plain axes or celts were common; these played an extremely important role in the daily life of men who lived in thickly grown forest areas where it was necessary to fell trees in order to clear fields for cultivation. The wood from these trees was indispensable for roofs, walls, and for hundreds of objects and implements of daily use. Thus, celts have been unearthed in great numbers, above all in the ritual offerings at La Venta; actually they are similar to those which have been fabricated throughout the entire world since Neolithic times. In Mexico their manufacture was to continue until the Aztec period. Forms vary slightly but the basic elements are always preserved, and among lithic instruments they are remarkable.

At the same time we have some Olmec celts which have ceased to be practical instruments: they are now ritual objects. Most of them, made of serpentine, are simple and perhaps try to simulate, through their color, those of jade, though the softness of serpentine makes them useless for cutting wood. These ritual objects, while retaining their customary form, were admirably carved with figures of the man-jaguar[109] and constitute one of the most characteristic elements of Olmec style. As they have been found scattered in very different sites all over Mesoamerica they may be Olmec objects—or they may be Olmecoid. Nevertheless, one must not forget that, since these stones are small and easily carried from place to place, the site where they were found is not significant, except on the rare occasions where they were unearthed in a scientific manner. But as one of them was found in Tomb E at La Venta[110] (pl. 38) it is evident that they form part of the Olmec heritage. Therefore, I will call them Olmec objects. Wicke has gathered eighteen examples[111] which, except for the one from La Venta, were not excavated scientifically. So it is impossible to attribute to them an exact date, a precise provenance, or a definite chronological order.

[108] Drucker, 1943: 87.

[109] Since Neolithic times some groups had special cults of celts. Regarding Mesoamerica, Covarrubias (1957: 71) remembers that—as in the Mixtec myth—the sky rests on the edge of an ax, and Caso (1965: 11) thinks that the celts possibly represented the thunderbolt.

[110] Drucker, 1952: pl. 56.

[111] Wicke, 1965: pl. 37. Piña Chán (1964: unnumbered plate) publishes another of gray stone. Except for the material the piece is characteristically Olmec. Its provenance is the coast of Veracruz.

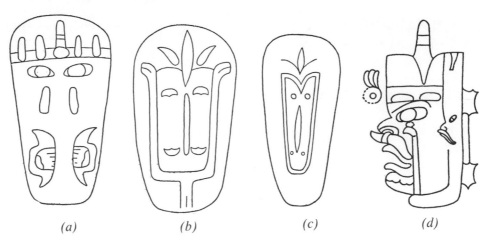

(a)   (b)   (c)   (d)

Fig. 11. Celts from La Venta.

Through seriation, however, Wicke has managed to classify the celts into two principal groups, within which an order of antiquity is given for each piece. He reaches the conclusion that these celts or ceremonial axes in general precede the great Olmec II period, because one of the latest of his first group is precisely that found in Tomb E of La Venta, which corresponds to that period. Therefore, the others should be earlier. But there is an objection to this conclusion: Tomb E belongs to Phase IV of that site,[112] the most recent in the Olmec II period. Even if one accepts the results of Wicke's seriation, it is possible that the earlier ceremonial celts correspond, rather, to phases I and III of La Venta, and are within the Olmec II epoch.

Besides these carved axes there are others only engraved with incised lines which form motifs. Those of La Venta (fig. 11) bear stylized human faces[113] or countenances of the man-jaguar[114] or other motifs. They are carved in different types of stone. Even though they are inferior to the stone sculptures, there is a marked stylistic relationship to them. On the other hand the great votive axes have not been found in the Olmec area; therefore I deduce that they are Olmecoid.

Among the implements discovered are the following: needles, hooks, spatulas, and awls (pl. 44). Besides jade and other stones the Olmecs imported amber and perhaps obsidian to make blades.[115] The last two were brought in in small quantities since they were not important to this culture.

[112] Drucker, Heizer, and Squier, 1959: 273.
[113] Drucker, 1952: fig. 47; and Drucker, Heizer, Squier, 1959: fig. 35c.
[114] *Ibid.*: figs. 35e, 36a, b, d, and 4θ.
[115] The obsidian comes from far away, from Cerro de las Navajas in Hidalgo (Heizer, personal communication). Green obsidian from this source was traded south to the Maya area and has been identified at the sites of Chichen Itza and Kaminaljuyu.

CERAMICS

The study of ceramics has at times become a simple game of classification and tabulation, losing sight of many important conclusions which could be obtained from the material to be analyzed. This situation forced Vaillant to state, with good reason, that in such a case archaeology is in danger of becoming an obscure branch of mathematics. Seen within its cultural context, however, and keeping in mind its true aim, ceramic classification is indispensable and is almost the only basis—at the present time—for establishing chronologies and understanding the relationships between different sites or areas in Mesoamerica. In this book I will not attempt a minute description of every ceramic type; this is the responsibility of highly specialized works. Ceramic studies will only be mentioned to the degree that they are necessary to the aims expressed above.

In the Olmec zone only the ceramics unearthed at La Venta and Tres Zapotes have been classified, and we have meager information regarding other sites. Ceramic ware from La Venta is similar to that of Tres Zapotes. This is extremely important, as it again proves that these two sites were at least partially contemporaneous. And what little we know of San Lorenzo indicates that it too was inhabited at the same time.[116] Above all, it permits us to speak not only of the ceramics of a single site but of "Olmec" ceramics as a whole. One of the aims of this book can be attained: that of studying, not the different sites which have been explored, but the culture which produced them.

It is only natural that there be contrasts in the ceramics of La Venta and Tres Zapotes; this is reassuring since—if absolute identity had been discovered—it would indicate errors on the part of the archaeologists. In fact, there are no two identical ceramic sites in Mesoamerica or anywhere else in the world, for that matter. Local specialization is typical of all human cultures and can be applied as much to objects as to ideas or to language. It has not been until our own times that this differentiation has come to take on a national character. From day to day the original intonation and accent of the provinces are being lost. Although numerous differences are noticeable within the same Indian language from region to region, dialectic differences are less obvious in Spanish. Great differences in Spanish pronunciation now occur only on national levels. This is due to transportation facilities, human mobility, and the widespread trade of our times in contrast with the sedentary ways and difficult communications of the past.

In general, Olmec ceramic ware is badly preserved because of the dampness and acidity of the soil, but, even so, it is evident that the

---

[116] Drucker, 1947: 6.

Olmecs were not great potters nor did they dedicate their interest and talent to this minor art, as Drucker has noted.

Olmec pottery, like most others, includes both coarse and fine pastes.[117]

(1) Coarse brown, which is the most abundant. Sherds of this type made up 42.2 percent of the total at La Venta and 54.4 percent at Tres Zapotes. At times it bears a red or white wash and on very rare occasions—late, I suspect—it is bichrome, since it associates the two colors. It first makes its appearance in the most ancient strata at both cities.

(2) Coarse buff makes up 23.8 percent of the total ceramic finds at La Venta. Because of differences in the methods of classification followed at Tres Zapotes, it was not recognized by archaeologists at that site, though it definitely exists there (Drucker, 1952: 89).

(3) Coarse white accounts for only 4 percent of the pottery at La Venta, but it is more abundant at Tres Zapotes. However, the type is not identical at the two sites, and therefore the comparison is not valid. It appears from the first stratum.

(4) Other coarse types of minor importance complete the total percentage.

The fine paste types are thinner, with a harder and more porous paste. Many variants of color are found, but orange, buff, gray, and black predominate. These fine paste types make up about one-quarter of all the pottery studied at La Venta and a quarter of that at Tres Zapotes as well. In the lowest strata of the latter site they are either scarce or nonexistent, but their number increases in the higher levels of the pit. That is, they belong rather to the end of the Middle Period at Tres Zapotes.

Two types, small in percentage, are important only because they are typical of the Olmec world. One of them is a gray or black ware with white blotching on the rims.[118] There are variants of this type both in La Venta and in Tres Zapotes, where it is also found in the earliest levels. The other type, with a white surface, is especially important also because of its widespread distribution. Although it changes from place to place, variants are found almost everywhere in the Olmec world. Probably the figurines with kaolin could be considered a development of this type.

In general terms it may be said that Olmec pottery is monochrome, since painted ware at La Venta accounts for only one out of every thousand of the total found. The fabrication is so simple that, rather than being painted, it seems stained with color.

The figures I have cited are percentages of all ceramics recorded for Period II. They give us, therefore, a general idea of known ceramics, but it is clear that they vary from stratum to stratum. Nevertheless, the study of the ceramic problem is not the aim of this book; I only wish to describe the Olmec complex without having to take into consideration the different strata, which are not significant in themselves since we are

---

[117] The characteristic coarse Olmec types seem to be:

[118] This result is achieved by a special firing technique. Curiously, we find it later in the Mixtec region.

dealing with one great epoch. Later we will analyze data that permits us to divide this long epoch into different periods.

In Olmec I Piña Chán has found the same types and some that differ. They are finer than the ones mentioned above, possibly because Olmec Period I produced a larger quantity of ceramics than Olmec Period II. Or it may be because the ceramics found in other explorations in this same epoch are so badly eroded that they give the impression of being coarser than they actually were in their time.[119]

Ceramic shapes are relatively varied but fall within a restricted pattern (pl. 45). For instance, we have the cylindrical bowls with turned or beveled simple rim; conical bowls or bowls with round bases; neckless ollas, vessels of composite silhouette, vases with annular flanges, and various types of jars, bottles, forms, and censers. Handles are rare except among the ollas, and the latter never have feet (actually, the only one found at La Venta was probably imported). The annular base is frequently found.

One should not forget that the number of complete or restorable ceramic pieces found at La Venta and Tres Zapotes is very small. From the former site we have fewer than two dozen, and from the latter (Olmec Period II) we have even fewer. This means that at the present time there is an enormous margin for error in our assumptions; at the same time it presents the hope that future excavations can amplify or modify our ideas regarding Olmec ceramics. Nevertheless, even though complete ceramic pieces are extremely scarce, potsherds are relatively abundant (24,000 of them have been studied at La Venta), though these are hardly comparable to the millions that have been collected at the great sites in the highlands of Mexico.

As a general rule decoration was incised on Olmec ware before firing.[120] The motifs are simple. It is curious that the finest and most beautiful ceramic ware is found at the sites belonging to the Colonial Olmecs and the Olmecoids and not in the Metropolitan area. This may be due to the fact that in other regions the Olmec style adapted itself to a more firmly rooted, ancient ceramic tradition,[121] and, as it was practically the only existing art form, all the interest of the people was directed toward it. This was not the case among the Olmecs proper nor among the people of such Olmecoid sites as Monte Alban or Izapa.

It is interesting that the Olmecs did not fabricate their ceramics for ceremonial purposes. I think that, aside from an exception or two, all

---

[119] Piña Chán, 1964, and personal communication.

[120] We occasionally find other types of decoration, such as modeling, among the effigy vessels, and rocker stamping or dotting in the coarser pottery.

[121] Nevertheless, Piña Chán found in La Venta—although in very fragmentary form—incised ceramics with motifs derived from the jaguar, more complex than those discovered previously.

was made for domestic use. By this I do not mean that ceremonialism was unimportant to the Olmecs, but that clay objects were not highly prized for ritual, judging by the few examples of ware of this type that have been unearthed. What a sharp contrast to later Mesoamerica!

If food was cooked in clay pots surely other types of household vessels were used, such as calabashes and gourds, a practice which continues to the present day. Maize and other seeds were ground on stone metates with long pestles,[122] but it is possible that the tortilla had not yet been invented. The tortilla, unleavened corn bread, was later to become the bread of Mesoamerican peoples and even today is the staple of Mexican diet. As a matter of fact, *comales*—griddles for baking tortillas—have been discovered from the late archaeological periods,[123] not in the Valley of Mexico but at Monte Alban I, where perhaps the only two complete specimens from ancient times have survived. Is it possible that this utensil indispensable for cooking the tasty tortilla was invented in the Valley of Oaxaca? The comal has almost died out in our present machine age.

Ceramics also provide some information on the amusements of the Olmecs. Certain clay discs 1 1/2 inches in diameter could have been markers for a game.[124]

It is certain that the courts for the ball game, which later were to become so common in Mesoamerica, did not exist at that time. It is possible, however, that the Olmecs practiced this sport in open fields— as it seems probable that the people of Teotihuacan did later. This must have been the case also among the Olmecoids—at Izapa, for example—where there are indications that the ball game existed. The rubber from which the balls were made is found from the Olmec area and gives its name to the area and to the inhabitants, even though this name may have been applied in later times. As Aguirre Beltrán (1955) has pointed out, several sites bear names related to heads or decapitation, and later we will see that there is an intimate connection between the ball game and decapitation. Piña Chán also corroborates this idea and suggests that the colossal heads may be monuments in honor of decapitated or immortalized champions.[125]

The most ancient of the arts, music, is modestly represented by a few ceramic whistles, ocarinas, simple flutes, and panpipes,[126] but I believe them all to be of a later period. It is possible that most Olmec musical instruments were fabricated from perishable materials. This again leads us to consider how little we know of the Olmec world. As

---

[122] Drucker, 1952: 144.
[123] Drucker, 1943: 101.
[124] *Ibid.*: 87, and Drucker, 1952: 143.
[125] Piña Chán, 1964: 48.
[126] Drucker, 1943: 88.

a matter of fact, the Olmecs must have used wood for their first sculptures and even for their architecture, since it was the only material they had at hand. And even though—at the expense of enormous labor—they managed to carve a few great monoliths and a few pieces of jade, most of the objects (for either ritual or daily use) were made of wood until the very end.[127] Everything has turned to dust because of the same destructive humidity which eliminated every trace of cloth, basketry, animal skins, and even bone and shell implements.

It seems an irony of fate that we can situate the Olmecs among other civilized peoples only through stone monuments and jade figurines. It was precisely that same stone and jade that was exotic to them because they came from far-off lands. So it is that again I lament the tremendous limitations suffered by the archaeologist. Without those stone and jade objects Olmec life and social organization could scarcely be conjectured, but this is also a proof of the marvelous possibilities of archaeology, which has managed to found serious hypotheses on such a scarcity of surviving evidence. The archaeologist's time and work have turned these meager remains into historical facts—with all the accuracy obtainable for our purposes.

[127] The famous wooden mask, miraculously preserved, now in the American Museum of Natural History, is the only object of this material that has survived. Although it is Olmecoid (for it comes from Guerrero), it suffices to give us an idea of what has been lost.

4

OLMEC SOCIETY

TRADE AND WAR

As I have mentioned, the Olmec way of life was based upon a farming economy—as Mesoamerica was to be throughout the entire course of its history—complemented by the products of hunting, fishing, and food gathering. It was probably due to the special conditions of the area that the gradual increase in population became possible. In time, at the end of the Olmec Period I, this led to demographic pressure, perhaps causing Olmec expansion toward territories that lay far beyond the Metropolitan zone. This expansion within the Mesoamerican sphere turned out to be as important and fruitful as Greek expansion under Alexander; the repercussions of Hellenistic expansion are comparable to the repercussions produced by a similar Olmec movement.

But Olmec economy could not be sustained for a long period nor carry out its vast expansion without another basis aside from agriculture and natural products. I believe that this second source of wealth was trade. We do not have direct evidence of trade, but we do have bases to suppose it: in numerous sites far from the Metropolitan zone Olmec objects have been discovered and the direct influence of this people can be felt. I will deal with these influences later; for the moment it is enough to make clear that their existence could only have been made possible by direct commercial contacts. It is indubitable that there were places outside the Metropolitan area which were inhabited by Olmecs and that there are other sites where Olmec culture apparently fused with an older and more modest local one in order to form from these two roots a more highly developed culture. These sites at times were isolated, such as Tlatilco, but frequently they occupied an entire area, such as the Valley of Oaxaca. Therefore, it is possible that there may have been regions where the Olmecs held a clearly defined but limited position, a sort of "commercial consulate" defended by soldiers. In other regions they occupied an entire area, perhaps thus forming separate and partially autonomous states, though depending culturally and perhaps to some extent politically on the Olmec homeland.

In explorations of the Metropolitan area—within the Olmec period —no discoveries have been made of manufactured objects from outside: on the contrary, everything seems to have been made at the site. On the other hand, we do find objects which are without any doubt Olmec—not Olmecoid—in such faraway places as Monte Alban, Tlatilco, and even Central America. These objects, small and precious, occasionally of jade, almost surely were made in the Olmec zone and exported.

Archaeology shows us that Olmec trade consisted not only of exporting manufactured objects but in importing natural products to be worked in the region itself. As we have seen, the great stones from which the monoliths were carved came, in many cases, from outside the Metropolitan area. Serpentine, andesite, schists, chromite, cinnabar,[1] and organic materials that have disintegrated, had to come from different and often distant zones, as has been shown for jade, which has many provenances. Thus it seems that the Olmecs imported raw materials—and probably seeds and other products that have not been preserved—and exported manufactured items.[2]

Everything seems to indicate that the imported pieces were of a considerable weight and size, while exported objects were small. The natural roads, the rivers, lent themselves admirably for such trade, since the main waterways flow from outside the Olmec area inward. Evidently, they constitute a centripetal force by means of which heaviest

[1] Heizer, 1962: 314.

[2] These relations between the Olmec world and other areas that to a certain extent formed part of this world—although only temporarily—seem to be contradicted by a theme that appears consistently in works by the authors who have dealt most extensively with the Olmecs and have carried out many of the important excavations in the area. For example, Drucker (1947: 8, and 1952: 232) claims that the Olmec culture developed without outside stimulus and that the region was isolated during the most important Olmec period, Middle Tres Zapotes—La Venta (Olmec II). I do not believe this to be true. Drucker's earlier point of view is explained by the chronological position in which he placed the Olmec culture. As he believed that it was contemporaneous with the Mesoamerican Classic and yet did not find reflections of the Classic in it, he assumed this isolation. In reality the Olmec culture is older than the Classic, and therefore could not contain Classic traits.

materials can be made to float downstream and only the small objects had to go against the current. This is contrary to what usually occurs in Mesoamerica, where the rivers generally flow from the center of a culture area toward the periphery.

If it is valid to judge by later conditions in Mesoamerica, trade does not necessarily indicate peace. On the contrary, Mesoamerican commerce seems intimately bound to conquest, and trade existed on a great scale among people who possessed armies to back the activities of the merchants. In later times it was this way; the Aztec merchant did not leave the limits of the empire unless he was accompanied by soldiers or unless he was a soldier himself. In general the pattern was to conquer or at least to occupy some fortified sites as a first step. From that nucleus a network of direct commercial transactions was established and tribute was exacted from subjected peoples—a policy which was intimately tied to the activity of the merchants. Without tribute and merchants one cannot understand the Aztec state, nor, probably, its forerunners in the highlands. We cannot be sure that the same situation prevailed in the Olmec period or that tribute was received from conquered peoples, since we are not even sure the Olmecs did conquer other peoples. I merely suggest the possibility.

We know nothing about Olmec armies or possible military feats. Aside from the historical fact that no state can stand for a long period without the support of military forces, ideas of warlike activity are indicated in Olmec art in a concrete way. For instance, on Altar 4 of La Venta (pl. 14) a human figure bound by a cord suggests a captive. Monument C at Tres Zapotes (fig. 7) shows scenes of war and combat. A trophy head is probably represented on Stela A from Tres Zapotes and on Stela D a kneeling figure also suggests that he is the victim of conquest. The representation of an obsidian-edged sword[3] would indicate the same. From stelae A and D of Tres Zapotes we know that the Olmecs possessed lances and knives.

As we will see later, it is possible that the Olmecs practiced human sacrifice. The latter was an institution—judging by later situations—associated with war and which did not exist in Mesoamerica without warlike activities. Perhaps the Olmec state initiated the pattern in which the war of conquest was to become a permanent factor.

Though it is true that there are few representations of warriors we must remember that these are not especially characteristic of Mesoamerica and, as Caso[4] has pointed out, even among the warlike Aztecs they are rare.

---

[3] Drucker, 1952: 202. Jiménez Moreno correctly believes that, although the *atlatl* or throwing stick does not appear in the representations, it must have been known (1959).

[4] Caso, 1965: 42.

THE STATE

It is only natural that the possible existence of the state as such among the Olmecs cannot be proved; we can only offer a few hypotheses based on archaeological remains. By its very definition the term "state" signifies a fairly elaborate society under conditions that are far more advanced than an earlier tribal organization. The concept of state also requires a fairly clear differentiation of social classes. I have already mentioned Olmec farmers, lapidaries, sculptors, and a number of other groups whose activities imply professional dedication.

Piña Chán[5] has listed some of these activities, which, because of their simplicity, do not require specialists nor professionals, since an individual could combine farming and pottery making—which was quite rudimentary—with the weaving of textiles, baskets, or mats; or with carpentry, the building of canoes, balsa rafts, or fishing implements; or with an endless number of similar crafts that do not necessarily indicate highly stratified society. The merchants would stand on a higher level, together with the warriors whose presence I have considered necessary in order to understand Olmec society.

Above these workers and specialists stood the supreme authority. Who was this authority? Was it constituted by one or by several individuals? We do not know the answer, but whatever the structure, we are no doubt dealing with a minority that was firmly established and acknowledged by the majority. Its authority must have been recognized as legitimate, as in the long run this seems to be the only kind of government that manages to stay in power. All societies possess some kind of social contract which governs them, and at least a sizable number of its members are in accord with this pattern. In a tribe the type of contract is still extremely simple; but to the degree that the community grows, difficulties in governing increase and the state becomes more complex. Imposition by force is never successful long and therefore the necessity of governing by a legitimate claim becomes obvious. Which man or men represented this legitimate claim among the Olmecs? Kings? High priests? We know that in later times in Mesoamerica the fusion of these two roles was common and that several states were controlled by priest-kings, masters of all power, of all rights, and responsible for all obligations. If this system prevailed among the people of Teotihuacan, among the Maya or Zapotecs (all of these heirs of the Olmecs to some extent), it is not improbable that this form of government may have originated among the Olmecs.

Heizer[6] has suggested, and I believe correctly, that these chieftains

[5] Piña Chán, 1964: 43–44.
[6] Heizer, 1962: 312–314.

were priests above all. He indicates that on the stelae the chests and ears of the priests represented are adorned with jade and that the same ornaments, made of the same material, were found in the tombs at La Venta, where the chieftains of the city had been buried. The idea is strengthened if we observe Monument 19 of La Venta (fig. 6), which represents a personage carrying a bag—probably for incense— in his hand. In all later Mesoamerican cultures the bag was to be the emblem of the priest.

But the possibility of priests as rulers becomes greater if we consider the extraordinary importance given to religion and ceremonialism, subjects which will be dealt with later. Perhaps the priests rose to a dominant position in an agricultural society when they became, among other things, experts on the calendar. In this way they may have been able to predict good days for sowing and harvesting, thus controlling to some extent climatic difficulties, even though the process may have been magical in part. The priests may also have been leaders who organized military and commercial expeditions and the building of monuments. Through the leadership of the hierarchy, the masses of the people obtained new products, a higher standard of living, and prestige; thus a mutually satisfactory relationship could be established between those who governed and those who were governed. We are dealing with the creative minority mentioned by Toynbee, the minority which always seems to move ahead in all the cultures of the world.

But in time the priests became more and more powerful and "divine," initiating that tremendous necrophilic tendency which was eventually to be the cause of the dissolution of the society dominated by it. Thus this priestly minority may have become more dominant than creative, causing unrest and destroying the people's desire to continue collaborating with an oppressive regime and excessive pomp. The moment to overthrow the hierarchy had arrived. Among the Olmecs this seems to have occurred toward the end of Period II.

This situation seems to point to the "tombs" of La Venta in which some of the leading chieftains were interred.[7] These tombs belong to Phase IV, the last at this site. They are the only Olmec tombs discovered up to the present time.[8]

---

[7] Farther on will be seen another indirect proof that the great tombs were dedicated to priests.

[8] All the interpretations of the importance of priest-kings have, as we have seen, a very flimsy basis. Michael Coe tells me, "I wonder how good the evidence is for priest-rulers among the Olmec. Priests as leaders are rare anywhere in the world, and among the Maya who are surely linked by culture if not by physical descent with the Olmec, there was no theocracy in recorded history—rather the priesthood was hereditary, but passed down in a 'younger brother' lineage ranking below that of the

Did this Metropolitan Olmec zone encompass a single state or several city-states, more or less independent, united in a league or a type of assembly,[9] as in the case of Greece? I am inclined to believe in the first possibility—with La Venta as the center—even though arguments in favor of this are meager. Drucker also feels that La Venta was the true Olmec capital wherein lay the tombs of the great chieftains. Heizer suggests that the site could have been the home of the "national treasury" of the Olmecs. I have already mentioned the possibility that it may have been a holy shrine but there are good reasons to suppose that La Venta was a capital, in spite of the fact that its geographic position is unspectacular and isolated. It is the only Olmec site where what might be called "royal tombs" are to be found. From La Venta come the greatest number and the best jade pieces[10] so far discovered. Furthermore, it is by far the most elaborately planned city, the one with the largest pyramid, carefully preserved and improved during at least four hundred years. As a detail I will add that it is at La Venta where there appear stelae that perhaps record visits of foreign rulers, such as on Stela 3. This would be more likely to occur in the capital of the state than in any other place.[11]

Important sites like Río Chiquito were to be prosperous but subject to others, as Stirling has observed.[12] He has also noted[13] the very direct and close communications between different Olmec sites, which seem to point to close bonds and therefore to one government for all of them, although obviously the similarity could be explained in other ways.

Similarities between La Venta and other sites of the Olmec area undoubtedly indicate a common basis that goes back to periods before the development of civilization, and especially to a common history,

---

ruler himself. The recent work on the Maya inscriptions by Tatiana Proskouriakoff casts some doubt on the importance of priests in Classic times as well." See Drucker, Heizer, and Squier, 1959: 127.

[9] Caso, 1965: 21.

[10] Drucker, Heizer, and Squier, 1959: 230.

[11] Wicke (1965: 122), basing his hypothesis on the succession of colossal heads whom he believes to represent dead kings, suggests that, on the contrary, three different cities served as the capital at different times. First would have been Tres Zapotes, then La Venta, and finally San Lorenzo. It can be said also that San Lorenzo represents the climax of Olmec art (Stirling, 1955: 22) and that the life of this site could have lasted a little longer than the end of La Venta. There is a possibility, therefore, of a change toward the end; when La Venta was abandoned, San Lorenzo might have become the chief city. Nevertheless, there are many arguments against this position. Coe has presented strong arguments indicating that San Lorenzo disappeared long before La Venta. For the reasons already expressed, I do not believe in Wicke's succession nor in that proposed by Kubler. For a very recent and important work on the subject see Clewlow, Cowan, O'Connell, and Benemann, 1967.

[12] Stirling, 1955: 23, and Stirling, 1961: 52. In 1968 this could hardly be said of San Lorenzo.

[13] Stirling, 1955: 22.

well established over a long period of time. This historical and cultural unity—long-lasting though it may have been—did not eliminate certain local differences. Or perhaps the opposite is true, that precisely because of the long duration of their parallel history certain differences grew up in each city—not basic differences, but distinguishable ones, a phenomenon that seems to come about over the course of time in all ancient cultures.

Nevertheless, it must not be forgotten that leagues of city-states seem to be one of the political characteristics of Mesoamerica, and therefore it is possible that they appeared in the Olmec period, as they later were part of the political picture in the two great regions which were heirs of the Olmecs: the Maya and the highland peoples.

With many reservations I have formed a provisional hypothesis: I believe that we are dealing with a theocratic state with an extremely important religious basis. Yet I feel that the name "theocracy" does not define this society unless we add the word "military": a military theocracy undoubtedly was the characteristic form of the great majority of Mesoamerican states. We still must discuss whether this state was an empire or not. This question can be settled only after we study the Olmecoid peoples and the Colonial Olmecs.

THE CALENDAR AND THE LONG COUNT

It is evident that a written calendar cannot exist without writing. Writing appeared, although in an incipient form—judging from what we know—in the Olmec II world. By Period III it had become more widespread; by that time there were more stone monuments or small objects bearing incised glyphs. There is no complete catalog of the glyphs or possible glyphs found among the Olmecs and Olmecoids, But M. D. Coe[14] has discussed some of them. It is clear that different peoples during the Olmec period inscribed on their monuments not only hieroglyphs but dates. Some may have been in the relatively simple system employed later by the Aztecs, in which dates could be indicated only within a span of 52 years, after which the system was repeated. Other inscriptions in the Olmec world, however, are made in the most complete and nearly perfect system of calculating time conceived in America, which is called the "Long Count." Until recently it was thought that this system was invented by the Maya and was the exclusive property of these people.

It must have dawned on the Olmecoids that a system in which dates were repeated every 52 years was confusing in the long run. It could

---

[14] M. D. Coe, 1965: 756–763.

be compared to our cryptic way of writing, for instance, '69. Does this refer to 1969, or 1869, or even 169? Of course at the moment of writing we know what is meant, but after many centuries it is not clear. The Long Count system is far more exact and equates basically to the one that has been followed by many civilized peoples. A starting point is fixed: for us it is the birth of Christ; for others it may be the Hegira or the first Olympiad. From this fixed date in the past, days are counted one by one in an unending succession. In order not to write huge numbers of days, periods are used which encompass a more or less large number of them: weeks, months, years, centuries. They must all be established in a most rigid form, since any change of periods or error would confuse the whole chronology.

The Mayas did establish a precise system. They set a date more than three thousand years in the past and counted the days from that starting point. They also divided this huge interval into periods. The basic one, the day, they called a *kin*. Twenty kins formed an *uinal* or month. Eighteen uinals made a *tun*, which we call a year. Twenty tuns made a *katun* and twenty katuns made a *baktun*, or 144,000 days. This is called the cycle and encompasses slightly fewer than 400 of our years. These numbers follow a vigesimal system (based on units of twenty), which was the one used in Mesoamerican mathematics. The one exception to the vigesimal system, that of 18 uinals making a tun or 360 days, certainly stems from the need of arriving as closely as possible to the real solar year of 365 days and a fraction.

Having discovered the value of the zero and being able therefore to write numbers by position, just as we do, the Mayas could write any number, no matter how enormous. Only three signs were necessary: a dot for one, a horizontal bar for five, and a special glyph for zero. Thus two would be two dots, six a bar and a dot, eleven two bars and a dot, and so on. After twenty, the second position would be used; thus twenty would be written by placing a dot in the second position and a zero in the first, just as we write 10. After 400 the third position would be used, just as we place two zeros after 1 to write 100. (In the calendar of course this third position would come after 360, as seen above).

With such a system no problem should arise in correlating Maya dates with our own, but unfortunately full Long Count notations were abandoned toward the end of the Classic Period. Although the matter has been thoroughly studied, scholars have not reached a definite solution, and a number of correlations have been proposed. The two most accepted ones—the others are mainly variants—are called Correlation A and Correlation B.

For our purposes the essential fact with respect to the two correlations is the 260-year difference in linking the Maya Long Count to our own calendar. In Correlation A the beginning point—certainly a mythical one, perhaps referring to the birth of gods—is fixed, in our computation, at October 4, 3373 B.C. Correlation B places the beginning point at August 13, 3113 B.C. of our calendar.

Although the Tuxtla statuette had been known since 1902 the importance of the date inscribed on it in "Long Count" was not really understood, until, on a warm January 16, 1939, Stirling found Stela C at Tres Zapotes[15] (pl. 46). This is only a fragment,[16] on one side of which there is a jaguar mask and on the other an inscription in the Long Count system, incomplete because of the fracture of the piece. From the beginning Stirling proposed (1940) that the reading of the count should be: 7 Baktuns, 16 Katuns, 6 Tuns, 16 Uinals, and 18 Kins, all of which is written thus: 7.16.6.16.18. The interpretation could not be verified, though, since all the Baktun is lacking and the dot that is necessary to reach the number 16 in the Katun is not complete. Evidence now shows that this dot did exist. On the other hand Baktun 7 is a reconstruction, the same as the month. At the beginning many specialists objected to this reading and its implications for two main reasons:

(a) They doubted that the inscription fell within the Maya counting system and assumed that it could have another day of origin which was not the same as that of the Maya calendar. In such a case it would not be possible to establish a correlation with the Christian calendar.

(b) They felt that it could refer not to a date contemporaneous with the erection of the stela but to a day in the remote past.[17]

Now, with new data strengthening Stirling's position, the consensus of opinion is inclined to accept the view that Stela C indicates a date within Baktun 7; it is now considered contemporaneous with its inscription. Therefore, it marks November 4, 291 B.C. according to Correlation A, and September 2, 31 B.C., according to Correlation B. Thus, Stela C reveals the oldest recorded Olmec date found up to now.

The sensational reading of the date of Stela C made it necessary to restudy other very ancient stelae whose dating had been considered impossible since they referred to periods prior to that accepted as the first inscription in stone in the "Long Count." It is almost a positive fact

---

[15] Stirling, 1939: 211–213.

[16] Williams and Heizer feel that the stela may not have been carved in Tres Zapotes; this would explain its poor condition but at the same time would present a series of problems regarding its origin.

[17] The most important study supporting these points of view (Thompson, 1941) presents many arguments against the contemporaneousness of the Baktun 7 dates.

that the first inscriptions were carved in wood and therefore have disappeared.

After the revelation of Stela C great importance was given to the Tuxtla statuette, whose provenance is a site near Tres Zapotes and therefore is also outside the Maya area (pl. 47). But it might not have been carved at Tuxtla, as it is a jade object, easy to carry because of its small size. The statuette represents a personage wearing a duck mask; on the front of the figure is a Long Count inscription with the date 8.6.2.4.17.[18] It indicates the date 98 B.C. or 162 B.C., according to the two principal correlations. There is another monument, Monument E of Tres Zapotes (fig. 12), which also bears an inscribed date.[19]

Outside the Olmec area are found Stela 1 of El Baul, Stela 2 of Colomba, and Stela 2 of Chiapa de Corzo, all of which have inscriptions

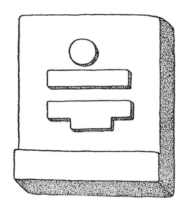

Fig. 12. Monument E, Tres Zapotes. Approximately 6 feet high.

[18] Holmes (1907); Stirling (1940); and M. D. Coe (1957). The style of this piece presents serious problems. Both Morley (1938) and Thompson (1941: 8–10, 27–29) came to the conclusion that it is not Maya, but neither could place it definitely in any other culture. It seems to me that this difficulty has been resolved since we have learned more about Olmec art; the statuette is strikingly similar to Monument 5 of Cerro de las Mesas (pl. 67), for example (see also Stirling, 1943: pl. 28). Nevertheless, Cerro de las Mesas is not only outside the Olmec area but is evidently not an Olmec site and is, in general, somewhat later, although some definitely Olmec objects have been found there, as we shall see further on. Probably both sculptures correspond to the Olmec III period. This would work out well chronologically, since the date of the statuette (even accepting it within the Long Count) is too late for it to be called an actual Olmec piece.

[19] This is the number 6 accompanied by a glyph carved in the rock. As the monument is lower than the level of the river, it could correspond to the Early Tres Zapotes period; this would mean that numbers and the calendar were invented in Olmec I (Drucker, 1943: 118). But, as Stirling suggests, the number could have been engraved when the river was in another position (1943: 220), or was dry, even for a short time. If this were true the monument would not have chronological value. This is my opinion. Another possible date is found on the Alvarado stela (fig. 8) (Thompson, 1941: 15).

from Baktun 7,[20] and which will be studied later. Research on these monuments proves that there is no doubt whatsoever regarding the correctness of the reading of Stela C of Tres Zapotes and that its date is contemporaneous with its erection. The same can be said of the Tuxtla statuette.

In the Olmec area there are some other inscriptions that, while they are not calendrical, do have glyphs, showing the use of a type of writing. Thus, on Monument 13 from La Venta (pl. 29) can be seen various hieroglyphs, among them one representing a foot, a glyph which was to be repeated in later epochs.[21] The personage on Monument 10 of San Lorenzo[22] displays a glyph on his chest (pl. 48). In other sculptures there are characters that also function as glyphs, for example the X that represents spots on the jaguar's skin.[23] In the same way a part of the jaguar, the claw or the mouth, represents the whole animal. This convention was to become common in Mesoamerican writing.

Other elements[24] are only decorative, but some seem to have been hieroglyphs since that early period, for we find them fulfilling this function in Olmecoid or later cultures. For example, the V with twisted points[25] becomes Glyph C in Monte Alban (see fig. 13). Drucker[26] has suggested that the Olmecs originated glyphs that the Maya were later to elaborate on, for instance, the squares with rounded corners, generally empty when they are Olmec but filled with motifs in Maya art.

All these data undoubtedly point to the existence of writing in the Olmec area, as well as the existence of a calendar which was the Mesoamerican prototype.

But a calendar of this kind would be impossible without the study of the movements of the sun, the moon, and of certain heavenly bodies. We can assume that the knowledge of the latter might have been a later acquisition, but it is undeniable that the Olmecs had discovered at least the length of the year and of the lunar month, and that they also computed time with the system of days that is characteristic of Mesoamerica. This calendar, which was probably intimately related to the agricul-

---

[20] Olmecoid glyphs or inscriptions have been found in many places, such as Cerro de las Mesas, Tonalá, Izapa, Chiapa, Padre Piedra, other sites in the Chiapas lowlands, and in Kaminaljuyu. In general they are later than La Venta, but some are contemporaneous. We will deal with these later, but they are mentioned here to demonstrate the diffusion of writing from an early date.

[21] Drucker (1952: 181 and fig. 61) and M. D. Coe (1965: 756) believe that these glyphs may indicate the name of the personage represented. Nevertheless, the foot glyph does not suggest a name, as it was used as a verb in later times.

[22] Stirling, 1955: 14.

[23] Medellín, 1960: 86; Covarrubias, 1957: 60 and fig. 21; M. D. Coe, 1965: 759.

[24] Covarrubias, 1942: 49; and Drucker, 1952: fig. 60.

[25] Drucker, 1952: fig. 60bb–gg.

[26] *Ibid.*: fig. 60h.

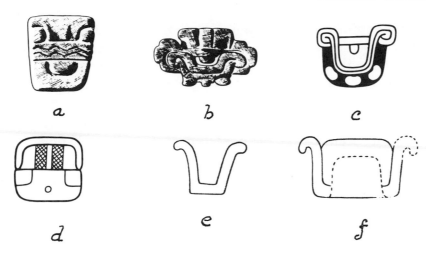

Fig. 13. Glyphs. (a and b) Oaxaca: Monte Alban. (c and d) Maya. (e and f) Olmec: altars 4 and 5 of La Venta.

tural cycle and to various types of ceremonies (as it undoubtedly was later)[27] was one of the most powerful elements in the hands of the priests since it gave them the possibility of directing agricultural life and perhaps, as occurred later, served as the basis of an astrology which determined the name given to the newborn.

It was only through a knowledge of astronomy that the Olmecs could orient their cities and monuments correctly. The rigorous orientation of Olmec cities, that obsession for order, the style of the great sculptures, the splendid tomb of La Venta, and the burial offerings of extremely valuable jade, the attire of the priests officiating in ceremonial acts represented on the monuments . . . all of these indicate the existence of the most characteristic trait of Mesoamerican civilization: ceremonialism, the vast importance given to rites and to religion in general.

RELIGION

THE GODS

Mesoamerican religion was polytheistic. The veneration of anthropomorphic gods associated with the cult of natural phenomena such as the sun was an important feature. But we know of no statues of gods among the Olmecs, or rather, we cannot be certain that any of the monoliths or figurines actually represent a deity. It seems evident that within the Olmec orbit and in the Preclassic period in general the concept

[27] Heizer, 1962: 314.

of formal divinities was just coming into being, with clearly recognizable attributes which were to be so characteristic from the Classic period on.

Heizer feels that there was a true Olmec pantheon of cosmological gods;[28] perhaps the latter existed, but we cannot accept the hypothesis, since definite representations are not known to exist. It is true that the figure sculptured on the marvelous Tres Zapotes box has been called a sun god,[29] but I am not at all convinced of this interpretation. Furthermore, the box is later than the Olmec II period. I believe that throughout the Olmec period worship was pointed directly to the jaguar—even the altars are jaguars[30]—and other deities had not yet appeared.

I doubt if the baby face type of figurine symbolizes a deity,[31] since it does not possess concrete attributes of its own, just as the Preclassic figurines do not.

On the other hand an old god comes from Laguna de los Cerros;[32] this evidently represents the old god of fire and is quite similar to that of Cerro de las Mesas, which is in the National Museum.[33] Both are quite late and correspond to the period I have called Post-Olmec, when influences of the central plateau were powerful and the Olmec zone was falling into decline as a great center and a creator of culture. Therefore, it would be more likely that this fire god represented a highland deity that had been imported to the Olmec region just as other influences had reached the area.

THE JAGUAR

Throughout the Olmec period the idea of animal-men is present, or of fantastic men-animals in which human traits are associated with those of one or more animals. Two or more animals are also found combined, thus forming a monster. With time this mythical beast was to embody religious concepts and would even become an anthropomorphic god.

All these variations revolve around the complicated concept of the *nahual*. This can be an animal mythically associated with a certain man so closely that his life depends upon that of the animal; if the animal dies, the man will surely die also. The nahual can be that of a god, that is, the animal form of his representation. Or it can be the symbol of something harmful and dangerous, although at other times it can be

---

[28] Heizer, 1960: 313.
[29] Stirling, 1943: 18.
[30] Flores Guerrero, 1962: 31.
[31] Weiant, 1943: 126–127.
[32] Medellín, 1960: 91.
[33] Drucker, 1943: pl. 8.

only mischievous, like a poltergeist. Even today the sorcerer continues to be, as he was in ancient times, capable of endless witchcraft, the one who steals things, who roams by night, and who lives surrounded by darkness.

In different periods and places of Mesoamerica there were animals like the serpent, the eagle, or the bat, which rose to special distinction and, associated with each other or with human beings, turned into nahuales. At times, when the nahual is inherent to a group, it is identified to some extent with a totem.[34]

Evidently the jaguar held the primacy among the Olmecs. In La Venta it could be at the same time the totem and the nahual of the supreme ruler. Today the jaguar seems to us—like almost all animals—a being that is fugitive, sometimes very large but rarely dangerous, and interesting mainly because of its beautiful spotted coat. A long time ago he symbolized terror and the mystery of the jungle, of life, of the other world. He was imbued with all forms: that of a deified animal, at times magnificently sculptured in jade[35] or in stone; at times he is seen complete, or only his face is stylized in masks (pl. 18); at other times he is a humanized jaguar (pl. 49), a man-jaguar (pl. 48), or a child-jaguar. Even today many popular legends related to the jaguar theme are common, like those collected by Covarrubias.[36]

Frequently we are not dealing with a simple jaguar, but with a monstrous jaguar far removed from a realistic representation.[37] Elements characteristic of man and of other animals have been added, mainly those of a bird and a serpent. Thus the jaguar is likely to have feathers over his eyes instead of eyebrows.[38] This association of a jaguar with feathers, that is, with a bird, is important furthermore because it is possibly the origin of the great god who also brings together a bird with another animal: Quetzalcoatl, the feathered serpent.[39] By then a bird—a quetzal or eagle—was to take the place of the lowland jaguar in the iconography of the high plateau of Mexico.

[34] The Popoloca of Veracruz still preserve strong beliefs regarding nahualism (Foster, 1940: 22–25).

[35] This is the case with the magnificent piece from Necaxa in the state of Puebla; though it is not from the Metropolitan area, it is undoubtedly Olmec (Covarrubias, 1957: facing p. 78).

[36] Covarrubias, 1944: 26.

[37] For example, at La Venta, as Drucker has demonstrated (1952: 192–194). Monument 41 at San Lorenzo is a four-sided column measuring 7 ft. 10 in. (part is broken off); "one surface is carved with a barbaric and very primitive Olmec relief of a were-jaguar, with smiling mouth and semicircular dimples on the cheeks. Its enormous left hand partly covers a withered right arm" (Coe, 1967, MS).

[38] As seems to be true of the rectangular appendages which appear above one of the mosaic masks at La Venta (Drucker, Heizer, and Squier, 1959: 93–94).

[39] There are legends that Quetzalcoatl was a native of the Papaloapan Basin.

Sometimes, as in the sarcophagus of La Venta, the jaguar mask not only has feathers for eyebrows, but also a bifid tongue, a feature found exclusively in the serpent (see pl. 18a). Be it as it may, in Olmec times we find the beginning of the combination of different animals to form one god, an idea that was to be basic in the Mesoamerican pantheon. It would be repeated in a thousand forms and in different combinations: animal bodies with human faces, or vice versa; men with masks or headdresses of animals, and two or more animals combined.

The jaguar cult was adopted by the Zapotecs and the Maya and by Teotihuacan, and it was preserved as late as the Aztec period, when the earth god Tepeyolohtli, symbol of the bowels of the earth and of the darkness of the night, was the feline who could eat the sun during an eclipse. In order to avoid this cataclysm it was necessary to frighten it by making a great deal of noise. Tepeyolohtli was a terrible god who lived in caves within the mountains, in the heart of the earth. Jade, because of its great value, also represents the heart of earth. The association of the jaguar and jade reveals another original Olmec concept that was to last until the end. Even after the Spanish conquest a certain jade figure of a bird-serpent was so precious that, it is said, it looked like "a transparent . . . emerald . . . which shone from its depths." It was made "with great exquisiteness," was called the "Heart of the People," and was guarded in an almost impenetrable part of the Achiutla mountains.[40]

Jade, then, was in Mesoamerica not valuable simply because of its rarity and beauty; it also had a symbolic value. It was the most precious of all materials, superior to gold itself (even when the latter appeared upon the scene a millennium later). Jade objects were offered in great ritual ceremonies and were placed in the tombs of priests. The association of jade with the heart of the earth or of the mountains and the heart of the people continued until the end and was to become eventually the symbol of the individual human heart. During the Aztec period a jade bead was placed in the mouth of the deceased.

It is quite possible that Olmec jaguars were always infantile beings,[41] probably connected with the *chaneques*—in which people still believe —who are "old dwarfs with faces of children," who chase women and bother people.[42] Chaneques live in waterfalls, cause illnesses, eat the human brain, foresee rain, and dominate wild animals and fish. They

[40] Burgoa, 1934: I:332.
[41] M. D. Coe, 1962: 85. Frequently the mouths of the man-jaguar do not have teeth, suggesting, therefore, a child and a young jaguar (Covarrubias, 1957: 56). The jaguar face used as a mask could be a predecessor of Xipe, the flayed god. As Covarrubias has noted, the swallowtail points typical of the headdress of this god are found in Olmec art (*ibid.*: 59).
[42] Covarrubias, 1957: 57.

are true poltergeists and "in order to appease them it is necessary to throw them buckets of water, the magic food."[43] The small figures which surround the central personages in stelae 2 and 3 of La Venta (see pl. 17) have been interpreted as chaneques because they carry canes, perhaps to break the clouds.[44] These are reminiscent of, and surely there is an intimate tie with, the *tlaloques* or *chacs* (assistants to the rain god, Tlaloc or Chac) who broke with a stick the jars (clouds) that contained water for rain; these tlaloques or chacs are, in part, identified with lightning. Covarrubias believes them to be celestial spirits of rain who became transformed into the rain god of the Classic period. These spirits are still found today in local folklore and frighten people, according to the Popolocas and Nahuas of southern Veracruz.[45] They are venerated, also, in caves.[46] Therefore, we have at least two clear associations of the chaneques: with children and water on one hand and with caves and mountains on the other.[47] As we have seen, the jaguar was associated with caves and mountains until the Aztec period, and had a child-jaguar face.

Covarrubias[48] has demonstrated the stylistic evolution from the Olmec jaguar to the rain god—Tlaloc, Cocijo, Chac, or Tajin—in later cultures (fig. 14). Caso[49] has called the Olmec jaguar, "a god who is probably an ancestor of Tlaloc." But the Aztec Tlaloc is no longer a feline; fundamentally his nahual is the serpent. The jaguar of the hot lowlands does not represent Tlaloc in the highlands, and this evolution seems to occur also in other cultures. This means that there was some change or rather a different emphasis in the component parts of the animal associated with the deity of rain; the serpent element, very weak in the beginning, later prevailed.[50]

[43] Aguirre Beltrán, 1955: 15.

[44] These, however, may have been only "companions" (Heizer, personal communication). Thompson (1965: 343) has described the Maya merchant gods with prominent clownlike noses, which remind us of the figures on the stelae of La Venta. The same author associates with this group a large ceramic figure with a clownlike nose from Veracruz–Oaxaca, now at the National Museum (personal communication).

[45] Foster, 1951: 170, and Foster, 1940: 27.

[46] Johnson, 1939: 147.

[47] The nahual sometimes takes on the disguise of a thunderbolt and, according to modern beliefs, creates a tempest (Foster, 1945: 184).

[48] Covarrubias, 1946: pl. 4.

[49] Caso, 1942: 44. Thompson is of the same opinion (1951: I:36). See also Wolf, 1959: 79.

[50] A figurine from Tres Zapotes has been compared (Weiant, 1943: 14, 97 and pl. 29) with the Cocijo of Period I of Monte Alban. There is no doubt that they are related but rather than Cocijo we seem to be dealing precisely with the jaguar, which was taken to Monte Alban by the Olmecs. The same is true of other representations, such as that on Monument 15 of La Venta (Drucker, 1952: fig. 64) and the Monte Alban clay tablets, which are Cocijos even more closely related to the Olmec jaguars

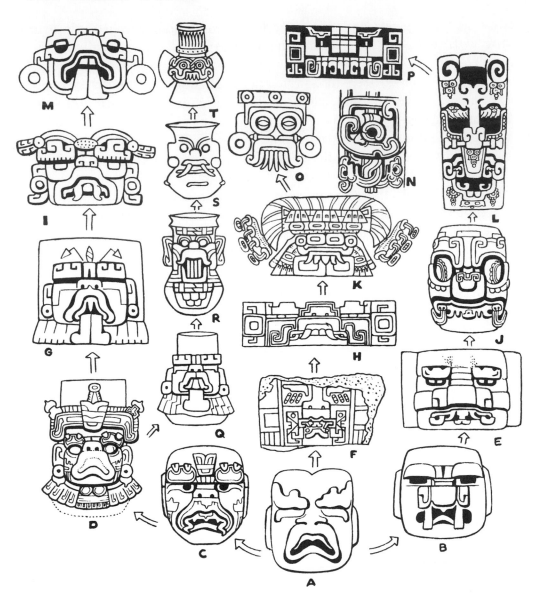

Fig. 14. Evolution of the mask of the rain god according to Covarrubias, 1946.

It seems doubtful to me that the jaguar was, among the Olmecs, a rain god or a water deity as Tlaloc was later. It would seem that the problem of rain—absolutely fundamental to the cultures of the dry highland region—would not be of such interest to the Olmecs since their prayers would be raised rather to petition less water.[51] Hence the

and which, by the way, at times show the forked tongue (e.g., Caso and Bernal, 1952: fig. 26).

[51] Heizer (personal communication) is correct, however, when he states "there is no denying the importance in the southeastern lowland of knowing all about rain—when it comes, how long it will last, when it will stop, etc."

serpent associated with water in the highland cultures would not be so important for the Olmecs. I believe that in its concept the jaguar, like jade, was identified more with the heart of the earth or with fertility,[52] but not necessarily with rain. The latter attribute was probably added later or perhaps came into being among the Olmecoid groups who lived in a different area and climate.

Kirchhoff states that since the jaguar was the god of early Mesoamerican cultures and the eagle the deity of more recent ones, there could be a certain historical memory in the symbolic struggle between the eagle knights and the jaguar knights of the Aztec period. This leads one to think of the possibility of the existence of jaguar-knights among the Olmecs, though the organization of these knights may have been elementary; this idea is based on the representation on monuments of men with jaguar helmets.

Another animal, perhaps with religious connections, is the "bird monster" studied by Drucker.[53] In general it has more of the appearance of a hieroglyph but is, however, highly reminiscent of certain fantastic birds of more recent peoples.

Mesoamerican religion puts considerable emphasis on the cardinal points, and associates each one with gods, trees, birds, colors, and so forth. In Aztec times the east was usually associated with blue-green, that is, jade. Perhaps this esoteric idea started in Olmec times. Such a possibility is suggested by the fact that when the Olmecs of La Venta made a sort of limiting clay marker or wall around a jaguar mosaic, they used mainly green clay. The marker or wall serves no practical function, and since the green clay is placed on the east side, it may indicate an association of green and east.[54]

The Olmecs may have observed a great calendric cycle of approximately a century, as there is evidence that the renovation of buildings at La Venta took place every 104 years.[55] There may have been a rite of breaking all the ceramics of each house (and perhaps of extinguish-

[52] For this theme see Thompson (1951: 36). Thompson (1954: 234) deals with the cult associated with corn. See also Wolf (1959), and Heizer (1960: 313), who sums up this point well. M. D. Coe (1965: 757) points out that the plants emerging from the V on the heads of the jaguars may be maize. Therefore, there already existed a connection between this animal and agriculture.

[53] 1952: 194 and figs. 9 and 12. The representation in fig. 9 is somewhat similar to the eagle or quetzal of Tetitla.

[54] Drucker, Heizer, and Squier, 1955: 103.

[55] Heizer, 1960. Nevertheless, as this same author points out in a personal letter, "It should be remembered that this figure of about one hundred years per phase at La Venta is not based upon a very accurate or precise internal site chronology. It is more a guess than a deduction. It is, in short, highly speculative, and the mere fact that my calculations provided an indication of phase-durations of about one century in length should not be taken as *proof* of any calendrical derivation. This may be so, but if it is true it will have to be demonstrated on other grounds."

ing the fires) at the end of the 52 years of the half-cycle. It could be that a reflection of this custom is found at Tres Zapotes[56] just as it appeared later in Mixtec sites like Coixtlahuaca[57] and Yagul[58] and among the Aztecs.

The beginning of another custom which was to prevail later was derived, perhaps, from Tres Zapotes also, where some telescoped stone tubes were found near burials.[59] In Oaxaca many tombs have these tubes (although made of clay here) in order to allow the escape of the soul. The idea is present in the crypt of the Temple of the Inscriptions in Palenque.

Another very important aspect of religion must be mentioned: sacrifice. The massive offerings at La Venta not only sacrificed valuable stones difficult to obtain but also human labor, the sweat and toil which was necessary to set them in place.[60] Perhaps these stones had a sacrificial symbolism, but regarding the culmination of all the sacrifices, the human, I have gathered some inferences.

At the top of Monument 1 of Laguna de los Cerros (pl. 12), there is a circular hole about 8 inches in diameter and 5 inches deep. "Unquestionably it served as a receptacle for some kind of liquid (water or blood), like the *cuauhxicallis* of the Toltec–Mexican period."[61] If this deduction is correct, it offers a fact of extreme importance. Another indication that could corroborate it is found in Monument D at Tres Zapotes. This is barrel shaped, with a cavity about 3 inches deep in the center. According to Stirling,[62] "it seems . . . likely that it was a sacrificial stone, as it would be of the correct dimensions for this purpose, and the basinlike bowl on the top would serve for collecting blood." The same function could have been fulfilled by the stone cylinders that are slightly hollowed out on top, with a well defined rim,[63] although the latter case is doubtful. It is curious that we do not find similar vessels again until much later, a fact that cannot be explained. Of course, the receptacles described above could have been used in sacrifices of animals, which seem to have taken place in Teotihuacan.

Various objects of jade, for example the famous Kunz axe (pl. 49a)

[56] Drucker, 1943: 28–29.
[57] Bernal, 1949.
[58] Bernal, manuscript in preparation.
[59] Weiant, 1943: 7.
[60] Drucker, Heizer, and Squier, 1959: 102, 132.
[61] Medellín, 1960: 87.
[62] Stirling, 1943: 21.
[63] Monument N at Tres Zapotes (Stirling, 1943: pl. 10a) (19 inches high and 22 in diameter) and Monument 14 at La Venta (Drucker, 1952: 182) are similar, curiously, to others belonging to different periods and to remote sites such as those found recently at Malinalco by Saénz.

in the American Museum of Natural History,[64] depict a person holding, at chest height, a knife borne in both hands. The importance given the object and the position of the man suggest that this is a sacrificial knife carried by a man-jaguar, perhaps the very priest disguised as a god, as is the case in later cultures. This undoubtedly is not a simple knife for domestic use but an object with true ritual significance, like the bag that the priests carried. The Olmec celt (pl. 49b) in the British Museum probably carried a knife originally also.

Although representations of human skulls are scarce, there is one made of rock crystal and a few others of clay from La Venta. They may provide an indication that human sacrifice was practiced, as it frequently was in the Olmec region at the time of the Spanish conquest.

Caso[65] accepts the possibility of human sacrifice among the Olmecs. He feels that children or dwarfs could have been the principal victims. His idea is strengthened if we remember the frequency with which dwarfs and children were represented in sculpture, which in a way deified them, as the victim was also made divine. At this time, however, it is not possible to reach a definite conclusion regarding sacrifice, just as we cannot affirm the existence of the practice among most of the groups of the Classic period.

[64] Saville, 1929: 267.
[65] Caso, 1965: 23.

5

PERIODS OF OLMEC HISTORY

I have left until now the attempt to place in chronological order the different elements of Olmec culture that I have examined in the foregoing pages. This discussion—conclusive here—could have been placed near the beginning of the book and would, perhaps, have clarified the concepts, but it seemed to me that it would be difficult for the reader to grasp the chronology of objects or of sites not yet described. It is evident that whatever time the Olmec culture took in being born, in growing, and in dying, it was made up of stages. A culture is never static. It will be necessary, therefore, to discuss the epochs through which the Olmec world passed and the dates of these epochs or periods.

At the beginning I made it clear that this book deals only with civilized Mesoamerica, therefore, periods prior to civilization will be mentioned only briefly when they constitute necessary antecedents.

The period that I call Olmec I (see chart) immediately precedes the beginning of this civilization and is its direct antecedent. But it in turn is based on a very long period during which the original challenges were slowly met successfully: man domesticated plants and learned how to make use of them; he began to live in permanent communities of settlements and villages; he made ceramics, wove cloth of cotton and of fibers, made baskets and mats, and polished stone. He was controlled by a social organization based on kinship. And, finally, he practiced magic.

This unspecialized culture, which took millennia to form, existed in vast regions of the American continent. In some limited areas, toward the

SEQUENCE OF CULTURES IN THE OLMEC AREA

Dates	Bernal	Drucker, Heizer, Squier, Weiant, etc.	Piña Chán	Coe
100 B.C. +	Post-Olmec	Lirios, San Marcos, Soncautla, Upper Tres Zapotes I (in part) and II		Villa Alta Postclassic
600–100 B.C.	Olmec III	Post-La Venta–Upper Tres Zapotes I (in part)	La Venta III	Palangana phase 600–400 B.C.
1200–600 B.C.	Olmec II	La Venta Phases I–IV, Middle Tres Zapotes	La Venta II (up to 200 B.C.)	San Lorenzo phase 1200–900 B.C.
1500–1200 B.C.	Olmec I	Pre-La Venta, Early Tres Zapotes	La Venta I	Pre-San Lorenzo before 1200 B.C.

end of the second millennium before the Christian era, regional styles began to emerge. The Olmec area was one of these, where a specialization began after 1500 B.C. which was to distinguish it from the rest. At that time the style that was to flower in this area from 1200 B.C. began to take shape, though modestly.

But we are confronted with this problem: after 1500 B.C. this style not only is found in the Olmec area but is also found in its transitional phase in different sites such as Tlatilco.[1] It would seem, therefore, that the Olmec style was not born in the area where it developed later but in a much wider region, actually in what was to be Mesoamerica centuries later, or perhaps in a region different from what we consider as Olmec, like Guerrero or Oaxaca. Many objects characteristic of Olmec style come from the latter areas.[2] On the other hand, Carbon 14 dating has become known only recently, and it has not yet been possible to determine the age of all the sites. Working before the discovery of Carbon 14 dating, Covarrubias believed (and Piña Chán also, at first) that this style originated in another place and that the Olmec zone was more an area of refuge. At the present time it is difficult to defend the latter theory because Carbon 14 dates indicate great antiquity for La Venta and San Lorenzo. Above all, in the Olmec zone the style that bears its name is the *only* one that appears at this period; that is, it is not mixed with outside influences. However, in the other regions Olmec-style objects are isolated and are associated or at least preceded by other objects that are obviously local and pertain to a different tradition.

[1] Piña Chán, 1958: 55.
[2] For a number of reasons it may be argued that the origin of the Olmec culture is not to be found in the "Olmec" area but in other areas: Guerrero, Puebla, or Oaxaca. Wicke (1965) feels that its origin was La Mixteca. Nevertheless, for the reasons I have given I believe in its local origin.

Later we will examine the Olmec-style structures and sculpture which represent true civilization and are found all over Mesoamerica. These are rarely datable; but when they are, they can be shown to be later than the Olmec II period and therefore cannot be an antecedent. For example, the figures from Huamelulpan in Oaxaca are contemporaneous, rather, with Monte Alban II; stelae with Baktun 7 Long Count dates in the Pacific watershed of Chiapas and Guatemala to the southeast are another example.

Monte Alban I, a site contemporaneous with Olmec II, also shows an advanced culture but is not really Olmec in the above sense, since there are innumerable different traits and those that are similar to the Olmec in no way explain all the Monte Alban I culture.

But there is still more. Throughout Mesoamerica, Olmec-type objects that appear in this period are mainly clay figurines—baby face, pretty woman, or hollow figurines[3]—all seeming to be more the result of the fusion of two styles: the Olmec and the local one.

Equally important are the Olmec traits we find scattered in various parts of Mesoamerica around 1200 B.C.; *not one* allows us to think of a civilization but of an advanced culture that had not reached the level of civilization. These traits include ceramic types, figurine forms, decorative motifs, and so on, but urban planning and the great sculptures had not yet come into being. So this first diffusion of Olmec style corresponds to a period prior to the efflorescence of La Venta.

It is more likely that even before the Olmec apogee some Olmec cultural traits had reached as far as the Valley of Mexico and other areas. It is hard to believe that this early diffusion was carried out in the same way as that which took place during the period 1200–600 B.C., since I feel that before this time there could not have been a strong Olmec army or a closely knit organization of merchants. But there is another form of influence typical of advanced cultures in many other parts of the world, which I believe existed here—the diffusion of a religious idea, in this case the jaguar cult. The baby face and hollow figurines are, actually, related to the jaguar. It is amazing that this animal could have been so important in the Valley of Mexico or in the highlands in general, where it was not found in the natural state. It seems feasible that during the years from 1500 to 1200 B.C. the jaguar cult was formed in the Olmec world and was then diffused as a religious idea. It is a definite fact that the cult was present in the area because we see its manifestations in La Venta as early as 1000, not as the first steps of an art or of a religion, but in its complete form. This undoubtedly means a previous period of elaboration, both ritual and artistic.

But to assure this point of view it is necessary to prove that antece-

[3] Piña Chán, 1964: 49.

dents of the culture which was to flower later existed in the Olmec area earlier than 1200 B.C. This seems to be exactly what occurred, in the three Olmec sites excavated, La Venta, San Lorenzo, and Tres Zapotes. In all places there are undeniable remains of a period preceding the culmination, remains corresponding to the pre-1200 B.C. period; and in these there appears the style, though not the technique, which was to predominate later.

In La Venta the existence of Olmec Period I is proved, although it is not yet well known. It is recognized because the inhabitants of Phase I at La Venta (in the terminology of Drucker, Heizer, and Squier, 1959) used clay which they removed from structures built before their time,[4] and also because the first buildings of Olmec II contained cultural materials that are obviously older, and therefore must have belonged to the creators of Olmec I. Furthermore, Piña Chán found evidence of this period still *in situ* in the pits he dug *underneath* a layer of sand[5] which revealed in three stratigraphic levels materials that were essentially ceramics and were undoubtedly earlier than the oldest known existing structures of Phase I which date from about 1000 B.C. There are, then, many probabilities that a ceremonial center existed in the Olmec I epoch which was later to be completely destroyed by people of the Olmec II period (Phase I) around the year 1000 B.C.[6] The most recent investigations at La Venta, carried out in January and February, 1968, produced evidence of pre-La Venta Phase I occupation of the area. This earlier occupation is not yet dated, but it is believed by the excavators that the age will be older than 1000 B.C. No stone sculpture or ceremonial architecture is demonstrably associated with this early period, and for this reason the culture conforms to the general requirements of Olmec I. Until these new data are analyzed and their Carbon 14 age determined nothing beyond this can be stated.

The situation at Tres Zapotes is far from clear; and while it is possible that the cultural materials (mainly pottery) from beneath the volcanic ash layer in Trench 26 are earlier than La Venta, opinions on the age and relationships of the sub-ash Tres Zapotes pottery differ. It will be necessary for more excavations to be carried out to collect additional study materials, as well as to secure Carbon 14 dates from Tres Zapotes, before we can be certain of the time span covered by the site.[7]

[4] Drucker, Heizer, and Squier, 1959: 268.

[5] Piña Chán, 1964: 18.

[6] Drucker, Heizer, and Squier, 1959: 38, 44. Berger, Graham, and Heizer, 1967 (revised dating of La Venta, 1000 B.C. to 600 B.C.).

[7] One radiocarbon age determination of what was assumed to be wood charcoal collected in 1967 from below the ash layer at Drucker's Trench 26 location gave an impossibly old date of 9000 B.C. Examination of the sample showed it to be mixed with asphalt. Coe, Diehl, and Stuiver (1967) report that one of their San Lorenzo samples was asphalt contaminated.

Good evidence of what can be considered Olmec I occurs at San Lorenzo in the form of Early Preclassic occupation deposits older than the San Lorenzo phase which has been dated by M. Coe at 1200–900 B.C.[8] The pre-San Lorenzo Phase deposits at the San Lorenzo site have not produced any stone sculpture, and at this time its content and dating do not contradict our viewing it as belonging to Olmec I.

We can, then, show that at both La Venta and San Lorenzo Olmec I is earlier than Olmec II. Also nearly certain is the fact that this Period II is a cultural continuation of the former. If we call Period II Olmec, it is correct to call Period I Olmec also, since we are dealing with the same people in different stages of their history.

Thus, I have called this "ancient ancestral pattern"[9] Olmec I. The Olmec II period, which we shall see now, signifies not a change of inhabitants but an extraordinary elaboration of the earlier village type. Here we have the main argument to reject the idea that the Olmec culture was created in another region. Its roots are in its own territory.

If Olmec II does not contain all the elements of a civilization, many traits are present in this period that are universally accepted as components of a civilization: monumental sculpture, planned and orientated cities, complex social organization with priests, merchants, and specialized workers, an economic surplus, and perhaps an imperial power that imposed its style on other areas. Many of these elements were to characterize civilizations which were to become heirs of the Olmecs.

The Olmec II period corresponds to the efflorescence of San Lorenzo and La Venta. It has been possible to distinguish four phases in the La Venta site up to now, but it should be clear that these four phases are not epochs or periods but subdivisions of a single one. They correspond to the four sequential reconstructions or enlargements of the monuments which are components of the ceremonial center of La Venta; vast offerings of carved stone were made during each period of construction. Each phase lasted approximately a century.[10] During Period II La Venta was occupied and was preserved in perfect condition.

The first phase at La Venta began about 1000 B.C. We can be sure that this date is approximately correct thanks to a number of Carbon 14 readings taken in La Venta.[11] During this time the center was completely

---

[8] Coe, 1967A, 1967B; Coe, Diehl, and Stuiver, 1967.

[9] Drucker, 1952: 230; see also Drucker, 1947: 6.

[10] Heizer, 1962: 311.

[11] In 1955 nine samples of wood charcoal were collected at La Venta. These were Carbon 14 dated in 1957, and the conclusion was reached by Drucker, Heizer, and Squier (1957) that La Venta Phase I began about 800 B.C. and Phase IV ended about 400 B.C. Archaeologists generally accepted this dating. Coe and Stuckenrath (1964) raised serious questions about the radiocarbon dating of La Venta, and two of the original 1955 samples were re-dated with the result that they gave age de-

planned, and it was probably then that one of the vast offerings of stones was made. The people possessed exquisite jades in both colors, blue-gray and emerald green (found in Offering 7), and used cinnabar as a pigment.

Possibly the custom of the offering-burial (almost surely a burial and not merely objects laid in the shape of the deceased) existed in this phase. It is probable that Olmec diffusion and perhaps conquest— begun, as we have seen, in the preceding period—was consolidated in this phase and was, actually, the basis of Phase II. This would explain why the Olmecs were able to carry out their splendid works as well as import many fine objects. As a result the Olmecs did not, at this time, have to depend exclusively on their own production but on the tribute of others and on commerce, which permitted expansion and a great cultural development. The Olmecs could, then, build their cities, carve their monoliths, and create their ceremonial center, all on a great scale.

In Phase II jaguar mosaics began to be made. There were more pieces of jade; small rock crystal objects made their appearance and, as is only natural, the ceremonial center was reconstructed. At this time the floors of white clay mixed with sand of the same color were laid. Perhaps they were painted in colors for a short time and then were made white again. Although it is not definite it is probable that some of the monoliths correspond to this phase.

The two final phases are the richest, for then most of the jades and many of the monolithic sculptures were carved. The great culmination of La Venta corresponds to these phases, especially to Phase IV, when Tomb A was constructed. By that time the city was at its zenith and, like ripe fruit, ready to fall.

The whole of this great period, traditionally called La Venta–Middle Tres Zapotes and which I call Olmec II, corresponds to the apogee of these two cities and also to the apogee of sculpture in the Río Chiquito sites. This flowering was evidently a result of the internal evolution of Olmec society and of its own art, although its wide diffusion would have brought direct contact with other peoples, especially in places colonized by Olmecs. By now this diffusion was based not only on religious ideas but also on political power joined to the economic growth in the region.

terminations several hundred years older (Heizer, 1964; Drucker and Heizer, 1965). In 1966 nine re-datings were performed, and the conclusion was reached that La Venta Phase I should be dated about 1000 B.C. and the end of Phase IV at about 600 B.C. The revised dating makes the age of the La Venta site occupation two centuries older than formerly believed. The information and basis for this conclusion is complex, and can be found in Berger, Graham, and Heizer, 1967. If this conclusion and Coe's dating are correct, Olmec II began earlier at San Lorenzo than at La Venta.

It is possible that Olmec Period II at Tres Zapotes was prolonged one or two centuries beyond that at La Venta. Piña Chán feels that the period should be extended as late as the year 200 B.C.[12] Actually, the following epoch at Tres Zapotes, the Upper period, is only partially Olmec, according to our definition of that culture, and partially more recent. It is necessary, therefore, to interpret the findings from the Upper Tres Zapotes period from a typological point of view—which is risky.[13]

It has been said that there is cultural continuity at Tres Zapotes.[14] Obviously this statement applies to the Early and Middle periods, but only part of the Upper period can be placed within that continuum. The new elements appearing throughout the rest of the period lack local antecedents, and their affiliation with the highlands is obvious. These foreign influences were felt strongly and the Olmec world ceased to predominate, to be the creator of ideas, falling to the level of many other groups culturally directed by outsiders. I feel that it is plausible that Olmecs—descendents of the original inhabitants—continued to live there and that something of their ancient culture was preserved, though transformed to such an extent by foreign elements that the later period can hardly be called Olmec. The same change occurred at La Venta,[15] about a century before the birth of Christ.

Before this final collapse, however, there was a period from about 600 B.C., the end of the great period, to 100 B.C., an epoch I have called Olmec III. It was a stage that became progressively decadent, in which objects reminiscent of the Classic Olmec style were still fabricated (they do not fit into any other culture), together with isolated examples showing the survival of the splendid ancient civilization. Not only were there survivals but it was in Olmec Period III that these people elaborated their last and perhaps most significant contribution to civilization: the Long Count.

It is curious that when Olmec art was first discovered and when it was thought that because of its perfection it necessarily must be art of the Classic period, Stela C from Tres Zapotes (pl. 18b), our first positive evidence of the use of the zero, seemed too early. Now we look upon it in precisely the opposite way. Within the Olmec efflorescence (approximately 1200 to 600 B.C.), the date of this stela would appear

---

[12] Piña Chán, 1964: 25, 28.

[13] The Soncautla Complex is of course not included; it belongs to a later period, as demonstrated by Drucker (1943: 102–107). Even less likely are the San Marcos and Lirios styles, which frankly are late. Even discarding all these intrusive elements, it is evident that Upper Tres Zapotes contains, at least in its final stages, a series of traits which are clearly Teotihuacan and therefore indubitably later than the Olmecs (*ibid.*: 120–122). By the way, the practice of cremation, common in Upper Tres Zapotes, is another trait which does not seem to be Olmec (*ibid.*: 147).

[14] Drucker, 1952: 258; Weiant, 1943.

[15] Drucker, Heizer, and Squier, 1959: 236–237.

to be too late, even though we employ Correlation A; it would, then, have to be placed within Olmec Period III. This is not our only reason for considering it to be late. Drucker points out that the jaguar mask on the other side of Stela C does not seem to have been understood by the artist who carved it.[16] Of course this does not prove that the stone is late, since such a misunderstanding may occur at any time, but usually this sort of thing occurs when an artist is repeating a dimly remembered trait. If we add the tears on the mask—a clear suggestion of the water god—and the presence of a forked tongue, also characteristic of later water gods and obviously a feature of the serpent, we have more elements showing the probable lateness of Stela C.

The forked tongue of the serpent, associated with jaguar elements, is typical of some Classic gods. Both elements form a sort of dragon very characteristic of Mesoamerican art and religion. If we observe the sides of Stela D at Tres Zapotes[17] we notice that they are carved with a kind of dragon (as denominated by Covarrubias),[18] its body made up of volutes. The volute is not an Olmec element,[19] and I have already mentioned how the box from Tres Zapotes, which is decorated with these scrolls (fig. 7), probably belongs to later times. Volutes perhaps represent clouds, and later may have been the origin of the plumed serpent,[20] which is not an Olmec element either.

Similar arguments could be brought up concerning the Tuxtla statuette (pl. 47), which bears the only other Long Count date found in the Olmec area. Here again, though the sculpture is assumed to be Olmec, the calendrical inscriptions are neither Maya nor do they fall within the Classic Olmec period. The Tuxtla statuette is a small and portable object and may have been imported from another region, presumably further to the south. This interesting piece of jade sculpture was found a few miles south of the present town of San Andrés Tuxtla in the heart of the Tuxtla mountains about sixty years ago. Nothing whatsoever is known about the circumstances of its discovery, and because of this obscurity we cannot really say anything certain about the specimen. It is generally assumed to be an Olmec piece because it was found in the Olmec area.

[16] Drucker, 1952: 205–208. Because of this he feels, contrary to my opinion, that the piece is older.

[17] Stirling, 1943: pls. 14b, c.

[18] Covarrubias, 1957: 63.

[19] Covarrubias had already noted (1944: 32) that two elements typical of later cultures are absent in Olmec art: the great fans of quetzal feathers and the combination of spiral motifs. Actually, the box and Monument C of Tres Zapotes (fig. 7) probably begin this latter type of decoration; that is another reason for considering them to be of a late period. Drucker (1952: 200) also has observed that, when there are feathers, they are not represented as they are later.

[20] Covarrubias, 1957.

We must not forget that no calendrical inscription has been found at San Lorenzo and La Venta, the principal center of the culture. This leads one to suppose that those which appear at Tres Zapotes and at Tuxtla belong to a later period. Stela C, therefore, would be late at Tres Zapotes, probably belonging to the Upper or at earliest to the end of the Middle period (if the latter laster longer there than at La Venta).[21]

It can be concluded that among the late Olmecs and Olmecoids it became a custom—though not frequently practiced—to carve dates using the Long Count system, which necessarily implies knowledge of the zero.[22] It is evident that these two recorded Olmec dates are earlier than the dates of the Maya stelae, as the earliest of the latter was carved shortly before the year 300 A.D. It follows, then, that the entire system of the Long Count—in stone—belongs to Olmec Period III, even though, as it must have required centuries to develop, it may have begun—in wood—in Period II. All of this leads us to accept Jiménez Moreno's pertinent statement: "Stela C at Tres Zapotes is something like the last will and testament of the La Venta culture."[23]

Summing up, I feel it is valid to believe that the final Olmec Period III extended from 600 to 100 B.C.[24] Nevertheless, by that time Olmec culture was not a focus of diffusion for all Mesoamerica, even though isolated spots, capable of giving birth to master works, continued to exist. Some of the monoliths described by Weyerstall and by Medellín[25] would fall within this epoch as do some of the famous dates recorded in the Long Count. Even though they had lost their cultural preemi-

[21] Drucker, Heizer, and Squier, 1959: 246–248.

[22] The sign for zero, apparently diffused by the Arabs, was unknown to the Greco-Roman world, although it was familiar with the concept. The zero originated in India, where it appears in inscriptions from the ninth century A.D., but literary sources indicate that without doubt it was known much earlier. Possibly the same phenomenon took place in Mesoamerica, where it was also known much earlier, but, since we do not possess literary sources, as in India, we can only know of its existence from the oldest inscription discovered.

[23] Jiménez Moreno, 1959: 1031. This author believes that the Long Count passed from the Maya to the late Olmecs, since earlier Maya stelae could have been made of wood and therefore would have disappeared. Thus, Stela C would not be the culmination of an internal development of the Olmec province but rather the assimilation of knowledge brought in from outside. He feels that perhaps the system is joined to the Maya language and that if Maya influences or the Maya themselves appear in various sites such as Monte Alban, Guerrero, and Xochicalco, they would appear also in the Olmec region. I believe that ancient associations existed between both areas (see, for example, Monument E-VII-Sub at Uaxactun) but that the influence was probably from Olmec to Maya. Those from the Maya to the Olmec zone are later, in what I have called the Post-Olmec period.

[24] Jiménez Moreno (1959: 1031) and Piña Chán (1964) propose 400–100 B.C. The date suggested by Kubler (1962) does not seem acceptable, since it goes back to the point of view, proved erroneous, that takes the Olmecs well into the Classic period.

[25] Weyerstall, 1932; Medellín, 1960.

nence the Olmecs were not dead and occasionally produced a master-piece within the old style. These hypotheses do not seem to be irrational, since we have numerous cases in history which demonstrate that moribund cultures can produce some of the fairest flowers at the moment of their death—as in the case of Aristotle.

It may also be said that this chronology and this point of view adapt themselves well to other dates which have been obtained from other contemporaneous sites in Mesoamerica.

It is only thus that we may accept the conclusion[26] that the efflorescence of La Venta and therefore of Middle Tres Zapotes ended around 600 B.C. But if we tried to place Stela C, or even worse the Tuxtla statuette, within that period, it would have to extend to the second century before our era—even if we accept Correlation A. Then Olmec Period III would have to be brought into the beginnings of the Christian era; this seems much too late. A basic error of the first chronologies placed Olmec culture within the Classic period. This led to the necessity of imagining that it formed a sort of cultural oasis which the influences of the Classic Maya culture or of the Classic highland cultures never reached. It also led to other peculiar interpretations disproved by more recent archaeology.

What was the cause of the decadence of the Olmecs? This question cannot be answered with absolute certainty, but the following ideas are plausible: there was pressure from other areas which by then had become highly developed; a revolution—such as Heizer has suggested—stripped an oppressive priesthood of its power. This seems to shed light on the excesses to which La Venta IV had become a victim when the monumental tomb was constructed. The step taken by the groups in power, from planners to oppressors—and the subsequent results—may well have been one of the causes of the dissolution of the great Mesoamerican empires. The Olmecs, who in so many ways were already true Mesoamericans, may have possessed these characteristics when they sowed the seeds of the type of society which, through history, was to produce these cyclical rises and falls of states. These cycles can perhaps explain the reason behind the Mesoamerican concept of history. M. Coe (1967B) interprets the breaking up of large numbers of sculptures at the end of the San Lorenzo period at the San Lorenzo site around 900 B.C. as a "revolutionary act" resulting from a "political crisis."

It seems evident, then, that the Olmecs were the first in North America to reach a grade of civilization, and that from them came many traits that were to become characteristic of Mesoamerica. It is not necessary to repeat them here, since I have mentioned them throughout this chap-

[26] Drucker, Heizer, and Squier, 1959, use the terminal date of 400 B.C.; but this has been changed to 600 B.C. as demonstrated in Berger, Graham, and Heizer, 1967.

ter, but I should like to note that they are divided into two groups. First are those traits not subject to discussion today, like the stelae, the altars, the system of the Long Count and the zero, monumental sculpture, carving in jade, the atlantes, the great heads, the stone sarcophagi, the Pharaonic tombs, buried stone mosaic floors, large adobe bricks, rock crystal skulls, concave mirrors, the idea of placing offerings beneath stelae, the platforms on terraces, the great earth pyramids, cities orientated astronomically, and so forth. Traits in the second group are elements inferred by us from archaeology, such as Mesoamerican-style commerce, the army, the state, and the empire, the social classes, and ceremonial religion.

It is possible that in dealing first with the Olmecs I have exaggerated their importance, or at least given this impression. I believe that the Olmecs were the first to reach the level we can call civilized, but there were other contemporaneous groups—or almost contemporaneous—who contributed extremely important elements, such as writing, which appears at Monte Alban earlier than in the Olmec world. On the other hand, in other areas groups emerged that also launched traditions to be distinctive in later times. Although these groups received Olmec elements, they carried them much further or initiated new elements which they then developed along channels separated from the main Olmec current. In this way the Maya world, for example, may be explained.

When the culture we have been describing disappeared, it left an immense legacy which was to be one of the main columns upon which the great civilization of later times was to be built. With the end of Olmec Period III, Olmec culture terminated and the area in which it flourished was never again to be of any importance. What had been the great cultural nucleus became a marginal zone. From this time on it was to contribute nothing to the cultural history of Mesoamerican civilization. However, before abandoning the theme I am going to make a brief summary of later archaeology since the evidence is that the region was inhabited permanently, just as it is inhabited in our own day, even though density of population has decreased.

At La Venta offerings posterior to Phase IV[27] have been discovered. It is believed that the site was abandoned long enough to permit sand and vegetation to cover the city.[28] The island was then reoccupied by an anonymous people who moved and mutilated[29] the monuments (at least

[27] *Ibid.*: 218–226.

[28] *Ibid.*: 246–248.

[29] I feel it is more plausible that this violent destruction was caused by new emigrants, perhaps the bearers of the "Classic Veracruz" culture, whose ceramics have been found by Medellín in many sites of this area and which both Piña Chán (1964) and Drucker and Heizer in 1955 found in the Torres site at La Venta.

twenty-four of the forty that we know) and dug holes, perhaps seeking—fortunately without complete success—the jade offerings. Certain evidence from the area of the North Pavement suggests that these people could have been either late Olmecs or their heirs, not strangers from outside. Later there seems to have been a slight renaissance, when modest pottery offerings were made in the sand which had covered the monuments. This seems to indicate a change of attitude: instead of being destroyers the new inhabitants honored the ancient site again and showed their respect to the old god. After this came an avalanche of classical influences from Teotihuacan and Veracruz, even though the Olmec territory did not lose its identity entirely. In the Torres site at La Venta[30] and in the upper stratum found by Piña Chán[31] lay polychrome ceramics contemporaneous with Classic Veracruz. Curiously, almost no Maya influence is visible.[32]

At Tres Zapotes there also are irrefutable proofs of later occupations and, as a matter of fact, Upper Tres Zapotes is one of them, showing obvious Teotihuacan influences and classical elements from Veracruz. Weiant[33] unearthed celts, yokes, and smiling figures. The Soncautla complex is even later. In the rest of the area are found ceramics and objects from the Classic and Toltec periods[34] and, finally, remains of what we know in history as the Aztec occupation. The same thing occurred at San Lorenzo. It is this succession of later peoples which belong to what I have here called Post-Olmec.

[30] Drucker, Heizer, and Squier, 1959: 237–246.

[31] Piña Chán, 1964: 18.

[32] Drucker, Heizer, and Squier (1959: 226) mention a fragment of plumbate pottery (with a lustrious metallic surface), which indicates late occupation.

[33] Weiant, 1943: 118.

[34] Medellín, 1960; Valenzuela, 1938, 1939, 1945.

PART TWO
OLMEC
MESOAMERICA

If we examine works of art outside the Metropolitan area we find numerous monuments and small objects that bear the Olmec stamp. All this abundant and important material will help us in understanding this first civilization in Mesoamerica.

When the archaeologist has studied the cultures contemporaneous to the Olmecs he will be ready to affirm that there are a number of different situations to be taken into consideration: (1) there are sites and objects that are identical with or very similar to those of the Metropolitan zone; (2) there are sites and objects within the Olmec style, but different from those of the Metropolitan area; (3) there are sites and objects related to the Metropolitan Olmec world which, however, retain their own style; and (4) there are sites and objects that are not related in any way to the Metropolitan Olmecs.

This fourth category will only be dealt with incidentally, since it refers to cultures that had not yet attained a level of civilization. Nevertheless, they are important as indications of the borders of the Olmec world. The other three categories will be the subject of the second part of this book.

I shall make little reference to isolated objects found throughout Mesoamerica which are Olmec or related to the Olmec, except for those objects or groups of objects which either are impossible to move or were found during controlled scientific explorations, or are notoriously abundant at one site. The smaller and isolated objects have circulated too much—either in ancient or in modern times—to be a useful basis for a study.[1] I have grouped the sites by areas in order to make them more easily studied.

[1] Unfortunately the provenance of a great many objects of Olmec style cannot be established with certainty because they were not excavated under controlled conditions and we therefore have no way of knowing which site produced or used them. These pieces are among the most beautiful and valuable ever produced by this culture. Today, severed from their historical roots, they are found in museums and private collections. The uncertainty as to their origin is due not only to the vandalism of site looters and the scarcely to be condoned practices of modern dealers but to the transporting of objects from one site to another in ancient times. They were moved precisely because they were highly valued, and perhaps were inherited from generation to generation.

6

THE LOWER AND MIDDLE PRECLASSIC

THE CENTRAL MEXICAN HIGHLANDS

This area may be dealt with as a whole since in ancient times it was a marginal region; in later times it was to become a focal area, with the development of the Teotihuacan culture.

Olmec culture occupied the valleys of Mexico and Puebla and was spread over the divisions known today as the states of Mexico, Tlaxcala, Puebla, and Hidalgo, and the Federal District (fig. 15). Here the highlands rise about 6000 feet above sea level and the entire area is ruggedly mountainous. As a matter of fact, these great mountains serve as an explanation of conditions through the area during later times. In the past the mountains were more heavily forested than they are today, and their main vegetation consisted of pines and oaks. The fauna, very similar to that of today, included the puma and the mountain lion, the deer, boar, bear, many other smaller animals, and numerous fowl. Fishing—in contrast to the Olmec area—was insignificant except in the lakes of the Valley of Mexico. On the other hand, food gathering must have been an occupation of considerable importance. By this time of course agriculture was generally practiced; the inhabitants surely possessed the dog as a domestic animal and may have kept the turkey as well. Be it as it may, these animals are not basic for human existence.

At the beginning of the Preclassic the climate of the Valley of Mexico seems to have been more humid, causing the lakes to rise. This would explain why the most ancient Preclassic site, El Arbolillo, stands higher

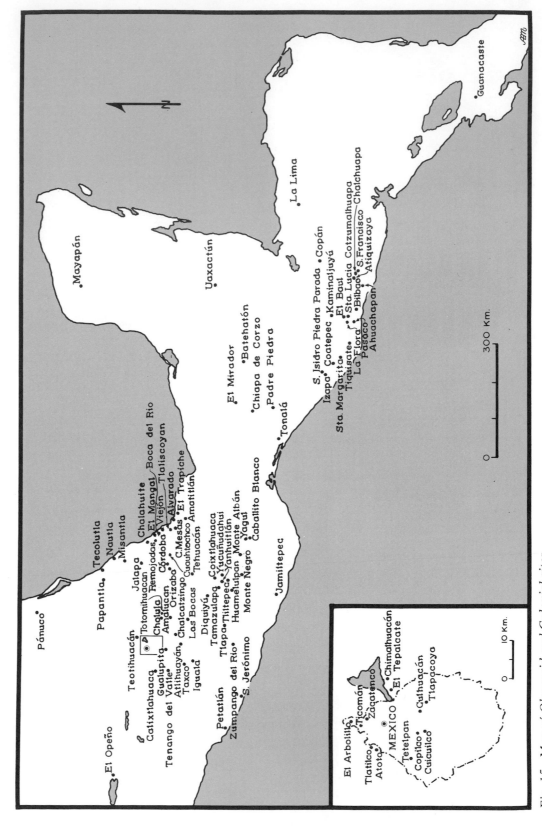

Fig. 15. Map of Olmecoid and Colonial sites.

on the slopes than do later sites such as Zacatenco. The Valley of Mexico with its great lakes seems to have been the pivot of the entire area, though the other regions also seem to have played an important role during the Preclassic.

Let us deal with the great periods known as the Lower and Middle Preclassic as a whole. It is evident that they are not the same and that there are important distinctions between them; still I will discuss them together because they are only antecedents of civilized history and therefore not the theme of this volume. They are necessary only to understand that which was to follow. As in the coastal gulf region, Olmec Period I is simply the threshold of the civilization which was to be initiated in Olmec Period II; in the highlands the periods known as Lower and Middle Preclassic are preparatory to the Upper Preclassic, and it is in this latter period that the civilized traits that were to form the Classic Period became apparent.

The Lower Preclassic dates back perhaps as far as 1700 B.C., when El Arbolillo, the first village of the area, seems to have been established.[1] Toward 1200 B.C. Zacatenco[2] and Tlatilco[3] began to be settled, together with other communities which are difficult to date because they have not been studied sufficiently. Around 1000 B.C. the second great period began: Middle Preclassic, which includes the phases called El Arbolillo II, Middle Zacatenco, Upper Tlatilco; Copilco and Tlapacoya were founded in the Valley of Mexico, Totimehuacan and Amalucan in the Valley of Puebla, and Calixtlahuaca in the region of Toluca. Indubitably many other villages were developing during this period, which was to last until about 500 B.C. It can be affirmed that, without taking into consideration Olmec influences, we are dealing with a culture with a basic unity. This was actually the local, Preclassic culture of the highlands.

The population density was extremely low. El Arbolillo and Zacatenco I were not populated by more than 200 inhabitants.[4] Because of high infant mortality it is to be doubted that a third of the children reached maturity; few inhabitants lived to be more than fifty. Little by little these conditions ameliorated.[5] It was in the Middle Preclassic that

[1] Vaillant, 1935.

[2] Vaillant, 1930.

[3] Piña Chán, 1958; Porter, 1953; Covarrubias, 1946. There are C-14 datings for these two sites which in general agree with the other data. Three for Tlatilco show the following: the oldest gives the date 1457 B.C. ± 250 (Johnson, 1951). The other two are M. 661, 982 B.C. ± 250, and M. 660, 568 B.C. ± 250 (Crane and Griffin, 1958). For Zacatenco we have C. 196 with the date 1360 B.C. ± 250 (Johnson, 1951: 7), which corresponds to Zacatenco I, and M. 662, which gives 492 B.C. (Crane and Griffin, 1958).

[4] Piña Chán, 1955: 25.

[5] Vaillant, 1935: 188.

Fig. 16. Ceramics from the Early Preclassic.

many new villages sprang up. During this time the Valley of Mexico may have contained between 3000 and 4000 inhabitants.[6]

Besides the three basic plants—corn, beans, and squash—the list of other cultivated plants is rather lengthy: amaranth, chili pepper;[7] numerous fruits and vegetables such as avocados, tomatoes, and the chayote of the cucumber family; tubers such as the sweet potato; and spicy herbs used in cooking. Cotton may have been known and cultivated in Morelos, as it was later, in Aztec times. The fiber of the century plant was used in the fabrication of textiles. Tobacco, which in the indigenous world was used more for medicinal purposes than for the pleasure of smoking, may have come later, since the oldest pipes that have been found are later than 1000 A.D.

Cereals were ground on metates which belong to a non-Olmec tradition, for they have a flange running around the top and therefore were worked with small grinding stones.[8] Frequently the metates have low supports. Many tools, simple but efficient, were made of stone, obsidian, deer antler, or bone.[9]

Basketry, textiles, wooden objects—all have disappeared except a few shapeless fragments.[10] The pottery, simple in form and technique, is well fashioned and reveals extensive earlier knowledge of the art of ceramics, although its origin in the area is still a mystery. A series of types, together with clay figurines, has allowed us to classify different stages in the Preclassic period.

[6] Piña Chán, 1955: 26.
[7] MacNeish, 1962: 38.
[8] Vaillant, 1930: pl. XLVI.
[9] Piña Chán, 1955: fig. 1.
[10] Vaillant, 1930: 38; Vaillant, 1931: 315; Vaillant, 1935: 250.

	1500 B.C.	1300	1100	900	700	500	300	100 B.C.
GREAT PERIODS	*Early Pre-Classic*			*Middle Pre-Classic*		*Late Pre-Classic*		
METROPOLITAN OLMEC AREA	OLMEC I		OLMEC II			OLMEC III		

CENTRAL HIGHLANDS
- ARBOLILLO I — ARBOLILLO II — TICOMAN
- ZACATENCO I (1360) — ZACATENCO II — ZACATENCO III (492)
- TLATILCO I (1457) — TLATILCO II (982)(568) — TEPALCATE
- COPILCO — CUICUILCO (82)
- TLAPACOYA I (650) — TLAPACOYA II
- TEHUACAN (Santa María) — TEOTIHUACAN I (483)(432)
- TOTIMEHUACAN
- AMALUCAN
- CALIXTLAHUACA I

MORELOS
- CHALCATZINGO
- GUALUPITA I — GUALUPITA II

VERACRUZ
- VIEJON
- TRAPICHE I — TRAPICHE II
- LOWER CERRO DE LAS MESAS I
- PANUCO I — PANUCO II

OAXACA
- SAN JOSE MOGOTE | GUADALUPE | MONTE ALBAN I (790)(390) — MONTE ALBAN II (273)(264)
- MONTE NEGRO — HUAMELULPAN
- YAGUL I — CABALLITO BLANCO

CHIAPAS
- CHIAPA I — CHIAPA II — CHIAPA III | CHIAPA IV | CHIAPA V
- IZAPA TONALA

GUATEMALA
- OCOS — CUADROS — CONCHAS I — CONCHAS II (La Victoria)
- ILUSIONES (Bilbao)
- EL BAUL I
- AREVALO — PROVIDENCIA — MIRAFLORES
- MAMON — CHICANEL (Uaxactun)

	1500 B.C.	1300	1100	900	700	500	300	100 B.C.

PERIODS OF MESOAMERICAN CULTURE (Numbers in parentheses indicate Carbon IV dates)

In the Early Preclassic polished black, blackish brown, polished white, and white on red were the principal types of ware (fig. 16). Decoration is based on incision, and shapes—vastly different from those of the Olmecs—include plates, jars with outflaring walls, forms with composite silhouette, bowls, and tripod plates with hollow conical supports. The base is usually hemispherical.[11]

[11] Piña Chán, 1958: 1:112.

127

All the figurines from this epoch are feminine, small (less than six inches high), and quite primitive (fig. 17). The sculptor modeled first the head and torso and then added arms and legs. The features and adornments were marked by pinching or by adding little pieces of clay. The figurine was then fired and frequently painted. They are rather naturalistic, but standards and fashions changed, producing styles that vary according to site and time.

Fig. 17. Figurines from the Early Preclassic.

The main types in the Early Preclassic are the ones Vaillant called C1 to C4 and F. Pieces of the C group are the ones most commonly found. They show a general trend but with clear distinctions between each subtype. C1 figurines are defined by their prominent lips and chin-lessness; the heads are large in proportion to the body. In C2 the fillets forming the features are smaller so that the planes of the face are more natural, as is the chin. Figurines of the C3 type have faces heavy in contour and oblong in outline, in contrast to the preceding group; the headdress is equally coarse and simple. C4 comprises figurines with a flat, thin head, conical in outline, and with features in relatively low relief.[12] Type F is the crudest of all. The head looks almost inhuman; the nose and the mouth fillets occupy a large space on the highly convex and prognathic face, and the brow recedes.[13]

[12] Vaillant, 1930.
[13] *Ibid.*: 128.

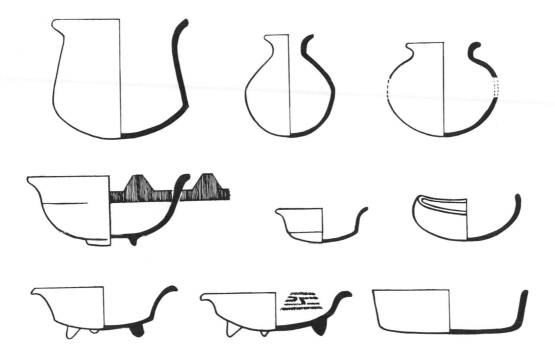

Fig. 18. Ceramic shapes from the Middle Preclassic.

In the Middle Preclassic many other pottery types appeared (fig. 18). The main ones are red on white, brown on yellow, polished red, thin black, and buff. Although decoration by incision was still common, two-color painted styles were abundant, as is evident in the names of the ceramic types. The flat base appeared, plus a number of other forms, some of which may be classified as "foreign."

The main non-Olmec types of figurines of the Middle Preclassic are B, I, K, and C5. The technique of construction is similar to the previous ones, but some features, especially the eyes, are made by incision and less by adding pieces of clay (pl. 51). Type B is the most abundant. "Body, head and legs are made as separate elements and combine into a flat whole, having a wide range in size. Anatomical proportions are only vaguely observed ... The eye is made by means of two broad ploughs and the nose and mouth fillets are small in comparison with the facial area."[14]

The heads of type I are flat in back and generally polished, while Type K has a round face, simple headdress, and mouth and eyes made by two

[14] Vaillant, 1935: 197.

gouges. All this gives it a frog-like appearance. C5 has a relatively large head with a plump and rounded face.[15]

These types of the Middle Preclassic are genetically related to those of the Early Preclassic. They represent the culture in the highland valleys that is not yet Olmec-influenced. Taken together they form a local tradition frequently called the C tradition,[16] in contrast with Olmec and Olmecoid figurines that form the D tradition.

All the figurines belonging to these periods are solid, and of course handmade. Rarely are they associated with burials; rather, they have been unearthed in cultivated fields or in house mounds. Perhaps they formed part of a fertility cult. They never represent deities. These little women are usually nude, although they frequently wear turbans or other headdresses, earplugs, bracelets, and anklets. Occasionally the more modest ones are clad in a loincloth or a short skirt.

Though the dead were buried (and as time progressed, with more abundant offerings), we can scarcely speak of the burials as tombs. We can only speak of graves without fixed orientation; the cadaver was never placed in a determined position.

Houses were mainly of wattle and daub, covered with thatched roofs, although stone foundations began to be used, as were clay floors, all of this pointing to the form architecture was to take in later times. The population had grown by the time of the Preclassic, but it is impossible to refer to it yet as anything but a village culture. We know nothing, actually, of the social and political organization of these peoples, nor of the existence of professional groups or specialists. Nevertheless, in view of what was to come, it is evident that vast transformations were under way and that if today we were in possession of all their artifacts we would discover some unsuspected traits.

The Olmecs penetrated this village world, and at certain places they transformed the highland cultures. The Olmecs were not the only immigrants, for others came from the west; but Olmec influence, limited to certain spots at the beginning, served as the most important catalyst to stimulate these peasant groups toward further progress, which in the Upper Preclassic led toward urbanism and the path to civilization.

For us, the most interesting site in the Valley of Mexico during the Middle Preclassic is definitely Tlatilco. This is the site where Olmec influence was greatest. Other sites, such as El Arbolillo and Zacatenco, continued their own course with some foreign influence. Even Atoto, close to Tlatilco, was only a village whose culture was still the typical peasant way of life of the Valley of Mexico.[17]

---

[15] Vaillant, 1930.
[16] Piña Chán, 1958; Covarrubias, 1957: pl. 8, left.
[17] Piña Chán, 1958: 73.

Tlatilco means in the Aztec language "Where Things Are Hidden," a most appropriate name. Since only burials have been found, we may surmise that the place was primarily a cemetery, but it was undoubtedly an inhabited site also. Its clay houses have left only the faintest traces of their existence, but numerous conical-shaped enclosures have been found. They are too small to be houses, but might have been used as kitchens. On the other hand, hundreds of burials have been unearthed. Many of the skeletons were deposited in an extended position, others flexed, all found at different levels. Most of the anthropological data referring to these skeletons has still not been published, so that it is not easy to discuss them fully. As we do not have Olmec skeletons with which to compare them, it is difficult to affirm whether we are dealing with the original inhabitants of the Valley of Mexico like those of Zacatenco or perhaps with migrants from the Gulf Coast.

The marvelous Tlatilco ceramics— and I am referring only to the Olmecoid types—bear traces of the Olmec culture. We find thick black pottery with engraved designs, black with white spots or with white rims (which reminds us immediately of one of the most typical traits of Olmec pottery), gray, and other types of minor occurrence. The use of the fine white clay, kaolin, is foreign to the Valley, since it comes from the Gulf Coast.[18]

An amazing variety of forms exists. Aside from those which are most general and frequent in Mesoamerica (and therefore do not characterize any site or epoch), such as the semispherical and conical bowls, many bottle forms appear at Tlatilco. At times the decoration of the latter is extraordinary. Forms vary from bowls of composite silhouette, neckless ollas, tall hourglass-shaped vases, vessels in the form of a shell, or with stirrup handle or a pedestal.[19] The anthropomorphic vessels (pl. 52) are astounding.[20] They include acrobats,[21] one figure in the form of a mask,[22] and zoomorphic vessels which are stylized armadillos, opossums, boars, fish, frogs, dogs, rabbits, and ducks.[23]

Incised or engraved lines which are added to hand-molded pottery to give form to the motif are a sort of "writing" characteristic of the Olmecs. In many cases these motifs are related to the jaguar, represented in a highly stylized fashion, showing his gums, claws, or spots. Occasionally other motifs appear, such as the water serpent or admira-

[18] *Ibid.*: 113.
[19] *Ibid.*: 76 to 84.
[20] Covarrubias, 1950: fig. on p. 160.
[21] Piña Chán, 1958: vol. 2, pls. 30 and 31, and Anton, 1961: pl. 2. Centuries later the same idea was reproduced in a marble celt (*Handbook of the Robert Woods Bliss Collection of Pre-Columbian Art*, 1963: pl. 92).
[22] Piña Chán, 1958: II, fig. 33.
[23] *Ibid.*: II, figs. 4 and 12.

bly worked human hands.[24] These same vessels bear cord or textile impressions and punctured or fingernail-impressed designs. Tlatilco seems to be the only site in the highlands containing a certain amount of rocker-stamped ceramics, made with an object rolled to and fro over the pot to leave imprints.[25]

Another infrequent type is perhaps a forerunner of "fresco" decoration: a thin coat of stucco is applied to the fired vessel and is then painted. Stucco work does not appear at Tlatilco, but the technique of inlaying colors—usually pink and green—suggests the cloisonné characteristic of Monte Alban II. This inlay appears at Tlatilco, perhaps full blown during the period of Olmec influence. Another novelty at Tlatilco is negative decoration—a technique similar to batik—which later was to thrive at many other sites.

The style of the abundant Tlatilco clay figurines is truly remarkable. Almost all represent women with short arms, tiny waists, bulbous legs, and extremely broad hips (pl. 53). These traits are not peculiar to Tlatilco pottery but were very widespread in the Preclassic. I believe that they represent not only fertility but an aesthetic ideal or a marked masculine taste. Thus, two thousand years later, according to the *Historia Tolteca Chichimeca*,[26] Huemac, last king of Tula, "asked for women and ordered the Nonoualcas to bring him 'a woman: and I order you that her hips be four palms in width . . .' " The king was then given a woman measuring four palms but he was still unsatisfied. "She still is not wide enough," said Huemac to the Nonoualcas. "Her hips are not so wide as I would like! Her hips barely measure four palms, and I want them wider." In Tlatilco, though, the figurines have incomparable figures, which perhaps would have appealed to Huemac more than the lady brought to him by the Nonoualcas.

The Tlatilco figurines are standing, seated, or move as if they were dancing (pl. 54). Many are nude, like the masculine ones from La Venta. They wear headdresses in a thousand forms, their bodies and faces are painted, and they are adorned with jewelry. At times they wear short skirts which seem to represent cloth or fibers, like Hawaiian skirts,[27] fitting over the hips rather than the waist. Hair was arranged in many forms and at times was painted red. The figurines which show us these traits represent, on the whole, tradition D.

Characteristic Olmec types are as fine and as beautiful in Tlatilco as are their counterparts in La Venta (see pl. 55). At times they are so similar that it would not be possible to tell their provenance had they

---

[24] *Ibid.*: 113.
[25] Porter, 1953: 37.
[26] *Historia Tolteca Chichimeca*, 1947: 69.
[27] Covarrubias, 1950: 157.

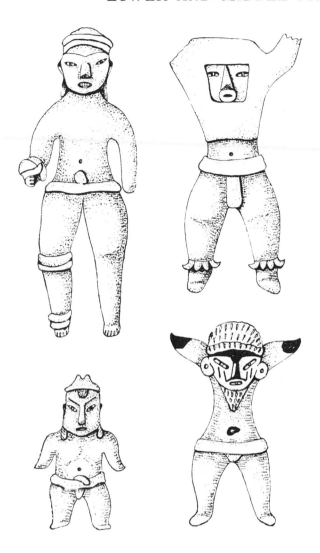

Fig. 19. Masculine figurines from Tlatilco.

not been found during explorations. There are, however, many Tlatilco figurine types not found in the Olmec region, like the feminine figures with one body and two heads or with two faces on one head. These are so modern that they remind us of the old saying—true in art although false in science—that there is nothing new under the sun.

The Middle Preclassic male figurines are interesting because they represent a direct Olmec idea; let us remember that male figurines were not made during the Preclassic in the non-Olmec-influenced sites of the highlands. They also show an entire gamut of attitudes and even of functions, which throw light on Tlatilco society (fig. 19). Bearded individuals appear; ball players (not found at La Venta) are represented (pl. 56), as are mysterious personages who have been classified as shamans

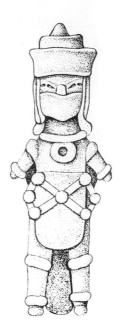

Fig. 20. Tlatilco figurine: shaman.

(fig. 20). Some, I believe, depict soldiers because they wear a type of armor,[28] while others—with masked faces—suggest certain aspects of religious life in the Preclassic, when undoubtedly there were not yet priests but an earlier combination of magician and witch doctor. At that time in Tlatilco there was no organized religion nor a professional priesthood. True priests could have existed at La Venta while at Tlatilco there were only shamans, precisely because the Olmecs had taken the step toward civilized urbanization, while Tlatilco—for all the brilliance of its works—had not yet reached that stage.

None of the figures actually represents a deity. Mesoamerican gods had not come into being among the Olmecs, although certain elements suggest that the appearance of the god of fire was near. Masks are amazing and always monstrous, like the two-faced one, half life and half death; it suggests the duality which is so basic in Mesoamerica but which can be understood only in later religious patterns.

Piña Chán[29] has pointed out that "the aquatic serpent, symbol of water, is combined in Tlatilco with the jaguar's claw, forming a kind of dragon-serpent-jaguar. Later this was transformed into the precious serpent of terrestrial water, associated with the complex of gods of celestial water such as Tlaloc, Chac, Cocijo, who bore jaguar-serpent traits, plus man-bird elements." I have already mentioned my doubts concerning a cult of rain in the Olmec region. But in the dry highlands rain is indispensable, and therefore it is not strange that agricultural

[28] Piña Chán, 1955: pls. on pp. 40–41.
[29] Piña Chán, 1964: 45.

134

peoples whose life depended upon it should seek rain anxiously. In this way we can explain the transformation of the jaguar god into a water god: Tlaloc.

Both in Tlatilco and in Morelos are found large hollow figurines made of white clay (well finished with kaolin) or of red clay, which are typical of the Olmec style. The same type of figurines, found outside of authorized explorations but whose provenance is quite certain, come from the region of the volcanoes Popocatepetl and Iztaccihuatl in Puebla and from Morelos[30] (see pl. 57). All are feminine, usually with short arms and heavy legs in the Tlatilco style.[31] The faces resemble type D.

But in the highlands the Olmec intrusion is seen not only in clay objects. Some stone figurines from Tlatilco are identical to those of the Metropolitan zone, as are "hematite mirrors, jade ornaments, cranial deformations, filed teeth . . . ,"[32] which are all imported traits. Some of these—like jade beads and earplugs and pendants in the form of a jaguar's eyetooth[33]—are also found in non-Olmecoid sites. These objects, or at least the material from which they were made (like hematite for the mirrors or kaolin), were imported from the Olmec region, although they may have been worked locally. The *yuguitos* or "little yokes" found at Tlatilco are unknown in the Metropolitan zone, although they appear at other Olmecoid sites (pl. 58). Yoke is a popular term for large yoke-shaped stones frequently carved with elaborate designs typical of Central Veracruz during the Classic period. They are possibly part of the ball game complex. In earlier, Olmec times, small yokes—*yuguitos*—appear in some Olmecoid sites. They may be an antecedent to the large ones, although if this is so, their function would be different.

Burials containing decapitated skeletons or parts of a human body associated with complete skeletons, both adult and infantile[34] have been found. This suggests the possibility of human sacrifice from a very early period. As we have seen, it is possible that this custom existed among the Metropolitan Olmecs who perhaps introduced the custom of sacrifice to Tlatilco.

[30] Caso, 1933: 577.

[31] These have been found in San Martín Texmelucan, Cholula, Huejotzingo, Ozumba, and Chalco in the states of Puebla and Mexico. Hay (1923) found others in Los Remedios. Some come from the state of Morelos, from such sites as Totolapa (Caso, 1933). Numerous figurines from Morelos were in the former Plancarte and Bourgeois collections (Vaillant and Vaillant, 1934: 28). A "magician" or warrior reminiscent of Tlatilco (*ibid.*: pls. 7, 8) is also from Gualupita, Morelos. Vaillant, who calls them D-III, illustrates other, very important, figurines he found at this site (*ibid.*: 50–53, figs. 14 and 15). These are the typical Olmec baby face figurines, which he calls C-IX. Some are great works of art (*ibid.*: pls. 14–2–3 and 15–1).

[32] Covarrubias, 1950: 161.

[33] Vaillant, 1930: pl. XL; Vaillant, 1931: 306 and 402; Vaillant, 1935: 244.

[34] Covarrubias, 1950: 160; Piña Chán, 164: 17.

These evident similarities are strengthened by chronology. A comparison of C 14 dates from Tlatilco with those obtained in La Venta show that they are strikingly similar. This provides another basis to believe that the two sites were contemporaneous and that the influence of the Olmecs in the highlands and their colonization of this area must have occurred during the same period.

But although "Tlatilco is the richest, most cosmopolitan, and surely the most important center of the Preclassic cultures in the Valley of Mexico,"[35] it does not reach the level of a metropolis. There is no architecture there, nor is there monumental stone sculpture, nor the beginnings of writing or of urban organization. In spite of the splendor of its ceramics, the beauty of its figurines, the sporadic appearance of jades, small stone sculpture, and mirrors, Tlatilco does not represent a city.

Tlatilco is clearly an Olmec colony. I say colony because the influences are so clear and so abundant, and are grouped in such a way that it is improbable that they are the result of commerce, but are due to the physical and permanent presence of Olmecs. Did their presence come about through a conquest? This is possible, because otherwise it is not understandable how this group—obviously different from the others— flourished there. There is no way to demonstrate this, however.

The physical presence of Olmecs in Tlatilco, unlike other sites only touched by Olmec influence, will allow us, perhaps, to distinguish between two types of expansion. I will call the first type that of Colonial Olmecs (as they seem to be), and the second Olmecoid.

While in many highland sites Olmec influence is insignificant, in Tlatilco it is remarkable; hence its extraordinary importance and its distinction. This is even more evident when we observe how local elements disappear in Tlatilco, to be replaced by Olmec ones. Tlatilco I is but a highland village; Tlatilco II is an Olmec colony. An adjacent site, Atoto, is a typical Preclassic village whose art is almost without Olmec traits. As Piña Chán[36] has stated, and I believe correctly:

Atoto presents the peculiarity of lacking almost all elements of Olmec origin—flat bases, scratched decoration, feline motifs, Type D figurines, etc.—to such an extent that there must be an explanation for this phenomenon.

At this time we believe it is due to the fact that when the Olmecs reached Tlatilco they were only a small group which had not yet begun to expand through the entire zone; while the Tlatilcans continued developing their same ceramic tradition the Olmecs continued with their own, though later. When the Olmecs were absorbed by the original population, the two traditions fused and from this mixture grew new pottery styles and new decorative techniques which were to be the cause of the great development of that site and which would produce the ceramic complexity, leading some to believe that Tlatilco corresponded to the Upper Preclassic.

[35] Covarrubias, 1950: 155.
[36] Piña Chán, 1958: 73.

The impact of a new cultural group in Tlatilco and the growing population must have led a conservative segment of the population to occupy Atoto Hill and continue to develop its own ceramic tradition, while the rest of the Tlatilcans mixed little by little with the newcomers and occupied mainly the zone included between the Hondo River and its branches, Los Cuartos and Totolica.

Thus the hill of Atoto remained on the fringe of the development that occurred in Tlatilco itself, although during the Middle Preclassic the two nuclei of population were contemporaneous and had a common origin.

Atoto is a Tlatilco without Olmecs.[37] We see, then, how the Olmecs eliminated in Tlatilco the older culture that was typical of the highlands. As time went on the Olmecs mixed with the local population to the point of ceasing to exist as a unity, which explains their disappearance at the end of the Middle Preclassic.

In Tlapacoya, also within the Valley of Mexico, some Olmec influences are visible. They correspond, probably, to the Middle Preclassic. Thus the polished white ceramics have a carved decoration with motifs similar to those of Tlatilco and of other Olmec sites of Morelos such as Chalcatzingo.[38] Also in Tlapacoya appear the conical formations characteristic of Tlatilco.[39]

Unquestionable Olmec influences are found at Tehuacan in the state of Puebla, especially during the Santa Maria phase (900–200 B.C.).[40] Ceramics with white or gray rims have been found; these are predominant at the end of this phase. There are also Type D figurines and other Olmec types, among them a large hollow figure.[41] At this time there appeared villages with temples together with other objects of clearly ceremonial function.

Various jade or clay objects come from other regions in the highlands. In the Puebla area, which was an Olmec center in a very broad sense, Olmec objects have been found at Totimehuacan and many

[37] Tolstoy and Guenette (1965: 35 and 77) also conclude that the Tlatilco burials containing Olmec pieces belong to the Atoto phase.

[38] Barba de Piña Chán, 1956: 63.

[39] At Tlapacoya only three small ceramic heads were found which can be associated with the Olmecs. This seems to indicate the latter's meager influence there (ibid.: 54). Two belong to D-I type, and another is said to be of an "Olmec type." Within the filling of Mound II two hematite mirrors were also discovered, another evidence of Olmec influence (ibid.: 124, fig. 18); the same may be said of some of the jade pieces. The Field Collection in Mexico City possesses a pair of female figures displaying a clear Olmec inspiration. They are from Tlapacoya but not discovered under scientific conditions (Piña Chán, 1964, pl. 10B). A Carbon 14 sample from Tomb 2 at Tlapacoya gives us the date 650 ± 250 (Crane and Griffin, 1958). A long jade object was also discovered at Teotihuacan, bearing incised drawings (Gamio, 1922: I, fig. 94). Another series of little-known sites in the central highlands of Mexico possibly reflect an Olmec influence (Piña Chán, 1964: maps 1 and 2).

[40] MacNeish, 1964: 6.

[41] MacNeish, 1964A: fig. 11; and MacNeish, 1962.

other localities.[42] Exceptionally important is Las Bocas, a site near Izucar, recently pillaged but not yet explored,[43] and Tepatlaxco, where sporadic finds have been made since the time of Seler (1890–1912). The jade head from Tenango del Valle[44] is worthy of mention, and many others of dubious provenance are known.[45] All these works of art seem to be from the latter part of the Olmec II period and possibly later. During the Upper Preclassic in the highlands, then, Olmec elements were preserved though dispersed. Some figurines from Ticoman are reminiscent of the Olmec style,[46] but the Olmec influence in the Valley of Mexico ends in Tlatilco. Known sites of the Upper Preclassic scarcely reflect this influence, and these sites returned—on a higher cultural level—to the local tradition. It was only later, in Teotihuacan, where some pale glimmerings of Olmec art reappeared. I cannot explain this eclipse and this hiatus, but it coincides quite clearly with the coastal style, which I have noted as characteristically Olmec. Its existence in the highlands did not continue longer than the end of the Middle Preclassic.

MORELOS

In Chalcatzingo in the district of Jonacatepec, at the foot of the Cerro de la Cantera, there are at least two large mounds. Findings from stratigraphic pits indicate that the site was occupied from the Preclassic to the Postclassic.

The most important elements in Chalcatzingo are two scenes engraved in the natural rocks of the hill. Both are true sculpture though in bas-relief. We can associate them with the stratigraphic pits only by their style, which is unquestionably Olmec, although—as I shall try to demonstrate—late Olmec. In spite of being considered petroglyphs because they are executed in living rock, their aesthetic quality and the technique of their carving removes them completely from the more primitive type of petroglyphic designs.

The first represents a personage seated on a bench with a box in his

[42] Particularly striking are the human figure in the Puebla Museum that Caso suggests comes from the area of Tehuacan (1965: 8), illustrated in Covarrubias, 1946: pl. 1; and the sculptured tiger from Necaxa (Vaillant, 1932; see also illustration in Covarrubias, 1957). In certain wares and large hollow figurines from the Ajalpan phase at Tehuacan, dated after 1500 B.C., MacNeish (1962: 39) noted similarities with Olmec objects.

[43] Illustrations of many of the objects found at this site appear in Michael Coe's excellent work *The Jaguar's Children*. In general Coe's conclusions are similar to mine regarding the style and Olmec expansion in central Mexico.

[44] Piña Chán, 1964: pl. 19.

[45] See, for instance, Lothrop, 1957: pl. 5.

[46] For instance, Vaillant, 1931: pl. LIX, lower part, 1.

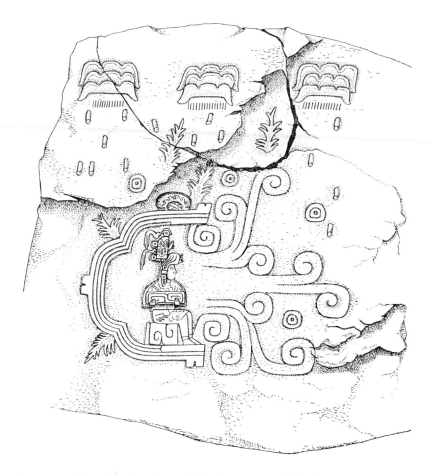

Fig. 21. Bas relief at Chalcatzingo. Height of cave, 57 inches.

hands[47] (fig. 21). It has been said that he is shown seated in a cave. I believe that this orifice could be, rather, the open mouth of a jaguar, symbolized by the cleft elements that end the parallel bands forming the mouth and by the glyph with the X mark, above, which, as we know, represents the spots of the animal. This continuation of the Olmec idea of portraying a person inside a niche, whether or not it be an animal's mouth, was to be extended more widely in the Maya world but apparently not in Teotihuacan. In the upper part of the Chalcatzingo relief, clouds and rain are indicated, and circular motifs representing jade, frequently symbolizing something precious, as is rain. The human figure, it seems to me, represents a great chieftain or priest rather than a god.

The second relief (fig. 22) consists of four human figures.[48] The three standing figures are dressed almost alike, but their headdresses are different and one wears a mask. The latter carries a branched staff in

[47] His dress has been fully described (Guzmán, 1934: 238–240).
[48] This relief has been described in detail by Piña Chán (1955: 24–25).

139

Fig. 22. Bas relief at Chalcatzingo. Height of first standing figure, 48 inches.

his hands, unlike the clubs carried by the other two, and he has his back turned to the others and to the nude captive, whose mask is also different from the others. Perhaps these differences indicate ranks or religious or political positions, a phenomenon that possibly occurs in the paintings of Teotihuacan. The ithyphallic captive suggests a fertility ceremony, which would make the theme of this relief similar to that previously described (fig. 21) but in a form that is extremely rare in Mesoamerica.

The impressive masks worn in the relief carving are an Olmecoid element rather than Olmec; we see them repeated with frequency in other sites. The figures in movement and the entire spirit of the scene—even though it be ceremonial—suggest an atmosphere that is not yet hieratic. Recently, three more carvings have been discovered in Chalcatzingo. One represents two men attacked by solar jaguars, another a man and a mythical serpent, and the last may be a tapir. They have been described amply by Cook de Leonard. Similar reliefs done in rock are occasionally found all along the Pacific watershed as far south as El Salvador.

In a small ravine to the north of the mounds Eulalia Guzmán[49] also found a fragment of a human figure in stone which is important because again it is Olmec in style and is amazingly similar to others from the Metropolitan area. In addition, there are some minor petroglyphs in the vicinity of Chalcatzingo.

Olmec influence in the ceramics can be noted in the earliest levels at Chalcatzingo. Cream or yellowish rims with black spots (similar to Olmec gray with white rims), the white lacquer type with "scraped or

[49] Guzmán, 1934: 248–250.

carved decoration, flat bottom, and bottle shape,"[50] and rocker stamped, D2, and baby face figurines, as well as jade beads and earplugs, are elements from both Olmec I and II.

At various sites in Morelos such as El Cortés, Atlihuayan,[51] and others —but especially Gualupita[52]—Olmec ceramics and figurines have appeared (pls. 59 and 60). Some of these predate the Olmec expansion and correspond to that generalized horizon from which Olmec culture sprang later, on the Gulf Coast. Because of this I believe it is pointless to deal in detail with similar sites, but the importance of this style in the earlier stratigraphic levels of the Morelos area should be emphasized.

It is evident, then, that in the highlands and in the lowland areas of Puebla and Morelos there was a strong influence from the main Olmec style, but not exclusively during the Middle Preclassic. This influence seems to have been exerted in two basic forms: in founding colonies such as Tlatilco, Chalcatzingo, Las Bocas, and perhaps Gualupita, and by means of commercial exchange—direct or indirect—in other places. It seems, however, that even with the importance of Tlatilco, the Valley of Mexico is not basically Olmec. The main Olmec strain is more obvious in the Puebla–Morelos area.

GUERRERO AND WESTERN MEXICO

The state of Guerrero, generally considered part of western Mexico from the archaeological point of view, is actually a separate area, more Mesoamerican, more important, and richer than the west. When Guerrero has become better known to archaeologists, it should be dealt with independently from the vast western area, for it has its own history. At the present time it remains almost completely unexplored from the scientific point of view, and at only a few sites have excavations of even

[50] Piña Chán, 1955: 23, 24.

[51] See Piña Chán, Romano, and Pareyón, 1952. The marvelous figure of a man wearing a jaguar skin on his back came from this site, but unfortunately the object was not excavated as part of a scientific exploration. (*Ibid.*: fig. 3; López González, 1953: 12; Covarrubias, 1957: fig. 61; Piña Chán, 1955: fig. 21.

[52] This was the first Preclassic site in Morelos to be explored in a satisfactory manner. Both the figurines and the ceramics found at Gualupita aided the authors in classifying the site into three periods. The first corresponds to the two first phases of the Preclassic. Gualupita II belongs to the Upper Preclassic. Gualupita III is very late (Vaillant and Vaillant, 1934: 127). At the time of excavation Olmec culture had not yet been defined, but the site was undoubtedly highly influenced by it. A magnificent baby face figurine was discovered in later explorations (Westheim, 1962: pl. 11). Judging by its size, it should be placed among the hollow figurines described by Caso (1935). These large hollow figures are not typically Olmec, since they are rarely found in the Metropolitan zone; rather, they are Olmecoid.

a minor scope been carried out. Surveys have been made on a somewhat larger scale; and although they are useful to determine in a preliminary manner the location of archaeological boundaries, they do not suffice to establish a chronology until excavations are made.

Near the center of the state there is a zone around Zumpango del Río from which a great number of objects come (although not from controlled explorations); they are mainly of jade or of fine stones and of unquestionable Olmec style. "They are so frequent and so important in this region that they cannot be considered trade objects."[53] They are found also, although in smaller quantities, to the north of Zumpango as far as the Iguala–Taxco region. Covarrubias classifies them in two groups: Olmec and Olmecoid.

The first includes "figurines, masks, colossal axes, 'little yokes,' plaques and pectorals with or without incised designs, 'little spoons,' jaguar teeth, various adornments, spherical and tubular beads, burins, awls, and so on, as well as some unique objects like a large jadeite hook or fishhook, pendants in the form of parts of the human body (a necklace of human legs from Zumpango, a realistic ear made of jadeite, the big toe of a foot), an alligator made of links of jadeite, a dwarf without the lower jawbone from Iguala, a pendant of a human figure with a duck mask, . . ."[54] (pl. 61). Some of these objects are not really Olmec in the sense that we have used earlier, but Olmecoid. Similar objects, such as the little yokes, have not been found in the Metropolitan zone. On the other hand they appear in Colonial Olmec sites like Tlatilco and most certainly are associated in general with this horizon and culture.

Olmecoid objects are, according to Covarrubias,[55] "of a coarser manufacture and poorer materials . . . This classification includes various types with a greater or lesser number of Olmec traits, such as the general one of the head in pear or avocado shape, superimposed on local styles. Nevertheless the most Olmec trait of these objects is the technique used in making them . . . Similar objects appear in the Cholula zone." Covarrubias feels that these Olmec objects showing a degeneration in style were made in later times (see pl. 62). I believe that they may have been, but it is also possible that they are contemporaneous, though they do not represent sites where the Olmecs were the original inhabitants but rather Olmecoid places; that is, where Olmec traits fused with local ones. This is what took place in other areas although to a different degree.

Indubitably in Guerrero there was a marked Olmec influence, to the point that Covarrubias thought that the style had been born there, be-

[53] Covarrubias, 1948: 86.
[54] *Ibid.*
[55] *Ibid.*: 87.

fore its efflorescence in Veracruz–Tabasco.[56] Olmec objects also come from sites on the Costa Grande (western coast of Guerrero) such as San Geronimo[57] or Soledad de Maciel near Petatlan.[58] We should not forget that the famous Olmec wooden mask—the only object of this material in this style that exists today—comes from a cave in Guerrero (pl. 63). If, on the other hand, in the Middle Balsas basin to the north the Olmec presence is fainter,[59] it becomes more marked along the border with Oaxaca. At places like Tlapa there are ceramics identical to the Olmecoid of the Valley of Oaxaca.

Piña Chán[60] believes the Olmec expansion into Guerrero occurred before 800 B.C. and therefore corresponds to our Olmec II. In principle I agree with this hypothesis, although I repeat that no stratigraphy has been demonstrated in the area and the material has been grouped only typologically. Rarely do these objects have a scientifically valid provenance.

I find no Olmec evidence in the rest of western Mexico, which means that these people did not reach that area. It has been said that the famous little sculpture of El Opeño, near Jacona, Michoacan (pl. 64), indicates that Olmec influence penetrated as far north as this region, so distant from the Metropolitan center, but it seems to me that the figure is Olmec only in the most vague way, if it is at all. It has a semicircular mouth with the corners turned down, but outside of this detail it does not appear to be in the least Olmec. It is of green stone, of primitive aspect, and is poorly carved.[61] Figurines reminiscent of Type D have been found in this zone also. My view is that the Olmecs never went farther north than the Balsas River—if they went that far—and did not penetrate to the Michoacan lakes region. This fact has extremely important implications; I believe that the basis of all the difference between western Mexico and the rest of Mesoamerica can be found here. Not having had the civilizing influence of the Olmecs, western Mexico remained permanently backward, a situation which began to alter only many centuries later with the establishing of the Tarascan empire in the fifteenth century.

[56] Covarrubias, 1956: 11.
[57] *Ibid.*: 15.
[58] Armillas, 1948: 75.
[59] *Ibid.*
[60] Piña Chán, 1964: map 2.
[61] Noguera, 1939: 588 and fig. 13. A stone piece, not unlike a yuguito and perhaps Olmecoid, is preserved at the Museo de las Artesanías in Guadalajara, Jalisco.

VERACRUZ

The region of the Gulf of Mexico northwest of the Papaloapan River and contiguous with the Olmec area is quite confusing because—contrary to what one would suppose—there are relatively few Olmec remains, and in some areas neither Olmec presence or influence has been discovered, even though its proximity and physical resemblance to the Olmec zone would lead one to expect this presence.

I refer, of course, to the Classic Olmec or Olmec II. In the preceding period a series of manifestations demonstrate that a fairly similar culture existed in the coastal region on both sides of the Papaloapan. Thus figurines of Types A, D and E[62] are found from Viejón to the north together with some ceramic types, such as that with the white rim which we have considered so characteristic of the Olmec world. Vessels and figurines from the lowest levels at Trapiche and Chalahuite[63] are the same as those from Olmec I.[64]

Aside from sites within the Olmec area, Medellín mentions the following places where ceramics with white rims have been found: underneath the *Teocalli* at Quauhtochco, in El Mangal, Cerro de las Mesas, Alvarado, Viejón, Tlalixcoyan, and Amatitlan. He also points out the presence of Type A figurines and even hollow figures with white slip.[65] It is not necessary to extend this list. It has been demonstrated that there was a horizon that probably began, also, around 1500 B.C. in the region of central Veracruz and that coincided with Olmec I. These two cultures shared similar traits, although they were not identical. This was the rather uniform ancient world which at that time extended from at least the Panuco region[66] to the southern border of the Olmecs; actually it could have been the same region—with only local variations—which embraced a large part of what was later to be the Maya area. The distribution of Early Preclassic objects corresponds in general with the distribution of the proto-Maya–Huastec language that I have already mentioned.

Medellín[67] has distinguished four zones in central Veracruz where,

---

[62] Type A figurines are defined as having "squat bodies in a seated posture, usually stubby limbs, a broad round face with nose and mouth fillets sunk into a central groove. The eye is made usually by two ploughs with a central perforation" (Vaillant, 1930: 120). Figurines of the E type are much finer, smaller, in different positions, and with a small, straight-waisted, flat, thin body. The female sex is indicated. The head, flat in the back, protrudes in the front into a bird-like prognathism. Type D has already been described.

[63] García Payón, 1950: 92 and 102.

[64] García Payón, 1952: 39–40.

[65] Medellín, 1960A: 14, 47, 185, 189; Piña Chán, 1964: 25.

[66] Ekholm, 1944.

[67] Medellín, 1960A.

during the Preclassic, "there are characteristic local elements which give a certain regional individuality." These zones are: the Nautla River basin, Xalapa region and the semiarid zone, another from Maltrata to somewhat east of Cordoba, and the region between the Blanco and Papaloapan rivers which, therefore, borders on the Olmec world.

These four zones not only possessed individual characteristics during a single period but during the entire 1200-year span before the Christian era. Only a part of this long period interests us.

Other facts must be added to Medellín's: numerous data found by García Payón add much to what is known about the semiarid zone and tell us something, especially, about two other areas—the Misantla region and northern Veracruz above the Tecolutla River. But in contrast to this more or less common background, what occurs in central and northern Veracruz during the Olmec II period?

Simplifying the explanation, and going from south to north, we see that first there is a vast region between the Papaloapan and the Cotaxtla rivers, known as the Mixtequilla. Here objects appear, some unquestionably Olmec, others vaguely Olmec, associated either with objects that are obviously from a later period, or with others that have nothing to do with this culture. The best-known site in this subarea is Cerro de las Mesas.

Cerro de las Mesas lies in swampland about sixteen miles east of Alvarado Bay. Physically it reminds one of Olmec sites because it also becomes an island during the rainy season. Its ruins are scattered over an enormous area of about twenty-five miles from east to west, in at least five main groups. Between these groups are many smaller mounds, indicating the existence of a very extensive ancient city. Planning does not seem to have been rigorous, but approximately square plazas are separated from one another by tall pyramids or by long, low mounds, in typical Mesoamerican fashion.[68]

This great center is not, evidently, contemporaneous with any of the Olmec periods already described. Undoubtedly construction took place during Olmec II and III, but most of the monuments are later. All of the Olmec elements correspond stratigraphically to Lower Cerro de las Mesas; this long period has been divided into I and II. Phase II, chronologically and for obvious associations, corresponds to the Classic period, since Teotihuacan influences are found here. Only Early Phase I seems to be contemporaneous with Olmec III. The associations are not so clear, however, for in the Lower II period of Cerro de las Mesas typically Olmec objects have been found: some stone monuments, jades, and certain types of ceramics.

Among the numerous monuments found up to the present time at

[68] Stirling, 1943: 31.

Fig. 23. Stela 9, Cerro de las Mesas.

Cerro de las Mesas, only stelae 4, 9, and 11 and monuments 2 and 5 are or could be Olmecoid. An Olmec flavor (although late) is found in Stela 4,[69] showing a personage seated on a bench and a glyph and a number 5 formed by dots (pl. 65). The very fact that the stela carries a calendar glyph—which never appears in Olmec II—places it tentatively in Olmec III. Because it is of the same style as Stela 11[70] and bears a general resemblance to this, it must be associated with it. Stirling, the discoverer of both stelae, feels that they are very late,[71] even later than the stelae of the Classic period.

Stela 9[72] (fig. 23) also has Olmecoid features and a certain similarity to the petroglyph at San Isidro Piedra Parada in Guatemala.[73] These figures are related, in a very general way, to the Izapa style, which is also Olmecoid and which I shall discuss later.

Monument 2 of Cerro de las Mesas (pl. 66) is a splendid head over five feet tall, carved in high relief.[74] Only because it is also a colossal head is it similar to the Olmec, for its general style is completely different; I believe that it is later. On the other hand, Monument 5 (pl. 67) has a general likeness to the rotund little Tuxtla statuette.[75] Therefore, it, like

[69] *Ibid.*: 34 and fig. 14c.
[70] *Ibid.*: fig. 12b and p. 43.
[71] *Ibid.*: 47.
[72] *Ibid.*: 42 and fig. 11a.
[73] Thompson, 1943: 104 and 111a.
[74] Stirling, 1943: 45.
[75] Stirling, 1941: 281.

Stela 4, can be placed in the Olmec III period.

It is risky to have chosen some sculptures and left out others because I feel that they are later, although all were found in a relatively small area. Actually, it is evident that they have been removed since ancient times from their original sites, for the plaza was reconstructed many times.[76] Thus their positions are not significant now. So the problem consists in whether these monuments can be attributed to Lower Cerro de las Mesas I period, which, as we have seen, is the only one that seems to correspond to Olmec III. This idea appeals to Drucker,[77] but there is no way of affirming it. Most of the buildings of the main group were constructed later, at the beginning of the Classic (Lower Cerro de las Mesas II), but as I have said, the stone monuments could have come from an earlier plaza.

The famous offering of 782 jade and stone pieces from the Lower II period was found in 1941. Most of the objects are made in varieties of jadeite, in a loose sense classified as jade. Many of the figurines and beads are of a soft, tan to buff stone. There are plaques, earspools, discs, celts, and miscellaneous objects[78] from various provenances and from different epochs.[79] The inhabitants of the Classic period may have included in this great offering (probably made for the dedication of the temple) not only contemporaneous objects but also others preserved as treasures for generations. As this heritage was admirably preserved I feel that perhaps it came from an earlier offering discovered during the excavation for the new offering. Here, as with the stone monuments, I have had to choose —typologically—a few examples from among many others that are later. Unfortunately they were found under conditions that did not allow a stratigraphic separation.[80]

Of these hundreds of pieces, however, we can be certain of the Olmec origin of only a few (pl. 68). Two are extraordinary because of the quality of the stone and of the carving: a pectoral in the form of a canoe, and a very fine jade figurine representing a dwarf.[81] Another figure is a hunchback or a man carrying a bundle on his back;[82] a last one may be a celt. It shows "a birdlike head with a heavy down turned beak reminis-

[76] "The two stelae (1 and 2) in Plaza I are the only ones at the site which undoubtedly are *in situ*" (Stirling, 1943: 33).

[77] Drucker, 1943: 85.

[78] Drucker, 1955.

[79] Stirling, 1941.

[80] Stirling, Rainey, and Stirling, 1960: 29. Years after the first discovery, another offering was found in Mound 2. It consisted of an olla which contained a figure of a kneeling rabbit, ten human figurines, and eight large polished axes placed with the sharp edges upward. All these are obviously Olmec. I believe they correspond to Phase III.

[81] Stirling, 1941; and Drucker, 1955.

[82] Drucker, 1955: pl. 28a.

Fig. 24. Stela from Cerro de la Piedra.

cent of that of the Olmec Bird-monster."[83] From another part of the site comes the splendid brazier representing Huehueteotl, old god of fire (pl. 69); although not characteristically Olmec, it is quite reminiscent of the style.[84]

The lowest levels of stratigraphic pits from Lower Cerro de las Mesas I contain some ceramic types and some figurines which correspond to Olmec II and early Olmec III. The ceramics are mainly of black clay with white spots or rims,[85] and some of the figurine types such as A and D are very similar to those of Tres Zapotes.[86] At Cerro de las Mesas they appear not only in the Lower I level but also in Lower II.

Cerro de las Mesas, therefore, is not an Olmec site. But in its earliest years it was influenced by the Olmec of Period III; thus in this phase we can consider it Olmecoid. Furthermore, since some of its stone monoliths are definitely Olmec, it seems evident that at a given moment the city was inhabited by Colonial Olmecs or, because of its nearness, was the object of late expansion of the Metropolitan area. At a nearby site,

[83] *Ibid.*: 59, fig. 7. It is less certain that these are Olmec: a skull (*ibid.*: pl. 28b), a plaque in the form of a fish (*ibid.*: fig. 4), another like a clam shell (*ibid.*: pl. 40a), and some awls that were, perhaps, for ceremonial use (*ibid.*: p. 58) and remind us of those from La Venta.

[84] Stirling, 1941: pl. II.

[85] Drucker, 1943: 44, 74, and 79 and pl. 20c.

[86] Drucker, 1943: 73.

the Cerro de la Piedra stela is undoubtedly Olmecoid[87] (fig. 24).

Farther to the northwest and inland there seem to be few Olmec remains in semiarid central Veracruz, between the Cotaxtla and the Actopan rivers. Probably the scarcity is due precisely to the great difference in habitat between these dry lands and the Metropolitan zone. Small quantities of Olmec II ceramics have been found here and a few more in places like Boca del Rio, and—outside the area—in Orizaba.[88] The best-known Preclassic site in this region, Remojadas,[89] is characterized by a marked regional individuality without the presence of Olmec elements.[90] The Early Remojadas culture, although very interesting, does not fall within our study, for it is unrelated to the Olmec.

On the other hand, on the coastal strip farther north, at least two sites are found near one another that I believe to be important in relation to the Olmec problem. They are Viejón and El Trapiche, and perhaps others exist in this region.

At Trapiche a very early level was found which I have already mentioned. Some of the vessels and figurines, as well as a hollow figure with white slip, appear to be Olmec I or from the general period, although others may be from Olmec II. At the present time it is not possible to identify clearly the objects at this site, but their appearance in important quantities suggests the possibility of an Olmec presence during Period II. Finds at Viejón strengthen this idea.

Viejón is a "vast and important" zone where the earliest remains in the Preclassic of central Veracruz have appeared.[91] But the large number of mounds and their size show that this site continued to prosper until a later period. The period of the efflorescence of Viejón is, I believe, fundamentally Olmec II, since everything corresponds to it. This is especially evident if we take into account the important stela (pl. 70) found there, on which "are represented two personages slightly larger than natural size, of quite pure Olmec style and markedly similar to the Chalcatzingo reliefs" (see fig. 22).[92] Especially striking is the fact that in both of these sculptures one of the persons carries what seems to be a cornstalk.

Also from Viejón,[93] where there are Olmec ceramics, comes a conical bowl with flat bottom and flanges decorated with notches. The motif,

[87] Medellín, 1960: pl. 6.

[88] Piña Chán, 1964: 25.

[89] Medellín, 1960A.

[90] Medellín reaches this conclusion by contrasting ceramics diagnostic of the Preclassic in central Veracruz (which are polished dark red, polished brown, red and brown with white slip, etc.) with the Olmec (black with white rim and spots, sandy brown with geometric figures, punctate design, bands, rocker stamping, etc.).

[91] Medellín, 1960A: 79–80.

[92] Medellín, 1960: 80, pl. 9.

[93] Medellín, 1960A: 13 and fig. 1.

executed in cinnabar (fig. 25), represents a jaguar that is unquestionably associated with the figurine from Atlihuayan, Morelos, of a personage covered with a jaguar skin (see pl. 59).

Fig. 25. Motif painted on a vessel from Viejón. Width 9 inches.

These data, although far from forming a coherent picture, suggest that this region was not only influenced by Olmec but was actually inhabited by them. As in other sites, among them Chalcatzingo and its zone, this seems to be the obvious explanation for the presence there of Olmec monoliths. I believe that Viejón is not an Olmecoid site but was actually occupied by Colonial Olmecs. The strong Viejón–Chalcatzingo resemblance, more evident than those of Viejón–La Venta or of Chalcatzingo–La Venta, suggest not only a colony, but a close relationship among the Olmec colonies. I think that a "Colonial Olmec" style could be defined as inspired by but not identical to the Metropolitan.

Medellín dates Viejón between 1000 and 500 B.C. This is very probable. Here, however, as in Trapiche and in the region in general, Olmec elements are not the only ones present, but appear mixed with local elements. The Olmec colony (if it was that) was surely built on top of earlier dwelling places, whose markers shared a common heritage with the Olmecs. Unlike the case of Tlatilco—where this common heritage did not exist—the Olmec colony did not displace the earlier peoples but both, colonizers and natives, continued living together, although it seems evident that the community was under the control of the immigrant Olmecs.

In the present-day district of Papantla—the area bounded by the Cazones River to the north and the Solteros River to the south—there seems to be nothing that would contribute data to our problem. This area was to be, of course, the most important of the Classic period.

In the Huastec area, the farthest north, Olmec influence can be traced; the data are more vague. Panuco II (called Prisco by MacNeish) is the period that interests us. Type A figurines from Panuco and, on a lesser scale, Types B and C, show clear relationships with those of the

Olmec II period. The same is true of some types of ceramics.[94] All this, however, does not prove a close connection because the similarities are found only in ceramics, and in the Huastec region (at least in the Panuco–Tuxpan zone) no sculpture of importance has been found, nor jades, nor other Olmec achievements. On the other hand, the ceramic similarities could come from a common basis—the general coastal pattern —found throughout the area before the rise of civilization.

Nevertheless, one general fact may be significant. In the Panuco II and IV periods are found more mounds and large sites than in any other period in the Tampico–Panuco area.[95] During Panuco II, MacNeish thinks there were towns in the region that had as many as five thousand inhabitants.[96] I do not believe that these were cities which, according to this scholar, appeared only in the Classic period, but this considerable density of urban population and these great sites did not exist before and rarely appeared later, suggesting influences from the Metropolitan center of that time around 500 B.C., or perhaps a little earlier.

Panuco II culture extended, as far as we know, through the coastal area, without invading the highlands.[97] Like the Olmec, it was a culture of low and hot lands; when it penetrated the mountain region it changed greatly.

Although there are certain suggestive elements in Panuco II, we cannot speak of Olmec establishments here nor of an Olmecoid culture, but only of distant relations. These might not have actually existed but might simply be manifestations of the common substratum that extended from the future Huastec region to the future Maya area.

OAXACA: MONTE ALBAN

PERIOD I

In Monte Alban from Period I and in the Valley of Oaxaca in general, unlike the other sites we have discussed up to now, the culture contemporaneous with Olmec II was of such importance and reached such heights that it requires a more complete study, even within the limitations of this volume. At least since the end of Monte Alban I we are dealing with a city that presents many of the characteristics of civilization.

[94] Ekholm, 1944: 445 and 426.
[95] MacNeish, 1954: 615.
[96] MacNeish, 1956: 145.
[97] Meade, 1953: 294.

Until recently we knew nothing about its local antecedents. Explorations had proved that in Monte Alban itself there is no culture prior to Period I[98] which is quite credible; but none had been found any place in the valley until Flannery discovered and dug various new sites. On two of them he has been able to distinguish two phases called San José Mogote and Guadalupe that are undoubtedly older than Monte Alban I. A good percentage of the ceramics is undoubtedly Olmec. Carbon 14 dates suggest that San José Mogote begins towards 1100 B.C. and Guadalupe towards 900 B.C. Thus we have for the first time local Olmec antecedents for the great developments at Monte Alban.

The two radiocarbon dates that we have come from the site of Monte Negro, probably contemporaneous with Monte Alban I, and give the date 649 B.C.[99] For the beginning of the Monte Alban I epoch, however, I prefer to select an earlier date since it appears probable that the Monte Negro samples are from late within the Monte Alban I period. Since the samples derive from the burned beams of Monte Negro Temple X, over which nothing was subsequently built, they undoubtedly correspond to the end of that city. We can assume, therefore, that Monte Alban I began around 900 B.C. In Yagul the matter is even clearer, for the date is derived from material associated with a typically Olmec brazier corresponding to Phase I-C, the end of Period I (pl. 71a).

This discovery is especially important, since it associates an object with very clear Olmec traits but of the general style of Oaxaca with the final phase of Monte Alban I and indicates that this phase corresponds to the end of Olmec II. Monte Negro belongs to the same period, as similar braziers are found there (pl. 71b and c). Thus it becomes evident that Phases A and B of this period are prior to Olmec presence, at least in a general sense, and in a certain way are independent of it. This is one more indication reinforcing my idea that Monte Alban and in general Culture I of Oaxaca—although contemporaneous with Olmec II—are not derived from the Metropolitan zone but from a local culture which only later became associated with the Olmec world. This explains why Monte Alban was more advanced in some aspects but behind in others compared with the Olmec, and of course the differences between the two.

---

[98] In the many stratigraphic pits excavated at this site, wares of Period I appear directly upon virgin earth—the Chernozen typical of Oaxaca. The same occurs at Yagul and probably at Cuilapan, though at these sites the depth of the pits leaves something to be desired. At thirty-nine sites in the Valley of Oaxaca, I found pottery belonging to this period, but we do not have clear stratigraphic data. Therefore it is impossible to ascertain if earlier strata exist.

[99] C. 424 gives us an average of 2600 ± 170 (at Monte Negro), and Humble Oil Refining Company indicates 390 ± 275 B.C. (at Yagul). See *Mexico City Collegian*, October 27, 1960.

Little remains of the architecture of Monte Alban I, though it is of stone. It is certainly more advanced than that of the Olmec area. At least the great square at Monte Alban was being planned and the few buildings we know from that period fall within the pattern that was to become permanent from Period II on. The general plan of the great square already existed, together with its orientation toward the cardinal points. The main building we are familiar with, the old Temple of the Dancing Figures or *danzantes*, is a great platform of only a single terrace. Its stone and earth nucleus forms vertical walls[100] dressed with large stone slabs of a more or less rectangular shape, placed lengthwise and held together with clay. Each row is separated from the one above by a line of smaller stones placed horizontally. The rows alternate in this way up to the upper platform, whose original height is unknown to us. A lower platform was attached to the front and to the center. This platform was reached by way of a staircase formed of large stone blocks lying in a horizontal position. The stairway, without balustrades, protrudes from the main body of the platform. A stairway of the same type leads from the lower platform to the upper part of the main structure. There are no remains of the temple that stood on top.[101] The roof must have been made of straw, though the floor is stuccoed and not made simply of earth.

The most remarkable aspect of the slabs that dress the building is the carved figures in motion, which has led to their being called "*danzantes*" or dancing figures. Each slab exhibits a single figure, always male, often accompanied by one or several hieroglyphs (pls. 72 and 73).

The danzantes from this period appear in "the most varied postures, one leg extended, lying on their backs, one or both legs flexed, lying on their stomachs, their hands raised as if swimming; some are seated with their legs open, some squat, some walk or run or leap, others genuflect or sit on the ground Oriental fashion but with one leg pulled in."[102] It is evident that these postures were often the result of an adaptation to the shape of the stone. The faces received a more elaborate treatment than the bodies and are carved in very low relief. Certain Negroid characteristics are present, such as thick lips, broad cheeks, and puffed eyes. The corners of the mouths often turn down, and nine of the dancing figures have avocado-shaped heads, reminiscent of the Olmec style.[103]

---

[100] In later times foundations were extremely weak, perhaps because the talud walls no longer required this support. This situation allowed earthquakes and the passing of time to destroy many buildings.

[101] From this period stone masonry columns exist which suggest a division at the entrance of the temple. This type of column is frequent at Monte Negro.

[102] Caso, 1946: 128.

[103] The study of bone remains unearthed during explorations in Oaxaca—together with a comparison of the bone structure of living natives of the area—have provided

Most of the figures are nude, though they wear ornaments and occasionally hats. The male sex is indicated in a realistic manner on one figure (pl. 73c). On the others the genital organs have been replaced by what might be tatooing or by curvilinear and flowery body paint. It has been suggested that this decoration may represent blood as a result of mutilation.[104]

The relationship between the danzantes and Olmec art has led to a number of controversies. Some deny any similarity;[105] others feel that the dancing figures of Monte Alban in spirit and detail[106] are "derived" from the Olmec.[107] Although it is evident that the danzantes are not characteristic of the Metropolitan Olmec style since they show many different elements, I believe that they bear important analogies and can be placed within the Olmec world.

Coe[108] has suggested that the danzantes are nude because they represent captives and are exhibited in the usual Mesoamerican manner of representing unfortunate prisoners. As we will see later, certain carvings on similar stones from Period II probably are testimonials to the successful campaigns of the lords of Monte Alban. They are again used for the dressing for a building, like those of the danzantes in Period I. The latter, therefore, may be forerunners of the Period II figures, and may represent—though in a different way—a similar idea: war and victory. The same meaning seems to be found on later stelae. Since many danzantes are accompanied by hieroglyphs and occasionally numbers,

---

us with interesting results. These are fairly accurate, since we have abundant material (personal communication, J. Romero). At Monte Alban, from Period I on, the same population (from a physical point of view) survived throughout all the succeeding periods. It is the same one found there today. The numerous skeletal remains discovered at Monte Alban indicate an average height of 5 feet 3 inches for adult males and approximately 4 feet 10 inches for females. The cranial index ranges from 80.45 upward; that is, they were a brachycephalic people. The facial index ranges from 44.78 to 56.72, the lower being more frequent. The medium nasal index is predominant. We have similar measurements for the Mixtecs, both ancient and modern. However, the skeletons discovered at Monte Negro are different: there the people were taller and dolichocephalic. The head measurements at Monte Alban are as aberrant in Mexico as those of the Pericu of Baja California.

[104] M. D. Coe, 1962: 95–96. From Monte Alban I period we find dental mutilations of the D4 type which last until the end of the culture. On the other hand, cranial deformation did not appear until Teotihuacan influence was felt. At Monte Negro, however, teeth were inlaid with hematite (at the time the practice existed only here and in the Mamon phase at Uaxactun), and together with erect tabular cranial deformation we find the practice (unique in Mexico) of tabular oblique deformation. At Monte Negro there seem to be cases of trepanation with regeneration; at Monte Alban such cases are known only after the beginning of Period III-B.

[105] Drucker, 1952: 226; Smith, 1963.

[106] Emmerich, 1963: 64.

[107] Covarrubias, 1957: 148; Acosta, 1942: 55.

[108] Coe, 1962: 95.

Fig. 26. Pectoral from La Venta. Length 2⅜ inches.

like the Period II slabs, these might indicate the name of the captured chieftain and the date.

At least four extraordinary polished jade pieces which are typically Olmec are danzantes if we consider their postures[109] (pl. 74). The features of a face on a breastplate from La Venta are similar to those of the Monte Alban carvings (fig. 26).[110] This adornment may have been imported from Oaxaca. These objects do not, however, imply Olmec influence in Oaxaca, though they demonstrate that the danzantes and La Venta were contemporaneous. A seal from Tres Zapotes may portray a danzante.[111]

There is no doubt that the ancient temple of the dancing figures, together with the stones attached to it, belongs to the oldest period discovered so far at Monte Alban. On certain vessels from the same period similar figures are depicted (see pl. 75). Stratigraphy also indicates the antiquity of this monument.[112]

[109] Regarding the first piece, Saville (1929: fig. 94) states that it proceeds from Oaxaca; Covarrubias (1946: 98), however, claims that it comes from Olinala, Guerrero. The second is believed to be from San Jerónimo, Guerrero, and the third is from Tepatlaxco, Puebla (Lothrop, 1957: pl. VI, no. 12). The last one was found in Tzintzuntzan in Michoacan (Piña Chán, 1960: photo 67) by Rubín de la Borbolla in a very late context. It may have been an heirloom, probably from Guerrero, that finally found its way into the Tarascan capital.

[110] Drucker, Heizer, and Squier, 1959: fig. 73.

[111] Weiant, 1943: fig. 50c.

[112] Caso, 1946: 118.

It also may be affirmed that the hieroglyphs and numerals which accompany the danzantes belong to Monte Alban I. Eleven of the glyphs belonging to this period are associated with numerals. Some numerals appear with the danzantes, and others are found on several stelae whose inscriptions are composed almost entirely of glyphs associated with numerals (see pl. 76). Their arrangement in columns suggests a local version of the Long Count, undeciphered up to now. The numerals are made up of bars and dots like those of Olmec III, but the glyphs are not the same.

As we have seen, both the danzantes (and therefore the glyphs) belong to Olmec II period, at a time when writing was unknown in the Metropolitan Olmec area. This is extremely significant because it would indicate that hieroglyphic writing in Oaxaca preceded the Olmec glyphs. Consequently, writing is to be found in Monte Alban earlier than in the Metropolitan zone. The only other possible case of early writing would be that of the stelae at Kaminaljuyu in Guatemala (if they are prior to the Miraflores period). If these are to be placed within Miraflores, they are more recent than those of Monte Alban, and we would be led to conclude that, based on our present-day knowledge, Monte Alban is the cradle of writing in Mesoamerica.

It is not only the cradle of writing, however. We have seen that the ancient temple of the danzantes was constructed of great blocks of stone and its floors were of stucco.[113] These things were unknown at contemporaneous Olmec sites. Furthermore, tombs appeared for the first time (at Monte Alban there are eight pertaining to this period). They are not simply holes dug into the earth but are actual structures. They are very simple, with none of the elaborations of later times; these tombs are rectangular excavations enclosed by stone walls and covered by flat roofs formed of stone slabs. A tomb of the same period from the nearby site of Yagul is built of adobe.

Pottery is rich, very abundant, and of fine quality. The most refined is usually gray, sometimes of a light hue, incised or modeled. With these techniques extremely beautiful vessels, representing men or animals, were produced (pl. 77). Some of them bear strong Olmec resemblances. Of the wares for everyday use the type known as C5 at Monte Alban—a cream paste with a white polish—is important, for it is akin to Olmec white. Other resemblances seem to be the technique of combining sculpturing and engraving on the same vessel; figures in movement (pl. 78); the composite silhouette; and the face of the fire god on braziers and of the rain god on bottle vessels. Characteristic of Monte Alban I ceramics are vessels of gray clay that is well strained and well fired,

---

[113] The earliest structure on the north platform displayed a serpent carved in stucco on its façade—perhaps the first appearance of this material in Mesoamerica.

Fig. 27. Gods from Period I of Monte Alban: Cocijo (Monte Negro T.1); figure with tiger on headdress (Las Sedas), and (below) god with serpent mask (Ocotlán). National Museum of Anthropology.

finely finished with a lustrous wash, cream clay with garnet-colored slip (besides the white I mentioned), sculptured decoration—frequently representing animals—which is applied to the vessel, vessels with the rim flaring backward, plates with wavy rims, basal or labial flanges, basket-shaped vessels, spout handles, bowls with three supports, griddles, and incense burners with handles without perforations. In Phase I-C begin to appear whistling jars, vessels in the form of gourds, spool supports without holes, al fresco decoration, finger impression as decoration, and cream ware with polished black wash. All these were to be characteristic of Period II.

Some ceramic associations, then, exist with the Olmec world. On the other hand almost none of the other traits are found; thus jades are rare in Period I of Monte Alban.

Another step that seems to have been taken for the first time in Oaxaca is the representation of gods. From this early period ten deities were sufficiently well characterized so that they can easily be identified: Cocijo (the rain god), a jaguar divinity, Quetzalcoatl, the young god with the helmet of a bird with the flat beak, Xipe, the opossum deity, perhaps the old god with the helmet of a bird with a broad beak, and the old god Two Tiger[114] (see fig. 27). There also appear several braziers with Olmec faces portraying the young god of fire, owl whistles, and a bizarre duck-billed god. It is not possible to identify any female deity.

This representation of gods is a fundamental characteristic of Meso-american ceremonialism. We have nothing like it at any site prior to or contemporaneous with Monte Alban I. It would almost seem that the gods were invented there.

The women portrayed in the figurines are nude, but the male deities wear mantles, loincloths, anklets, perhaps sandals, and are crowned with bands, helmets, and hats. They are adorned with practically all the ornaments for personal use worn by the people of Mesoamerica; facial and body paint are common, as is tattooing. Masks are used together with beards (perhaps false) (fig. 28), and teeth are mutilated and in-laid with pyrite.[115]

The prevailing style of Monte Alban, therefore, can be considered to be a variant of the Olmec and may be called the "dancing figure style," since this typical motif is to be found not only in stone but in clay and in minor objects. I believe that it falls within the general Olmec tradition, but in no way can it be said that Monte Alban was merely a Colonial site, such as Tlatilco: it was the center of a vast area, not only refusing to imitate others but leading in such important aspects as writing, the calendar, and architecture. Its Olmec connections would commence with Olmec I. The Oaxaca style with its sphere of influence cannot be called "Colonial Olmec" but Olmecoid in a sense. Monte Alban possessed a creativity and an individuality of its own.

Indirect relationships between the Olmec world and Monte Alban probably existed after Olmec I. These did not come from the Metropolitan zone but south across the Isthmus of Tehuantepec and along the coastal plains, from there to ascend to the Valley of Oaxaca. These contacts may have been via the Ixtlan mountain range, though the Olmecs were not "mountain" people in general.

In the time of Monte Alban I Oaxaca could not have been divided in the basic Zapotec and Mixtec areas, nor could any of the regions in-

[114] Caso and Bernal, 1952.
[115] Romero, 1958: 100.

Fig. 28. Bat mask of jade from Monte Alban. Height 11⅜ inches. National Museum of Anthropology.

habited by later peoples be identified as cultural units. A single culture covered the entire area, though with different degrees of intensity. So it is that at several sites in the Mixteca area we find remains of a culture similar to that of Monte Alban I. Examples are Coixtlahuaca,[116] Monte Negro, Yucuñudahui,[117] Tamazulapan,[118] and even Tehuacan.[119] Several sites in the lower or coastal Mixteca,[120] the Ithmus, and the Chinantla in northern Oaxaca show the same resemblance.[121] Other sites closer to Veracruz have stronger connections with the Metropolitan Olmec zone.[122]

[116] A whistling jar from Coixtlahuaca is identical with one from Monte Alban.
[117] Caso, 1938: 50.
[118] *Excavations in the Mixteca Alta*: 17, 48–49.
[119] Noguera, 1940: 18.
[120] De Cicco and Brockington, 1956; Piña Chán, 1960.
[121] Delgado, 1961: 95–96, and 1956.
[122] Cline, 1959; Delgado, 1960.

In the higher or mountain Mixteca, statues have been found that undoubtedly belong to the Olmec style. One is from Huamelulpan and perhaps corresponds to this epoch (pl. 79), and another is from Diquiqú. Ceramic pieces, above all braziers displaying the face of the young god of fire, have been unearthed at Monte Negro[123] and are similar to those from Monte Alban. Though Monte Negro is a planned site, it is still a village and its culture is not especially advanced. Other ceramics from the area are similar only in a general way to Monte Alban I, but their origin is rather to be found in the ancestral culture common to the entire horizon.

In the coastal Mixteca area Olmec reminiscences are still vague, for little excavation has been done there. Nevertheless, we can mention a statue from Jamiltepec[124] and some ceramic ware pertaining to Monte Alban I period. It is quite possible that the area played an important role in ancient times.

PERIOD II

Period II is apparent in fewer places than Period I or the following phases. In the Valley of Oaxaca it appears at Caballito Blanco and at twenty-four other sites, almost all of which are large. Apparently the most important site in the higher Mixteca at this time was Huamelulpan,[125] where the archaeological zone is relatively large and where the partially explored mound has revealed a staircase bordered by enormous rectangular stone blocks bearing hieroglyphs and numerals in the Monte Alban II style. The pottery in the mound seems to be of the same period or the end of Period I. And a tomb found accidentally at Tliltepec (Cerro del Jazmin), near Yanhuitlan, contained numerous vessels which, though different from those of Monte Alban II, are similar in some aspects. These finds constitute practically all the evidence we have for Period II outside of Monte Alban. They are so scarce and incomplete that without our knowledge of this splendid city we might be led to believe that it had never existed. I have the impression (though I cannot prove it at the present time) that many sites in the Valley of Oaxaca passed directly from Phase I-C to the transition epoch II–III. These sites, then, continued to live in culture I, while at Monte Alban and many other places in the Valley Period II was developing. It is evident that this point may only be proved or refuted through intensive explorations at the sites where Period II appears. For the moment our classification of Period II

[123] Caso and Bernal, 1952: 326–333.
[124] De Cicco and Brockington, 1956: figs. 4–5.
[125] Caso and Gamio, 1961.

must necessarily be based mainly on evidence at Monte Alban.

Phase I-C is an antecedent—practically a transition—to Period II. Some elements began to arrive in this phase which were to characterize the period. The bearers of the culture of Period II brought or invented many traits of their own but continued to utilize others which were typical of the previous period. Therefore, though undoubtedly a new and different culture was evolving, it preserved much of its forerunner. The carriers of Period II culture (at least at Monte Alban) were an aristocracy made up of chieftains or priests who imposed their own ideas upon others. At the same time they did not constitute a majority sufficiently strong to wipe out the ancient culture, which continued to thrive among the masses. Period II seems to have flourished in relatively few sites in the Valley of Oaxaca and in almost none outside. Basically these seem to have been ceremonial centers, places where an aristocratic minority could have resided without having directly influenced the smaller villages, which may have only gradually acquired some of the new traits. The process may have been so slow that the first Teotihuacan influences may have arrived before the older traits had been assimilated. Actually, I believe that Period III-A is a final fusion of Periods I and II combined with Teotihuacan features.

By this time Monte Alban—at least its principal square—had been completely planned. During this period the square was leveled by eliminating the rocky protuberances and by filling in the hollows.[126] This was a titanic feat. Thus the builders managed to mold a perfectly flat surface some 1500 feet above the Valley of Oaxaca. It measures 3000 by 1300 feet and around it stand the monuments—built little by little—which were to surround the great plaza. The Monte Alban II people also constructed a ball court, though we cannot define its type because of its poor state of preservation.

Few structures of this period remain, but the ones we are familiar with show the tendency both to preserve several forms from the previous epoch and to invent new styles. Strong vertical walls continued to be constructed, built of massive stones frequently incised with figures. Staircases continued to be attached and to lack balustrades.

But the new masters of Monte Alban created many innovations. Together with the earlier system of staircases, new ones were constructed with balustrades. Vertical walls often end in inclined cornices. At times a sunken wall panel appears, decorated with a line of discs that touch one another, the probable antecedent of the *tablero*. This becomes more probable in view of the appearance of the battered wall element we know

---

[126] This is proved by the appearance of numerous offerings belonging to Period II under the stucco of the plaza. Among them is found the famous jade bat mask (fig.

as the *talud*, which is almost invariably accompanied by the tablero. In contrast to the buildings of Teotihuacan this talud is formed by a succession of small steps, plastered with an extremely thick coat of stucco.

By this time stucco was not only known but was used in abundance, as much on the talud as on cornices, walls, and floors. In the staircases the system of large stones was gradually exchanged for one of small rows of stones alternating with others even smaller. Both lines of stones, covered with stucco, formed a stair in the same manner in which the taluds were constructed.

At least one temple with two rooms of adobe walls on a stone foundation has survived. The entrance was divided by two columns of stone masonry, thus forming three doorways.

Undoubtedly Mound J is the most important structure that remains from this period. It is curious both because of its arrowhead shape and the engravings that decorate its walls. There have been many conjectures about its functions. A covered passageway cuts through the entire building. This passageway and its orientation (northeast–southwest) contrast with the rest of the buildings, and it has been surmised that the edifice may have been an astronomical observatory.

The rear of the building is dressed with large stones similar to those of the temple of the danzantes (fig. 29). Though they are also engraved,

Fig. 29. Motifs from tablets on Mound J, Monte Alban. (a) Tablet 4. (b) Tablet 106. (c) Tablet 14.

(a)

(b)

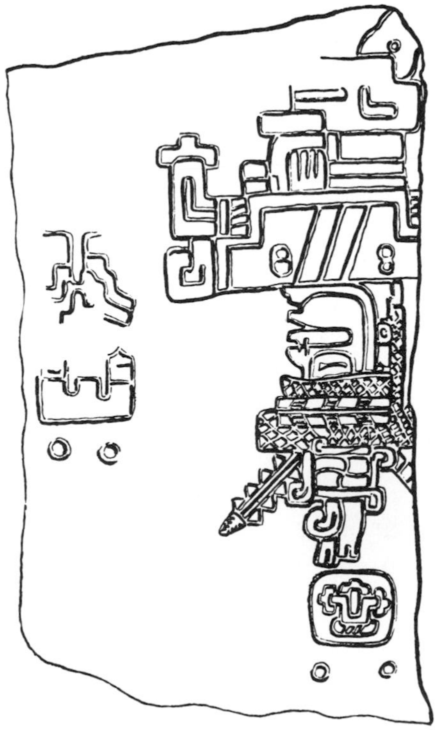

the motifs are different. On each stone slab may be found "(*a*) a human head facing downward, always on the same scale; (*b*) the 'hill glyph,' which indicates a place; (*c*) a combination of hieroglyphs that probably signify the name of a place; (*d*) an inscription that, in its most complete form, constitutes a year, month, and day, plus other symbols we have not been able to decipher."[127] All of these carvings may indicate a number of conquests carried out by the inhabitants of Monte Alban, and the building may be a sort of gallery of victories which in Rome would have been represented by a triumphal arch. I have already mentioned the possible symbolic relationship of these glyphs with the dancing figures of Period I.

Whatever the case may be, it is evident that the heads, headdresses, ornaments, and chin straps are surprisingly similar to Olmec art, even though they also present considerable differences.[128] Because we have more inscriptions from this epoch than from Monte Alban I, or perhaps because they are more detailed, we find a large number of new glyphs next to the old ones. Some stand alone and others are associated with numerals; that is, they are of a calendrical nature.[129] Stone Monu-

[127] Caso, 1946: 131.

[128] *Ibid.*: fig. 58 and unnumbered figure preceding it.

[129] See Caso (1946) for a complete study of writing and the calendar at Monte Alban I and II.

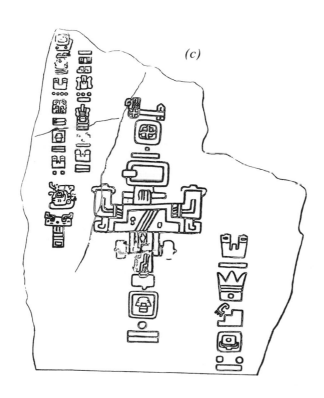

(c)

Fig. 30. Urns depicting gods from Period II of Monte Alban: Cocijo (Cuilapan); companion (Monte Alban); god with serpent mask (Monte Alban). National Museum of Anthropology.

ment 14, though not unique, is especially interesting, since it exhibits true columns of hieroglyphs and numbers which can be compared to Maya-style inscriptions, though unfortunately they have not yet been deciphered.

In spite of such patent differences I believe that the glyph system of Monte Alban belongs to the general world of the Olmecs, although the Valley of Oaxaca was not only one of the true Olmec centers but was the center itself of invention and diffusion. It should be remembered, by the way, that the inscriptions are not a good chronological indicator since once form and meaning become established the glyph tends to live on. Thus, we find almost identical glyphs reproduced a thousand years later.

Mound J at Monte Alban is not unique, however. A similar monument has been discovered at Caballito Blanco near Yagul. Though it is smaller, less elaborate, and contains no incised stone slabs, its form is the same. Ceramics found there belong to Period II.[130] A Carbon 14 age determination gave the date 264 B.C. ± 120.

On the whole, though fundamental differences cannot be denied, at Monte Alban II we have antecedents of what was to be the Zapotec architecture of later periods.

Twenty-one tombs from Monte Alban II are known to us, and among them—together with simple rectangular structures—there appear plain façades and entrances which occasionally lead to an antechamber. Niches are set into some of the walls; they are frequently plastered with a

[130] John Paddock, verbal information.

164

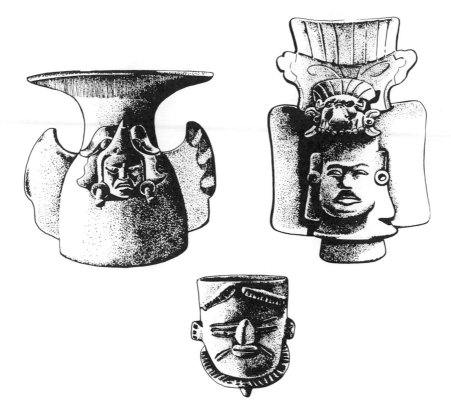

Fig. 31. Gods from Period II of Monte Alban: young god with bird helmet (Monte Alban), National Museum of Anthropology; god with tiger head and wide-billed bird mask (Frisell Collection); Xipe (?) (Monte Alban), National Museum of Anthropology.

coat of stucco and occasionally painted al fresco. The arched ceiling appears as well as the flat one.

We are acquainted with fifteen deities from this epoch (see fig. 30). One of them is feminine: the goddess 11 Death. (Gods and men were named according to the day of their birth, thus 11 Death means that she was thought to have been born on that day of the calendar.) Another figurine may represent the goddess 8Z. By this time women were shown fully garbed. Male clothing had become extremely elaborate and headdresses more complicated, with chin straps, feathers, bows, and ribbons which fell to the neck.

The gods usually appear on the urns which are so typical of the area and were gradually to become more abundant. Actually, some are not urns strictly speaking, but rather are clay statues, for they do not form a vessel. In this category are the three figures from Tomb 113[131] (fig. 31), which, by the way, are among the most Olmec of the pieces of the period.

The magnificent modeled ceramics of Period I disappeared, to be

[131] Caso and Bernal, 1952: figs. 498–500.

Fig. 32. Clay boxes from Monte Alban. Height 21⅛ inches (with lid).

replaced by the more geometric and impersonal style which characterizes Period II. For the first time appeared the *xicalcoliuhqui* or fret design—one of the most typical decorative-symbolic elements not only of Oaxaca but of Mesoamerica (pl. 80). Also present are flower motifs, representations of human bones, and the trilobate ornament which, as a terminal element, was so typical of Zapotec art. Multicolored fresco decorations were also applied.

Many new wares began to appear, or perhaps old forms from Phase I-C became more popular: four-legged vessels, jars with gourd-shaped necks, vessels with lids of different shapes, and the large clay boxes decorated with glyphs representing water or the eye of a reptile, a design that was to become frequent in later times (fig. 32).

Monte Alban II, therefore, still preserved its Olmecoid substratum, which it had inherited in part from the earlier inhabitants of the site and in part from the area that had spawned the aristocratic bearers of Monte Alban II culture. This area may have been Chiapas or the Guatemalan highlands or perhaps the highlands by way of Chiapas. Tombs 2 and 3 at Chiapa de Corzo contained several vessels strikingly similar to those of Monte Alban II. The newcomers added certain Olmec influences which were still alive but which did not necessarily proceed from the Metropolitan zone. This becomes more apparent when we consider that Monte Alban II corresponds both to Olmec III and even to a later time—when the Metropolitan zone was losing its importance.

A question is now pertinent. If the culture of the Valley of Oaxaca in Periods I and II, represented mainly by Monte Alban, is so important and seems to have pushed forward to such an extent, why should it not be considered the axis of the Olmec world? Why should we not consider it the mother culture? Actually, several reasons seem to argue against it. It was a culture which did not diffuse and whose products, style, and knowledge rarely left its confines. I cannot claim to understand the reasons for this but archaeology indicates clearly that it is so. It may be supposed therefore that much was imported from outside and that Monte Alban is only an extraordinarily distinguished heir.

THE CENTRAL DEPRESSION OF CHIAPAS

The Isthmus of Tehuantepec unites the Olmec area with the Chiapas depression and the Pacific watershed. It is a region which attracted the Olmecs, for no mountains cut across it and the climate was tropical. In the central depression and, generally speaking, in the entire state of Chiapas, Olmec remains or others related to it appear constantly, though—as in other regions of Central America—they do not constitute the basis or majority of archaeological finds. We are dealing with a culture related to the Olmec, though with its own peculiar features.

Black ceramics with white rims or spots appear quite frequently. At other sites such as San Agustin and on the Pacific coast of Chiapas the same ware has been found in scientific explorations.[132] At Santa Cruz[133] it is clearly associated with other types belonging to the Olmec complex. At Mirador abundant Olmec figurines have been unearthed.[134]

Even more obviously Olmec is the stela of Padre Piedra, which bears a representation of a standing personage; another man seems to be kneeling in front of him (fig. 33). It stands seven feet tall in its present state and originally was even larger. It can be of only local fabrication.[135] This stela may have been associated with ceramics corresponding to Periods I and II of Chiapa de Corzo, which are Olmecoid. Another low relief on a rock near Batehaton[136] (fig. 34) is also markedly Olmec in style, and other Olmec objects are to be found at numerous sites such as Simojovel and Ocozocuautla.[137]

Chiapa de Corzo is the only site that has been explored thoroughly.

[132] Navarrete, 1959: 4, 11, and fig. 5f.
[133] Sanders, 1961: 51.
[134] Peterson, 1963: 11–13 and figs. 137–138.
[135] Navarette, 1960: 10–11 and figs. 11, 12, 46b and c.
[136] Cordan, 1963: facing p. 72.
[137] Piña Chán, 1964: 25.

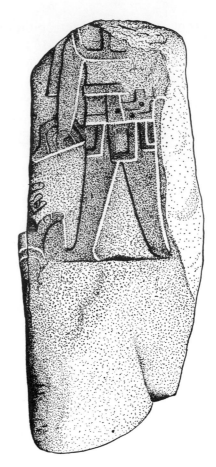

Fig. 33. Bas relief on stela from Padre Piedra, Chiapas. Height 7 feet, 2 inches.

It is evident there that in the earlier periods (Dili Phase, 1000–550 B.C.) there are certain Olmec elements which by no means belong to the basic culture.[138] Some difficulties arise in correlating with precision the periods at Chiapa de Corzo with Olmec II, since Chiapa I would seem earlier. Late Chiapa II and early Chiapa III would largely correspond to Olmec II. Periods late III, IV, and V are to be connected with Olmec III,[139] but discoveries do not correspond exactly to that pattern. The most important group of objects related to our discussion of the Olmecs consists of four admirably carved bones[140] (fig. 35) found in Tomb I. This tomb, however, belongs to the Chiapa VI period, thought to correspond to 100–1 B.C., which is rather late. There is no doubt that the bones resemble the style of the Kaminaljuya stela and of some elements at Monte Alban I, but their most evident relationship is with La

[138] Lowe (1962: 195) proposes the following dates for the earliest ceramic periods in Chiapas: I: 1400–1000 B.C.; II: 1000–550 B.C.; III: 550–450 B.C.; IV: 450–250 B.C.; V: 250–100 B.C.; VI: 100 B.C. – A.D. 1.

[139] Sanders, 1961: 52.

[140] Agrinier, 1960.

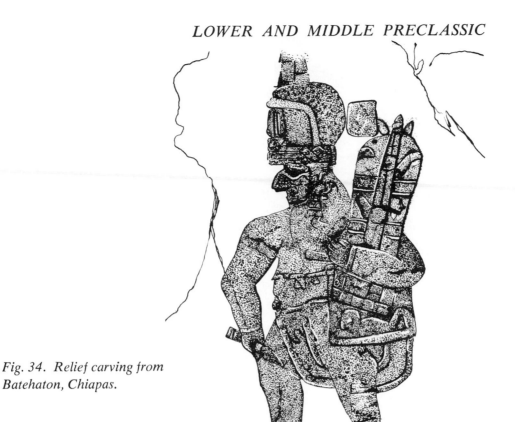

*Fig. 34. Relief carving from
Batehaton, Chiapas.*

Venta[141] and with Izapa, another city which lies within the imperial
Olmec world.

A most important discovery was the find, in 1961, of stela fragments
at Chiapa de Corzo. Though shattered and incomplete, they suggest associations with Izapa and Tres Zapotes; I consider them to fall within
Olmec III. One of them, Stela 2, is especially interesting because it
bears an inscription in the Long Count (pl. 81). Unfortunately incomplete (a sort of curse seems to hover over these dates), it has lost its
Baktun glyph totally and even the Katun is doubtful. Its probable reconstruction, however,[142] is 7.16.3.2.13. In other words, we now have
the possibility of adding another stela from Cycle 7 to our short but
sensational list. If this be the case, Stela 2 from Chiapa de Corzo would
be the oldest Mesoamerican inscription found so far, three years and
nine months older than Stela C at Tres Zapotes. It would correspond
to December 7, 35 B.C. according to Correlation B, and to 294 B.C. according to Correlation A.

[141] *Ibid.*: 22.
[142] Lowe, 1962: 194.

Fig. 35. Motifs carved on bones. Chiapa de Corzo, Chiapas.

THE PACIFIC WATERSHED OF CHIAPAS—GUATEMALA

This area is similar in many aspects to the Olmec though it lacks swamps and great river systems. Obvious physical differences are present within it—occasional tall jungles as well as savannas. Nevertheless, I will consider all this coastal region which spreads from Tehuantepec to El Salvador as a single unit, since the traces of Olmec culture found there bear striking similarities among themselves.

The coast of Chiapas is extremely narrow; perhaps because of the lack of exploration in this very limited area, we know little about its archaeology. On the other hand, where the coast widens, the land reveals the remains of an entire and highly important culture, though almost completely unknown to us. The known sites extend from Tonalá in Chiapas as far as Chalchuapa in El Salvador. At times this coastal region had important relationships with the Guatemalan highlands, with the central depression of Chiapas, and with the Central Maya area.

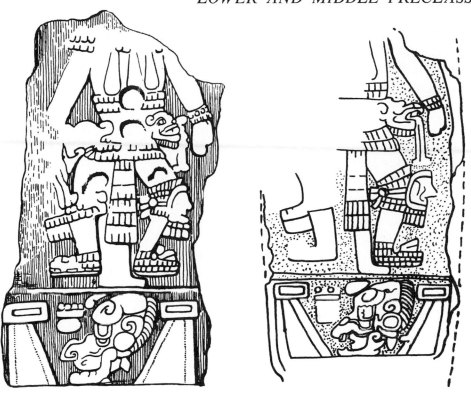

Fig. 36. Stela at Tonalá. Height 63 inches.

Judging by our present knowledge, the Chiapas area we are now dealing with was dominated by two important cities: Tonalá and Izapa. The larger, Tonalá, has hardly been explored though it has been mapped, thus revealing its extent and the importance of its structures. Several of the monoliths discovered there suggest an Olmec association: Monument 5, Petroglyph 1, and Stela 9,[143] which are similar to the relief at Padre Piedra (see pls. 82–84).

A stela, bearing numerals in the bar and dot system, stands today at the railroad station in Tonalá[144] (fig. 36). The number may refer to a 7 or a 9 but does not belong to an Initial Series, that is, a notation in the Long Count computation. It is part of a glyph indicating a day or a month. Another stela which at one time stood in the square of the same town is similar to the style found in the Pacific watershed of Guatemala.[145] I believe Ferdon to be right when he expresses the belief that Tonalá possessed its own style, undoubtedly influenced by the Olmec.

[143] Ferdon, 1953: 103–104, pls. 20a, d, and e, and 23b.
[144] See Palacios, 1928: fig. 24, and Satterthwaite, 1943: 128–129 and fig. 1c.
[145] Seler Sachs, 1900: 111.

This may not have been the principal influence; that may be sought toward the south in Izapa or on the Guatemalan coast.

In the second of the Chiapas coastal sites, Izapa (almost on the Mexico–Guatemala border), we also find several structures, though none is spectacular. There are earth mounds like their Olmec counterparts, but their construction also involved river stones and occasionally cut slabs. At this site stone was not lacking. The buildings are distributed in a rather irregular pattern around plazas without rigorous planning. All of these things suggest the Olmec style, though Izapa probably continued to be inhabited until later times.

Izapa stands out because of its stone sculptures. Twenty-two stelae, nineteen altars, and other monuments have been found. I do not believe that all are contemporaneous, though most of them are related to the Olmec style and are extraordinarily similar to other monuments found between Tonalá and Guatemala.

The frequent association of stelae and altars at Izapa is notable. At only one site in the Metropolitan zone—Tres Zapotes—do we find a similar situation. Such associations appear at other Olmecoid sites such as Tonalá and also constitute a trait of the later Maya art style. The stelae at Izapa (see pl. 85) belong to a much more baroque and florid style than those in the pure Olmec manner, though they are undoubtedly related. Without going into details which have already been published,[146] it is evident that they are associated with the sculptures of El Baul and San Isidro Piedra Parada in Guatemala[147] and even with the Tonalá culture.

Stelae 1, 3, and 6 of Izapa are, for example, reminiscent of the Metropolitan style but indubitably different and are more closely associated with Guatemala (see pl. 86). Stela 21 at the same site (pl. 87) represents the moment at which a person is decapitated by his conqueror.[148] This may easily refer to the ball game which, as we have seen, is not represented in the Metropolitan area but is frequently found among the Olmecoids. Monument 2 of Izapa, showing a human figure within the open jaws of a jaguar (fig. 37), is also reminiscent of a theme characteristic of Olmec art.

Coe[149] has pointed out many important differences between the Izapa and Olmec styles. These differences are unquestionable, and they indicate that the "Guatemala–Chiapas province" of the Olmec world was different from that of the Metropolitan area. Sometimes at Tres Zapotes we seem to see influences from Izapa. It is comparable to Rome influencing Greece.

[146] Stirling, 1943.
[147] Thompson, 1943.
[148] Orellana, 1955.
[149] Coe, 1965: 772.

Fig. 37. Monument 2, Izapa.

Recent excavations in Izapa have demonstrated that a ceramic period existed there which was associated with the Olmecoid stelae that correspond precisely with those of Chiapa de Corzo. The stylistic study of the stone monuments, then, is corroborated with the stratigraphy, although it is probable that Izapa, like many of the sites mentioned here, corresponds to the end of Olmec II and to III, even though its relations with the Metropolitan area may have begun in Olmec I. Actually, it seems that this entire region formed a great Olmecoid province in the sense that the Olmecs took an active part in its development, although the Olmec style is by no means the only one found there. In general terms it may be said that the local inhabitants formed part of the Olmec I world and branched out from there, at times in association with the Olmec II and III people and at times on their own. From this independence and also from this relationship, perhaps, the Maya world came into being.

Farther south, in the Pacific watershed of Guatemala and El Salvador, we are acquainted mainly with large and immovable structures. This lends them a special importance, since the place where they were found must be their birthplace.

As usually happens in the Olmec world, the sites, though many are huge,[150] have little important stone architecture.[151] In general, this material was rarely used; for example, at Bilbao[152] the buildings belonging to the Ilusiones phase (400–100 B.C.) contain no stone in their construction. This might indicate one more relationship with the Metropolitan Olmecs. Few objects can be dated. Only from a stylistic point of view (with all the perils this implies) may several of these groups be considered Olmecoid.

Perhaps the most notable remains are the heads, also colossal (pl. 88). Their size connects them with the Olmecs, in spite of differences in style. The most important heads are found at Monte Alto.[153] As Parsons and Jenson have shown, these stone monuments were associated with mounds.[154] Actually two of the heads at Monte Alto (the larger is fourteen feet high) form part of a group of other sculptures.[155] One was placed with its head to the northwest and the other facing southwest. They do not obey, therefore, the northward orientation which, as we have seen, prevailed among the colossal heads in the Metropolitan area.

A third colossal head at Monte Alto is somewhat different from the others in that it wears a jaguar mask in a striking Olmecoid style[156] (pl. 88b). As Richardson has noted, it strongly resembles the famous masks at Uaxactun which I will discuss later. The same author[157] shows seven jaguar heads of different sizes, all of them large, from the departments of Ahuachapan and Santa Ana in El Salvador. With some differences they undoubtedly constitute a continuation of the Olmec style. Finally, another head appears at El Palmar,[158] and Habel[159] mentions five large heads in the Sonsonate region in El Salvador. Though I am not acquainted with the stratigraphic position of any of these pieces, it is probable that they indicate a sequence that evolved over a long period. They may be a survival of the Olmec style in this area, even though I

[150] Shook, 1951: 99.

[151] Thompson, 1943: 109.

[152] Parsons (1965: 94). Carbon dating indicates 510 B.C. ± 130. Parsons prefers the later date, but I believe that 500 B.C. could be considered the beginning of this period.

[153] Villacorta and Villacorta, 1930, and Richardson, 1940: pl. XVIIIa and b. Clewlow, Cowan, O'Connell, and Benemann, 1967: App. II discusses the Olmec colossal heads in relation to others from Mesoamerica.

[154] Parsons and Jenson, 1965: map, p. 137.

[155] Richardson, 1940: 396.

[156] Ibid.: 397, pl. XVIIIc; Parsons, 1965: pls. 7 and 8.

[157] Richardson, 1940: figs. 33 and 34; some published previously by Spinden, 1915: 472–473, fig. 78.

[158] Richardson, 1940: 396.

[159] Habel, 1878: 32.

do not believe that the style lasted there much longer than at other sites, when, at the end of Period III, it too fused with other cultures.

The colossal head at El Baul (pl. 89a) is strikingly different and does not fit into the Olmec style at all nor into the period I am describing. Rather, it resembles later pieces such as the figures adorning some plumbate vessels (pl. 89b). This was Dieseldorff's opinion.[160]

More within the Olmec style are the seated human figures. Some bear a remarkable resemblance—are almost identical—to those of the Metropolitan area, and others, though differing from each other, undoubtedly form part of the same style. This does not necessarily mean that all are contemporaneous; it seems more probable that some are older, since they range from an extremely coarse art to another style which is reminiscent of "the Wrestler" from Uxpanapa (pl. 27).

Eighty-five pieces[161] are known from southern Guatemala, indicating that we are not dealing with an isolated element but with a common one. They share the same characteristics: asexual bodies, frequently chubby, some of them nude or wearing only a loincloth; occasionally, like one figure from Bilbao, they are frankly baby-faced[162] (pl. 90). The typical cranial crest appears, characteristic of some Metropolitan Olmec sculpture.[163] A sculpture from Tiquisate (pl. 91) is remarkably beautiful, though it is incomplete.[164]

A fairly frequent variant shows a paunchy individual. This type of figure is found from San Isidro Piedra Parada to Pasaco in the Pacific drainage area and is also common in the highlands; we have no fewer than a dozen examples from Kaminaljuyu. They are probably related to some sculptures from Yucatan.[165] Lothrop[166] gives a good description of the Guatemalan pieces as: "figures sculptured in the round with fat bodies, thick short necks . . . and with large heads—the whole very crudely yet vigorously carved. . . . The legs often curve around the base of the barrel-like body, and are parallel to the ground, while the arms are clasped against the sides with elbows bent" (see pl. 92). At that time (1926) Lothrop thought that the figures belonged to ancient times, but the excavations at Kaminaljuyu have not confirmed his

---

[160] Dieseldorff, 1926: fig. 155. His plate shows this great head. The most common type of plumbate vessel (Shepard, 1948, figs. 18 and 19; also p. 29) is undoubtedly that following the style of the El Baul head. Shepard actually connects them with a plumbate vessel published by Seler, 1908: III; 624, or pl. 24b, p. 108 of the English edition (BAE-B, 28). J. Eric Thompson is of the same opinion (1941: 47).

[161] Parsons and Jenson, 1965: 137.

[162] *Ibid.*: fig. 14.

[163] See also that of Obero; Richardson, 1940: pl. XVIIIe.

[164] Shook, 1950: 63. The exact site is called Sin Cabezas.

[165] Parsons and Jenson, 1965: 138.

[166] Lothrop, 1926: 164.

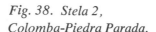

*Fig. 38. Stela 2,
Colomba-Piedra Parada.*

opinion. These objects are from the Miraflores period or perhaps earlier.

Larger in size but similar are three enormous rocks carved in human likenesses which stand at Monte Alto.[167] Here—even more so than the previous examples—the form of the natural stone has been respected. Only the necessary minimum was hewn in order to turn the rock into a ponderous seated man (pl. 93). Although the face is not especially Olmec, the general style of the pieces conforms to Olmec norms. One of them, furthermore, lifts his head up and looks at the sky, a feature found among some of the Metropolitan sculptures.[168]

Although none of the aforementioned sculptures (except those of Kaminaljuyu) has been actually dated, those of Monte Alto have been at least partly unearthed, and their evidence leads us to "postulate that occupation of Monte Alto was at its peak between the sixth and fourth centuries before Christ . . . though it is distinctly possible that some of the boulder sculptures could have been carved as early as 1000 B.C."[169]

In this area of the Pacific watershed many stelae are also found. At this time we are interested in those which may possibly have dates from

[167] Parsons and Jenson, 1965: figs. 10, 11, and 12.

[168] I agree with Richardson (1940: 398) that both the Guatemalan colossal heads and full figure sculptures originated with the "same people" and that their focus seemed to be the lowlands of the Pacific slopes. A great human statue at La Flora, department of Escuintla, has some traits that are reminiscent of the Olmec (*ibid.*: pl. XIXc).

[169] Parsons and Jenson, 1965: 143; Shook (1950) believes those of Tiquisate to be posterior. We have seen that those of Kaminaljuyu belong, at the latest, to the Miraflores period.

THE DATING OF STELAE
AND THE TUXTLA STATUETTE

		Maya Date	Christian Date, Correlation B	Christian Date, Correlation A
Chiapa de Corzo	Stela 2	7.16.3.2.13	December 7, 35 B.C.	June 19, 295 B.C.
Tres Zapotes	Stela C	7.16.6.16.18	September 2, 31 B.C.	November 4, 291 B.C.
El Baul	Stela 1	7.19.15.7.12	March 4, 36 A.D.	December 10, 222 B.C.
Colomba–Santa Margarita	Stela 2	7.?.?.?.?.		
Tuxtla statuette		8.6.2.4.17	March 14, 162 A.D.	November 22, 97 B.C.

Baktun 7, for these would be chronologically close to the Tres Zapotes stela and the Tuxtla statuette, and earlier than the Classic Maya world. Two such stelae are known: Stela 1 of El Baul and Stela 2 of Santa Margarita Colomba. Both of these are in poor condition and therefore cannot be clearly understood. They have been the cause of much controversy, and the reading of their dates is still hypothetical.

Stela 1 of El Baul (pl. 94) has been known in scientific circles since 1924,[170] but it was not until 1936 that Walter Lehmann reconstructed the inscription as 7.19.7.8.12 Eb.[171] In a well-known work, Eric Thompson (1941) discarded Lehmann's reading on the basis of calendrical and stylistic arguments, even though he later withdrew some of his arguments, especially those having to do with style and based partly on Waterman's ideas. In 1950 Proskouriakoff[172] contributed some important ideas regarding the stylistic position of the stela. She found it to be quite ancient, though not so ancient as Baktun 7. A little earlier (1948) Thompson himself had recognized the similarity between Stela 1 and the Izapa monuments—which are also very old. In the excavations Thompson made in the region (Thompson, 1948) he refers to a very early period, prior to the San Francisco phase and corresponding to the Esperanza phase of Kaminaljuyu, which is represented by Miraflores ceramics. It is possible (though not proven at Izapa) that the stela pertains to that horizon. Coe sums up this matter very well[173] when he claims that the correct reading is 7.19.15.7.12, 12 Eb, and that the date is contemporaneous with the sculpture itself. It would then be only fifty years later than Stela C at Tres Zapotes.

The date on Stela 2 of Colomba, which is also called Santa Margarita or Stela 2 at Piedra Parada,[174] is even less legible (fig. 38). The

[170] Waterman, 1929.

[171] If not Maya, it would correspond to *malinalli*—grass—in the calendars of central Mexico. (Lehmann, 1936–1939: 186).

[172] Proskouriakoff (1950: 175) agrees that, according to stylistic data, both the Olmecoid pieces from El Baul and those of Izapa are early.

[173] M. D. Coe, 1957.

[174] *Ibid.*: 604. This is the same piece that Lehmann calls the Schlubach stone.

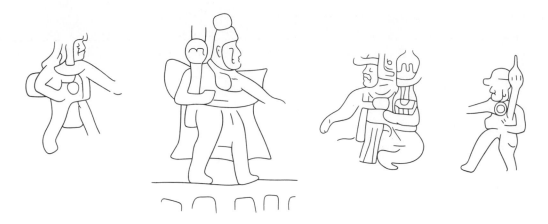

Fig. 39. Bas relief carving at Las Victorias, El Salvador. Total length slightly under 13 feet.

only part of the inscribed date that is clear is a number 7, which perhaps begins the reading; therefore it is possible that this piece belongs to Baktun 7.[175]

The two Guatemalan stelae are quite different in style, but both are covered with volutes in the curvilinear style of the Tres Zapotes box, Monument C (fig. 7), which we have considered to be from Olmec Period III. If we compare the two Guatemalan stelae with monuments from the Miraflores period at Kaminaljuyu, with the Izapa stones (which are also Preclassic), with some of the details at Monte Alban I, and with the origins of Maya art, we can affirm that they belong to Olmec III and that it was the late Olmecs who, for the first time, used the zero and the Long Count.

Other carvings in the region are not accompanied by glyphs, but their style is similar. Some indicate relationships with the Olmec. For example, a low stone relief on a boulder from Piedra Parada[176] (pl. 95) has Olmec features; the carving of the figure and its position are very similar to the dancing figures of Monte Alban I. On the other hand, Stela 1 (pl. 96) also from Piedra Parada,[177] is very much like the Izapa style, thus marking another connection between these Guatemalan stones and the two Olmecoid sites of Monte Alban and Izapa. Furthermore, Stela 1 at Piedra Parada, Stela 1 at El Baul (pl. 94), and the Alvarado stela (fig. 8)—the latter within the Metropolitan Olmec zone—show the main figure standing on a decorated pedestal. This may be another link between Olmecs and Olmecoids.

Another bas relief is at Las Victorias, in Chalchuapa, El Salvador

[175] See Lehmann, 1926: 76; Thompson, 1943: 110b; M. D. Coe, 1957.
[176] Thompson, 1943: p. 111a.
[177] *Ibid.*: 101 and 110a.

(fig. 39). The living rock is engraved with a person on each of its four sides. Three are standing and one is seated. All carry objects in their hands. Curiously—in view of its great distance from the Metropolitan zone—the style is one of the most characteristically Olmec in the entire Pacific watershed.[178]

Finally, although I cannot be positive that it pertains to this period, I cannot overlook one of the outstanding sculptures of Mesoamerica: the monumental tiger of El Baul[179] (pl. 97).

Although it has been published a number of times, I had not realized how impressive it is until I saw it. It stands today in a garden behind a caretaker's house, although it would be a major ornament to any museum. The ferocious feline face contrasts with the ears and seated body, all obviously humanized. There is a sort of cape on the shoulders and over it seems to be a collar with a knot in front. This would suggest a late date, since collared jaguars are frequent in the Toltec period, but the rest of the sculpture suggests a much older date.

From La Victoria—one of the few explored sites on Guatemala's Pacific coast—the first phase, Ocos, seems to correspond to Olmec I. The second phase, Conchas I and II, corresponds to Olmec II; many Preclassic aspects appear here which establish a connection, though slight, since no important ceremonial development is found at La Victoria.[180]

THE GUATEMALAN HIGHLANDS

Here the Olmec presence is less clear and less frequent. I have mentioned the abundant chubby figures in stone at Kaminaljuyu.[181] The structures, tombs, and ceramics there demonstrate Olmec influence, although possibly not directly from the Metropolitan area but from the Pacific watershed.

Kaminaljuyu was a great center. About two hundred mounds stand in an area of two square miles, but these are from a later period. We do not know their size in 500 B.C. The Miraflores phase of Kaminaljuyu,

---

[178] Boggs, 1950: 85–92. Boggs sugests (1944 and 1950) that this Chalchuapa petroglyph may be related stylistically to the "Virgin" of Tazumal, which is preserved today in the National Museum of El Salvador. Frankly, I do not find any Olmec influence in the style of the "Virgin." Also, Lehmann (1939: 47) states that it is inscribed with Maya glyphs.

[179] Richardson, 1940: pl. XIXa.

[180] M. D. Coe, 1961. Coe writes that the ceramics collected by Drucker in 1940 at La Venta are identical to those of the Conchas period in Guatemala: many types of white pottery, much of it fugitive (that is, painted after firing), especially flat-bottomed bowls with double-line incisions, and neckless ollas (*tecomates*) made of red clay. They are, therefore, to be placed in the Middle Preclassic (800–300 B.C.).

[181] Lothrop, 1926.

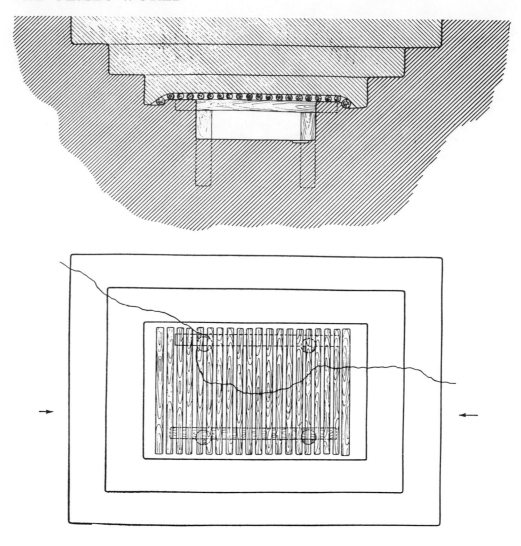

Fig. 40. Section and plan, restored, of Tomb I at Kaminaljuyu. Length of outer trench, 31 feet.

which is still difficult to situate in time, seems to have begun around 400 B.C. In this phase are found more traits related to the Olmec but especially to Monte Alban I culture. Thus there are vessels with wavy rims and with animal heads and tails, figurines with heavy legs, and incised kaolin pottery like that of Veracruz or the Mexican highlands, and which in Monte Alban was to be called Type C5.

In the Kaminaljuyu region it is now possible to distinguish various periods prior to Miraflores, which is the first, apparently, showing some relationship with the Olmecs. The large Mound E-III-3, about 65.5 feet high and with a diameter of 230 to 300 feet, was constructed entirely of adobe, with earth, sand, clay. Stone was not used at all, nor was it used in any of the other buildings from this period or from earlier ones. Stuc-

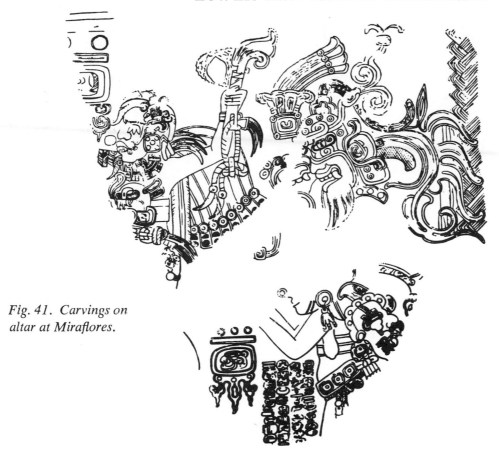

Fig. 41. Carvings on altar at Miraflores.

co was not utilized either.[182] In other words, except for the difference of the natural available elements, this could be a Metropolitan Olmec structure.

Two large tombs were found here, excavated in the upper platform of the edifice. Steps were left on all sides (three to one tomb, four to the other) which allowed access to the central and most sunken part of the tomb. The principal skeleton was buried on a wooden litter, and enormous offerings were placed both on the litter and on the steps. Four posts supported the roof beams, which were surely placed there after the burial (fig. 40). Finally everything was filled in and a platform was built on top. The weight of the fill caused the roof to cave in within a few years.[183] The burials indicate that this was a very advanced culture, probably with a great chieftain at its head, and an extraordinary richness of offerings. Not only in the tombs themselves but throughout the mound there was an incredible abundance of ceramics—perhaps fifteen million sherds.

Olmec reminiscences, we see, are only of a general order here. It is

[182] Shook and Kidder, 1952: 41–46.
[183] *Ibid.*: 56–65.

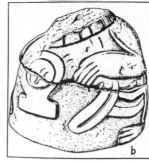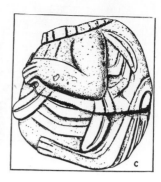

Fig. 42. Olmecoid figure at Copan.

clear that the Miraflores period is the result of an evolution of an an-cient local culture with few contributions from outside.

From the Miraflores phase itself we have a splendid stela (pl. 98) and an altar (fig. 41), both adorned with hieroglyphs.[184] Although nei-ther is completely Olmec they have elements of this art style. They con-stitute another demonstration of the existence of an advanced culture contemporaneous with the end of Olmec II and with Olmec III, but with independent features.[185]

On the other side of Guatemala, on the Atlantic coast—where later the marvelous Maya city of Copan was to come into existence—there are some indications of the Olmec presence. Underneath Stela 4 at Copan two headless sculptures were found, four feet tall, which look like the human representations from the Pacific coast, although they are different in some respects: they are shown clothed, and we could al-most say that this sculpture begins to be Mayanized; at least it is not typically Olmec[186] (fig. 42).

In the North Guatemalan jungles of the Peten, except for vague re-lationships with ceramics and with some minor objects, what is most striking (and has been discussed heatedly for years) is the possible re-lationship between a structure at Uaxactun (see pl. 99) and the Olmec style. This is the pyramid called E VII Sub. This poetic name was given the building because it was found underneath another of later construc-tion, in Structure VII of Group E in Uaxactun. The pyramidal platform, completely stuccoed (a trait later than Olmec II but rare even in III), is decorated on its two upper terraces with great jaguar masks, also of

[184] Caso, 1965: fig. 7c, and Kidder and Chinchilla, 1959: 46.

[185] Shook, who discovered both pieces, tells me that they lay under fourteen adobe floors and that they were associated with ceramic ware from a period not later than Miraflores.

[186] See Dieseldorff, 1926–33; II: 27; Stromsvik, 1941: 76; and Richardson, 1940: fig. 37. A seated figure from La Unión, department of Copan, is made of ser-pentine, has slanted eyes and a thick mouth, and although not Olmec does have the general feeling of this art, especially in the body, arms, and legs. The figure is in the museum at Copan.

0 10 INCHES   0 20 CMS   0 10 INCHES   0 20 CMS

Fig. 43. Masks at Uaxactun. Right: Mask 13, west façade, middle row. Left: Mask 16, south side, same row.

stucco. These have similarities to the mask on Stela C at Tres Zapotes, whose date falls within the Olmec III period. The Uaxactun masks correspond to the Chicanel period of that city, generally considered to cover from 700 to 100 B.C. The chronology of these two monuments, therefore, does not offer a major problem.[187]

Morley agreed on the stylistic similarity between the two monuments but not on the sequence.[188] In reality the eight masks on the first terrace are quite different from the ten on the second and third terraces.[189] The former are more serpentine, while the latter (fig. 43) are frankly jaguar-like and of course more like the Olmec jaguars. I believe that Drucker is right[190] when he states that there were two periods of influences flowing from Maya to Olmec and vice versa; these masks would have been the result of the second and later current and can probably be correlated with Olmec III period, since they are from the Chicanel period in Uaxactun and their main likeness is to Stela C at Tres Zapotes. This type of architectural mask was later to develop greatly in the Maya world.

Furthermore, the Uaxactun masks are important as proof of the relative contemporaneity of Olmec III and the Chicanel period of Peten. Once more they demonstrate that the Olmec world preceded the Maya, since in the Chicanel (Preclassic) period of Uaxactun there were associations with Olmec III, that is, with the end of the Olmec culture. Recent data suggest the same for other sites in the Peten.

Further north, Drucker[191] sees Olmecoid traits in very crude sculp-

---

[187] See Stirling, 1940: 5; Drucker, 1952: 220.
[188] Morley, 1938: IV: 316.
[189] Ricketson and Ricketson, 1937: figs. 39 to 50.
[190] Drucker, 1952: 221.
[191] *Ibid.*: 224–225.

ture from Yucatan, published by Andrews.[192] I agree that they represent a style that is not Maya, but I do not feel that they are very Olmec, though they may be a very late degeneration of the Olmec style. Actually, from Yucatan we are acquainted only with some small Olmec figurines purchased in Merida.[193] This locale has no significance, as they could have been taken there by modern merchants; Merida is a market for antiques. The existence of the little stone head from Mayapan can be explained as an object that was preserved and buried[194] (pl. 100). I believe, really, that Olmec influence in Yucatan is practically nonexistent; this can be very important in explaining why the later Teotihuacan empire, with all its power, never reached Yucatan. To a considerable degree Teotihuacan was following the outline of expansion which the Olmecs had begun. If the Olmecs did not reach Yucatan, we can understand why the Teotihuacanos did not reach it either. It would not be until more than a thousand years later that the Toltec empire would succeed in occupying or influencing that area, something which the Aztecs themselves never did.

At Tancah in Quintana Roo, where the earliest phase corresponds to the late Preclassic,[195] I find nothing Olmec, nor do I in the Belize Valley.[196]

Objects that are small (and therefore easily carried from one place to another) are of little historical value when found in an isolated manner, but they tend to reinforce the presence of a style when discovered in certain quantities in an area. I shall list here only some whose provenance is definite. This does not mean, however, that in ancient times they were not transported from one site to another.

I believe Drucker is right when he sees an Olmec style in braziers from Kaminaljuyu.[197] One, especially (pl. 101), is similar to the Monte Alban I and II braziers. A squatting figurine with a hole in its head, from the department of Quiché in the western highlands of Guatemala, is reminiscent of the Olmec.[198] Another figurine, probably from Coatepec, near the Pacific coast, is of jadeite with a buccal mask and forked tongue.[199]

Like the Coatepec piece, a seated human figure 11.5 inches tall, found at Uaxactun, also has a general Olmec aspect, although the details do not conform to this style. It corresponds to the Tzakol period (about 300 A.D.) and therefore is post-Olmec; it could be either of late

[192] Andrews, 1939, 1941.
[193] Kidder, 1942: 39d, e, f.
[194] Smith and Ruppert, 1953: fig. 9c.
[195] Sanders, 1960: 209–212 and chart 3.
[196] Willey, Bullard, Glass, and Gifford, 1965.
[197] Drucker, 1952: 222; Kidder, Jennings, and Shook, 1946: fig. 201.
[198] Lothrop, 1936: fig. 105.
[199] Kidder, 1942: 37 and fig. 40d.

manufacture or an inherited object.[200]

From El Baul comes a splendid head which was probably part of a complete figure.[201] In the La Aurora Museum there is a jade celt which was formerly in the Dieseldorff collection, and a large seated masculine figure made of jadeite with incisions on the fingers, eyebrows, and cheeks. Both of these are suggestive of the Olmec style.

A jade figure, certainly Olmec, was found (although not scientifically) in La Lima in the department of Cortés, Llano de Sul, Honduras. It represents a kneeling man[202] (pl. 102). And from Guanacaste province in Costa Rica comes a winged personage of the baby-face type in bluish green jade[203] (pl. 103). This is reminiscent, perhaps, of the wings on a figure from Las Victorias near Chalchuapa, in El Salvador.[204]

Figures of ball players and a plaque engraved with a jaguar, executed in Olmec style, come from El Salvador, in the area between Chalchuapan and Atiquizaya, near the Guatemalan border.[205] In the La Aurora Museum are exhibited, aside from the above mentioned pieces, some objects which remind one of the Olmec style, such as two seated stone figures (nos. 2006 and 2028). A stela from Kaminaljuyu depicting a man-jaguar is also found in this museum.

A summary of what we have seen suggests that the entire area—including the Metropolitan Olmec zone—was more or less a single cultural entity during the Olmec I period, with deviations only in ceramics or in the minor arts. When civilization became a fact in the Metropolitan area, traces of it scattered throughout the rest of the region. In some places this influence is clearly marked; in others it is weak. In smaller regions a special and partially independent style evolved, preserving only remnants of the Olmec. The main regions of this style, with internal divergences, are the Valley of Oaxaca and the area that seems to extend along the Pacific coast from Tonalá in Chiapas to El Salvador. Both areas, in many aspects, took the lead. In its different local characteristics the Chiapas–Guatemala style (which we are coming to know somewhat better, though only in Izapa and in the Escuintla region) could be a tie between the Olmec and the Maya. This does not mean, however, that the Maya is derived exclusively from this Chiapas–Guatemala style, for it has its own roots, especially in the Peten and in the central zone—and these roots are precisely those which stem from the numerous non-Olmec objects from these regions in the Preclassic Mamon and Chicanel periods.

[200] Kidder, 1947: 47–48 and figs. 37 and 74.
[201] Shook, 1956.
[202] Stone, 1957: 123 and fig. 84b; Anton, 1961: pl. 9; or Kelemen, 1943: II, pl. 253c.
[203] Lines, 1941: I: 117–122, and 1942: 54; Covarrubias, 1946: fig. 18.
[204] M. D. Coe, 1965: 766.
[205] *Ibid.*: 766.

7

OLMECS AND OLMECOIDS: A SUMMARY

The study of the Metropolitan Olmec zone and a view of other areas where the Olmec presence is either marked or perceptible will allow us to propose hypotheses regarding the first Mesoamerican civilization, the extent of the area itself, its character in ancient times, its significance, and the heritage it bequeathed to later peoples.

At certain sites there are Olmec monuments or remains that are either immovable or of such a nature that they must have been made locally; in other sites or areas Olmec objects have been found that were not necessarily produced there but could have been brought by trade and could even have been preserved for a long time as an inheritance. The difference between these situations is important, of course, for reconstructing the Olmec culture in general and its probable expansion. Both types of sites are included because they show approximately how far this influence reached; they allow us to estimate the continental area occupied by this first civilization.

It is a fact that for the first time in history this region of the North American continent was distinguished from the rest as the area that took the step toward civilization, while the other regions continued and were to continue almost in their totality—until their discovery by Europeans—in a culturally inferior state. The area that took the step is, in general, the same one we call Mesoamerica. Olmec Mesoamerica was smaller than the future Mesoamerica of Teotihuacan, the Maya, Toltecs, and Aztecs, but fundamentally it was the same. The southern frontier underwent fewer changes than the northern. Except for the very late expansion of Otomangue peoples to Nicaragua and Costa Rica, the border was fixed at western Honduras and El Salvador. In the north, on the Atlantic side, Mesoamerica reached from the Panuco River south through the central valleys of Mexico, Morelos, and eastern Guerrero. It stretched eastward along the Gulf through Veracruz and Tabasco. Only Yucatan, which we have seen presents scarce Olmec traces, could be excluded from this entire area. All of western and north-central Mexico were still outside of Mesoamerica.[1]

With the important exception of Yucatan, then, the Olmec world formed what would be nuclear Mesoamerica. Except in the final pre-Conquest period, the west was a marginal cultural area.

It seems evident that the Olmec horizon inaugurated Mesoamerica just as it gave birth to so many concrete and visible traits (that is to say, those that can be demonstrated archaeologically) which were to be characteristic of Mesoamerica. In the foregoing pages I have tried to point out many of these, referring to their survival in later cultures. These visible traits, aside from their basic importance for our knowledge of the development and essence of Mesoamerica, allow us—with somewhat more assurance—to assume that the Olmec world also initiated features that are not visible and therefore cannot be demonstrated through archaeology, but that were to continue as characteristic of the final period of Mesoamerica, which we know best. For example, in order to study religion or the priesthood, ceremonialism, the state, and perhaps the empire in Olmec times, we may be able to take advantage of both recent ethnographic data and information from written sources, which are relatively modern. But this must be done with great care, and in general the method is valid only when there is some archaeological indication that suggests the possibility.

In order to follow this line of thought we must accept the idea that the Olmecs constituted civilization, and that in Mesoamerica there has been but one civilization, although the forms have changed in time and in space. If the Olmec world was precivilized or if its civilization was not the same in essence as that of the Aztecs at the end of the pre-Conquest period, or if in Mesoamerica there was more than one civilization either in time or in space—then the correlation between Olmecs and later peoples is false. If we carefully study its entirety and its details we will see that the background always seems to be the same, and the basic elements the same. From now on I will not speak of a Maya or Teotihuacan or Aztec civilization. I believe they are all the same. The Maya or the people of Teotihuacan or the Aztecs only represent different cultures within a civilization, just as western Christianity is but one

---

[1] See Caso's map, 1965. See also Covarrubias, 1946: 155. The El Opeño problem has already been discussed (see p. 143 above).

civilization in spite of differences that exist between Spanish, German, or English cultures. Thus, although I accept Toynbee's concept of civilization, I differ from him in that I believe that in Mesoamerica we are dealing with one civilization and not with several.[2]

It might be thought that this duration for one civilization is too long, since it would extend from 1200 B.C. to the sixteenth century A.D.—twenty-eight centuries. This would not be an isolated instance in the history of civilizations, for Egypt and China had even longer time spans.

If we are to assert the common origin of Mesoamerica, its validity as a cultural area, its continuity and therefore its parallel history, we must be able to demonstrate these through archaeology. I believe that, in spite of the many lacunae that must yet be filled, in spite of numerous doubts regarding the correct interpretation of the facts, at least a few serious hypotheses may be constructed which tend to validate our argument.

Which patterns did Olmec expansion follow from the small Metropolitan area to its most remote sites? I believe that it was carried out in several ways: essentially through the growth of an Olmec state which was obliged, in order to survive, to embark on a clearly imperialistic endeavor—as was to occur in the states of central Mexico later on. Thus the Olmecs not only engendered Mesoamerica but also brought forth the first Mesoamerican empire, whose remains are still visible. It is impossible to be certain, however, whether the empire expanded through military activity or colonization or through commerce and religious diffusion, or—as is more probable—through a combination of these imperialistic patterns. It seems clear that the Olmecs established the pattern which, through the centuries, was to be followed by other expansionist Mesoamerican cultures. The Olmecs broke the paths which were to be followed by merchants of a later age; they became aware for the first time of regions beyond their own, which were to be occupied by other soldiers and other elites who were to disseminate their own inventions and establish one religious pattern.

In the early precivilization background, before 1200 B.C., clear local differences were visible, and curiously enough elements existed which did not appear in the Metropolitian zone. Thus the list of traits formulated by Piña Chán[3] is not made up exclusively of Olmec elements, since some of them are not to be found within the Metropolitan area.

We have seen how that common basis, from which centuries later the Olmec style and world were to emerge, extended at least from the Pacific coast of Guatemala (Ocós Phase at La Victoria) as far as the Panuco River. Around 1200 B.C. the beginnings of a true civilization were

---

[2] Bernal, 1960.
[3] Piña Chán, 1964: 25.

born in what we have called the Metropolitan Olmec area, and from that time on the Olmecs began to import materials from the outlying regions. These areas—even the most backward—had ancient cultural ties with the central zone, since both had possessed over the centuries a similar culture, though certainly not an identical one. The new relationships between the more advanced Metropolitan zone and its more backward relatives were generally based on commerce and possibly on tribute as a result of conquest.

It was not essential for an empire in Mesoamerica to possess a large urban concentration.[4] In my opinion, the Olmec was by no means a solid empire; that is, it never achieved geographic unity but was notable for its regional differences. For example, Remojadas, which was relatively close to the Olmec center and which possessed an entirely different culture unaffected by the Olmec,[5] suggests that Olmec expansion left cultural islands and never achieved a massive territorial expansion.

On the other hand, the Olmecs seem to have founded true colonies in some areas such as Morelos or Puebla, perhaps in the central part of present-day Guerrero, at Tlatilco in the Valley of Mexico, and in the area of El Viejón in Veracruz.[6] Some of these colonies occupied a vast zone; others, like Tlatilco, occupied a single site. I have called these people the Colonial Olmecs. Certain colonies, especially the larger ones, probably were ruled by a small military and religious Olmec elite, which dominated the local people; others, such as Tlatilco and perhaps Morelos, suggest, rather, a true Olmec population, though the latter was increasingly more influenced by inferior local cultures.

In other areas, less precisely defined, we are aware of only a more remote Olmec influence, one that is less concrete and abundant. These are the Olmecoid groups. In this case the local culture predominates and that of the Olmecs is simply an additional contribution, though in part both are derived from a lower and older common culture. Typical Olmecoids areas are Oaxaca and the Pacific slopes. Here we are dealing not with an Olmec civilization dominating peoples of a lower culture, but with two branches of the same civilization, in contact with one another and both standing at the same level, though the Metropolitan Olmec culture was the more influential.

The influence exerted by some of the local groups over others (without the intervention of the Metropolitan area) should also be taken into consideration. This would explain the diffusion among some Colonials and Olmecs of distinctive traits which do not appear in the Metropolitan area. Among these are certain ceramic types, burial systems such as

---

[4] Caso, 1965: 17.
[5] Medellín, 1960A.
[6] Stirling, 1961: 44, and Drucker, Heizer, and Squier, 1959: 251.

those of Tlatilco and, above all, a great number of elements that do not correspond to Olmec Period II. These, which appear only in Period III in the Metropolitan zone, seem to be earlier in other areas. The most extraordinary element is that of writing, the calendar, dot and bar numerals—which I believe to have appeared first at Monte Alban, even though in a confused form. The system becomes more fixed at Tres Zapotes and at other sites bearing dates which belong to Cycle 7. Thus there exists not only a centripetal expansion but a centrifugal movement. At many sites these local traits seem derived in part from the common substratum from which the Olmecs themselves proceeded. For instance, no traces of the ball game exist in the Metropolitan area. We do find them, however, at places such as Chalcatzingo and Tlatilco (if the *yuguitos* point to the ball game).[7] Pathological representations of children have been discovered in Veracruz and Guerrero but not in the Metropolitan area.[8] Another example is that of the stirrup spout found on the ceramics. Among the known hieroglyphs are some such as the X-shaped cross (if the latter is a glyph) which appears on many Olmec and Olmecoid objects of Periods II and III.[9] Other glyphs, such as those of Monte Alban, are different.

This presents another problem of great interest. The period of efflorescence of the Olmec world outside the Metropolitan area corresponds precisely to the period of decadence in the central zone. Olmec Period III seems to have produced the largest number of elaborations everywhere, but these no longer emerged from the central zone directly but were the result of the evolution of the culture in separate areas—all more or less connected with the Metropolitan Olmecs.

Perhaps this situation can be explained not only through the causes which are usually associated with the history of empires but through one of the essential characteristics of Olmec expansion: its religiosity. More than any other way, the Olmec style was exported in association with the jaguar cult and its ceremonialism. Thus the Olmec colonies are colored by missionary aspects such as conversion or proselytism; a germ of differentiation between the masses and the hierarchy is also present.[10] In fact, and due to the causes which have been described here, the Met-

---

[7] We are dealing with the ball game played perhaps without a field and with bats—very different from the well-known type of ball game which was to be played later. The older type was to be continued at Teotihuacan (see Aveleyra, 1964). "Yuguitos," or "little yokes" (thought to have been worn as protection) have been discovered at other sites besides Tlatilco. Some representations suggest the game (Smith, 1963: 141 and figs. 57, 163–164, 171; and Piña Chán, 1964: 40 and 43–44; see also Stern, 1948). Decapitated ball players also appear on a stela at Izapa, a theme that was to be continued in later times at sites such as Aparicio, Tajín, and Chichen.

[8] Delgado, 1965.

[9] M. D. Coe, 1965: 759.

[10] See Heizer, 1962: 313–314; Thompson, 1950: 6; and W. R. Coe, 1959.

ropolitan culture—besides presenting more urban aspects—is partially different from the culture of the other sites which received her influence, since the original culture fuses with local elements or evolves into others that may stem from the fusion.

Let us return to the basic theme of this chapter—the origin and first manifestations of Mesoamerican civilization. Perhaps I have overemphasized the preeminence of the Metropolitan Olmec area. On the other hand, I have attempted to show the importance of a few sites and areas beyond the Metropolitan which became highly developed in the same era; I refer especially to the Pacific slopes of Chiapas-Guatemala, the highlands of Guatemala, and the Valley of Oaxaca. In these three zones we find great buildings, which only in Oaxaca are of stone; a fabrication of objects which indicates considerable evolution; an advanced social organization; the use of writing and the calendar in stone monuments—often remarkable, especially on the Pacific slopes and in the Guatemalan highlands. The stone monuments of Monte Alban are especially important, because they indicate a relatively extensive use of writing and calendrical numerals rather than because of their beauty.

Generally speaking—and not necessarily from an aesthetic point of view—I agree with Willey when he writes, "I am inclined to see the Olmec style, if not the earliest of all of these, at least the earliest to mature to greatness."[11] Actually I believe it was in the Olmec area that not one or two of the elements of civilization appeared but rather a whole combination of these traits which justify our calling this entire horizon the Olmec world. Perhaps a better name might be the world of the Olmecs–Monte Alban–Chiapas-Guatemala. This denomination, however, is somewhat impractical, though it sheds light on one significant aspect, not only of the Olmec world but of all Mesoamerica.

When I speak of an "Olmec horizon" I am not using the term "horizon" in a strict sense. I mean it in a sense similar to that used by Kroeber[12] or Willey,[13] since I include within it not only one clearly defined style but several others, which, though different, are related. In order to prove the contemporancity of these styles, their interrelationship has to be proved. This is one of the basic things I have tried to do in this book. I think there is little doubt that all the cultural manifestations of the different areas here reviewed, in the epoch chosen for this book, are more or less contemporaneous, and more or less similar, forming a great period or horizon that is Pan-Mesoamerican. Another basic point is that the relationship between these areas existed precisely because they had all reached a certain level of development and together formed an early stage of Mesoamerican civilization.

[11] Willey, 1964: 145.
[12] Kroeber, 1944: 108–111.
[13] Willey, 1948: 8.

Coe[14] believes that "it is fairly certain that we are *not* dealing with a horizon style" because objects of Olmec style are, in some areas, either absent or restricted to a few trade pieces. I agree with Coe if we apply the term horizon style very strictly and if we do not include within it the many variants of style which, as I have tried to show, formed a unit—the Olmec world. These variants are the result of several causes, essentially I believe, of the different social and political situations existing in the Olmec world. Thus my Colonial Olmecs and Olmecoids.

It is evident that we must ignore the concept (which, by the way, has fallen into disuse though still accepted by many) that the Valley of Mexico was the cultural center of Mesoamerica. It was to become that in a far later period, but it surely did not fill that role in Olmec times, since a civilized way of life was still alien to it—the beauty of the Tlatilco figurines notwithstanding. The Valley of Mexico was frankly marginal and backward. It was to stand out only with the emergence of Teotihuacan, which gathered all the dispersed cultural currents and converted the highlands into one of the leading cultures of Mesoamerica.

In Mesoamerica, in contrast to the Andean area, each region preserved a large part of its cultural independence, since many traits never fused or passed (except in small doses) from one region to another. This characteristic seems to apply at any given moment. Therefore, the less pronounced the horizon style, the more individuality we find in the local styles. Even so, contemporaneous styles are more closely related among themselves than with earlier or later styles. In spite of all their evident differences, a more basic relationship exists between the Olmec style and that of the other cultures described in this chapter, than among all these and any later forms. Even the Maya canons, which occasionally remind us of Izapa, are more distant from Izapa than the Olmec is, no matter how great the differences between La Venta and Izapa. The same may be said of other sites such as Monte Alban, where Periods I and II share more similarities among themselves and some other cultures within the Olmec horizon than with posterior periods in the same city.

I have already spoken of the differentiation between the people and the hierarchy. This is part of the vast problem of the existence of class-differentiated groups in Mesoamerica. As Eric Thompson has pointed out, it is evident that among the Classic Maya of a later period there existed, side by side with the uninstructed peasantry, a hierarchy that reserved all knowledge for itself. This was to be, in later times, the situation in Tenochtitlan. Did such a fundamental division exist among the Olmecs? We cannot answer this question with certainty, but it seems reasonably probable.[15]

[14] M. D. Coe, 1965: 771.
[15] See Heizer, 1961: 52ff.

OLMECS AND OLMECOIDS: A SUMMARY

To sum up: the world of the Olmecs and Olmecoids formed Meso-america and set patterns of civilization that were to distinguish this area from all other parts of the Americas.

The end of the Olmec world is not an end but a beginning. It leads directly into the Classic world of Teotihuacan, Monte Alban, Tajín, and the Maya. These people were to absorb the Olmec inheritance and push civilization to far higher levels. They would reach a new ledge on the rocky ascent to civilization. Archaeology has already uncovered enough so that the fascinating history of these later cultures can be sketched and made understandable. If life allows, I hope to write it some day.

BIBLIOGRAPHY

ABBREVIATIONS USED

AA	American Anthropologist.
AmA	American Antiquity.
AMNM	Anales del Museo Nacional de México.
BAE-B	Bureau of American Ethnology, Washington. Bulletin.
CIAM-B	Centro de Investigaciones Antropológicas de México. Boletín.
CIW-	Carnegie Institution of Washington:
C	Contributions
P	Publications
CR	Current Reports
INAH-DMP	Instituto Nacional de Antropología e Historia. México. Dirección de Monumentos Prehispánicos.
NGM	National Geographic Magazine.

NWAF-P	New World Archaeological Foundation. Publications.
NMAAE	Carnegie Institution of Washington. Notes on Middle American Archaeology and Ethnology.
PMAE-M	Peabody Museum of American Archaeology and Ethnology. Memoirs.
RMEA	Sociedad Mexicana de Antropología. Revista Mexicana de Estudios Antropológicos (antes Históricos).
SMA-	Sociedad Mexicana de Antropología. Reuniones de Mesa Redonda:
MO	Mayas y Olmecas
SMGE-B	Sociedad Mexicana de Geografía y Estadística. Boletín.

Acosta, Jorge
    1942   Rasgos Olmecas en Monte Albán. SMA-MO, pp. 55–56.
Agrinier, Pierre
    1960   The carved human femurs from tomb 1, Chiapa de Corzo. NWAF-P, 6, no. 5.

Aguirre Beltrán, Gonzalo
  1955   Gente del país del Hule. Universidad de México, vol. X, no. 3.
Andrews, E. Wyllys
  1939   A group of related sculptures from Yucatan. CIW-C, V; 71–85.
  1941   Pustunich, Campeche. *In* Los Mayas Antiguos, pp. 127–135.
Anton, Ferdinand
  1961   Mexiko. Indianerkunst aus Präkolumbischerzeit. München.
Armillas, Pedro
  1948   Arqueología del Occidente de Guerrero. *In* El Occidente de México,
            Sociedad Mexicana de Antropología, pp. 74–76. México.
Aveleyra, Luis
  1964   La estela teotihuacana de la Ventilla. Cuadernos del Museo Nacional
            de Antropología, 1. México.
Barba de Piña Chán, Beatriz
  1956   Tlapacoya: un sitio preclásico de transición. Acta Anthropológica, vol.
            2–1. México.
Bastian, A.
  1882   Steinskulpturen aus Guatemala. Königliche Museum zu Berlin.
Batres, Leopoldo
  1905   La lápida arqueológica de Tepaxtlaco–Orizaba. México.
  1908   Civilización prehistórica de las riberas del Papaloapan y Costa de Sota-
            vento. México.
Berger, Rainer, John A. Graham, and Robert F. Heizer
  1967   A reconsideration of the age of the La Venta site. Contributions of the
            University of California Archaeological Research Facility, 3: 1–24.
            Berkeley.
Berlin, Heinrich
  1953   Archaeological reconnaissance in Tabasco. CIW-CR, no. 7: 102–135.
  1955   Selected pottery from Tabasco. NMAAE, V–126: 83–87.
  1956   Late pottery horizons of Tabasco, México. CIW-C, LIX.
Bernal, Ignacio
  1947   Straw hats. Tlalocan, II: 287–288.
  1949   Exploraciones en Coixtlahuaca. RMEA, X: 5–76.
  1958   Exploraciones en Cuilapan de Guerrero. INAH-DMP, 7. México.
  1960   Toynbee y Mesoamérica. Estudios de Cultura Nahuatl, 2: 43–58.
Beyer, Hermann
  1927   *Review of* Blom and La Farge, Tribes and temples. El México Antiguo,
            II: 305–313.
Blom, F., and O. La Farge
  1926   *see* Tribes and Temples
Boggs, Stanley H.
  1944   Excavations in central and western El Salvador, *In* John M. Longyear
            III, Archaeological investigations in El Salvador. PMAE-M, IV–2.
  1950   "Olmec" pictographs in the Las Victorias group, Chalchuapa archaeo-
            logical Zone, El Salvador. NMAAE, 99: 85–92.
Burgoa, Fray Francisco de
  1934   Geográfica descripción. Publicaciones del Archivo General de la
  (1674)   Nación, vols. XXV–XXVI. México.
Burkitt, R.
  1933   Two stones in Guatemala. Anthropos, XXVIII: 9–26.

Cangas y Quiñones, Suero de
  1928   Descripción de la villa del Espíritu Santo. RMEA, II: 176–180.
Caso, Alfonso
  1933   Idolos huecos de barro de tipo arcaico. AMNM, época IV, vol. VIII: 578–582.
  1938   Exploraciones en Oaxaca. Quinta y sexta temporadas. Instituto Panamericano de Geografía e Historia, Pub. 34. México.
  1942   Definición y extensión del complejo "Olmeca." SMA-MO, pp. 43–46.
  1946   Calendario y escritura de las antiguas culturas de Monte Albán. *In* Obras completas de Miguel O. de Mendizabal, I: 113–144.
  1965   Existió un imperio olmeca? Memorias del Colegio Nacional, V–3: 1–52.
Caso, Alfonso, and Ignacio Bernal
  1952   Urnas de Oaxaca. INAH, Memorias II. México.
Chavero, Alfredo
  1883   Historia Antigua. *In* México a través de los siglos, vol. 1.
Chevalier, F., and L. Huguet
  1958   Peuplement et mise en valeur du tropique mexicain. *In* Miscelanea P. Rivet, octogenario dicata, pp. 395–438. México.
Childe, V. G.
  1950   The urban revolution. Town Planning Review, 21: 3–17. University of Liverpool.
Clewlow, C. William, Richard A. Cowan, James F. O'Connell, and Carlos Benemann
  1967   Colossal heads of the Olmec culture. Contributions of the University of California Archaeological Research Facility, 4. Berkeley.
Cline, Howard F.
  1959   A preliminary report on Chinantec archaeology. Congreso Internacional de Americanistas, XXXIII–2: 158–170. San José, Costa Rica.
Coe, Michael D.
  1957   Cycle 7 monuments in Middle America, a Reconsideration. AA, LIX: 597–611.
  1961   La Victoria, and early site on the Pacific coast of Guatemala. PMAE Papers, vol. LIII.
  1962   Mexico. Ancient Peoples and Places Series. London.
  1965   The Olmec style and its distribution. Handbook of Middle American Indians, 3: 739–775.
  1965A   Jaguar's Children: Pre-Classic Central Mexico. Museum of Primitive Art, New York.
  1966   Exploraciones arqueológicas en San Lorenzo Tenochtitlan, Veracruz. INAH-DMP Boletín no. 24: 21–25.
  1967   San Lorenzo and the Olmec civilization. MS.
  1967A   La segunda temporada en San Lorenzo Tenochtitlan, Veracruz. Boletín del INAH, No. 28, June: 1–10.
  1967B   Solving a monumental mystery. Discovery, 3: 21–26.
Coe, Michael D., Richard A. Diehl, and Minze Stuiver
  1967   Olmec civilization, Veracruz, Mexico: Dating of the San Lorenzo phase. Science, 155: 1399–1401.
Coe, William R.
  1959   Piedras Negras archaeology: artifacts, caches, and burials. University Museum, Philadelphia.

Coe, William R., and Robert Stuckenrath
  1964   Review of [Excavations at] La Venta, Tabasco, 1955, and its relevance
          to the Olmec problem. Kroeber Anthropological Society Papers, 31:
          1–43.

Comas, Juan
  1942   El problema de la existencia de un tipo racial olmeca. SMA-MO, pp.
          69–70.
  1945   Osteometría olmeca (Informe preliminar sobre los restos hallados en
          Cerro de las Mesas, Estado de Veracruz, México). Anales del Instituto
          de Etnografía Americana, Universidad del Cuyo, VI: 169–218.

Conklin, Harold C.
  1963   The study of shifting cultivation. Union Panamericana, Estudios y
          Monografías, XI (VI in English ed.). Washington.

Cook de Leonard, Carmen
  1967   Sculptures and rock carvings at Chalcatzingo, Morelos. Contributions
          of the University of California Archaeological Research Facility, 3:
          57–84. Berkeley.

Cordan, Wolfgang
  1963   Secret of the Forest. London.

Corona, Gustavo
  1962   El luchador olmeca. INAH, Boletin, 10: 12–13. México.

Covarrubias, Miguel
  1942   Origen y desarrollo del estilo artístico "Olmeca." SMA-MO, pp. 46–49.
  1944   La Venta: colossal heads and jaguar gods. DYN, 6: 24–33.
  1946   El arte "Olmeca" o de La Venta. Cuadernos Americanos, V–4: 153–
          179.
  1946A   Mexico South. New York.
  1948   Tipología de la industria de piedra tallada y pulida de la cuenca del Río
          Mezcala. *In* El Occidente de México, Sociedad Mexicana de Antropo-
          logía, pp. 86–90. México.
  1950   Tlatilco: el arte y la cultura preclásica del Valle de México. Cuadernos
          Americanos, IX–3: 149–162.
  1956   Mezcala: Ancient Mexican Sculpture. New York.
  1957   Indian Art of Mexico and Central America. New York.

Crane, H. R., and J. B. Griffin
  1958   Radiocarbon Dates III. University of Michigan. (Mimeo.)

Curtis, Garniss H.
  1959   The petrology of artifacts and architectural stone at La Venta. *In*
          Drucker, Heizer, and Squier, pp. 284–289.

Dahlgren, Barbro
  1953   Etnografía prehispánica de la costa del Golfo. RMEA, XIII–2–3: 145–
          156. México.

Dávalos Hurtado, E., and J. M. Ortiz de Zárate
  1953   La plástica indígena y la patología. RMEA, XIII–2–3: 95–104.

De Cicco, Gabriel, and Donald Brockington
  1956   Reconocimiento arqueológico en el Suroeste de Oaxaca. INAH-DMP,
          6. México.

Delgado, Agustín
  1956   La arqueología de la Chinantla. Tlatoani, X: 29–33. México.
  1960   Exploraciones en la Chinantla. RMEA, XVI: 105–123.

1961 La secuencia arqueológica en el istmo de Tehuantepec. *In* Los Mayas del Sur y sus relaciones con los Nahuas meridionales. SMA, pp. 93–104. México.

1965 Infantile and jaguar traits in Olmec Sculpture, Archaeology, 18, 1: 55–62.

Dieseldorff, E. P.

1926 Kunst und Religion der Mayavölker im alten und heutigen

1933 Mittelamerika. 3 vols. Berlin and Hamburg.

Disselhoff, Hans Dietrich

1952 Eine mexikanische Grunstein-Maske aus der "Kunstkammer" der Bayrischen Herzoge. Ethnos, XVII: 130–141.

Drucker, Philip

1943 Ceramic stratigraphy at Cerro de las Mesas, Veracruz. BAE-B, 141.

1943A Ceramic sequences at Tres Zapotes, Veracruz. BAE-B, 140.

1947 Some implications of the ceramic complex of La Venta. Smithsonian Institution, Miscellaneous Collections, CVII–8.

1952 La Venta, Tabasco: a study of Olmec ceramics and art. BAE-B, 153.

1952 Middle Tres Zapotes and the Pre-Classic ceramic sequence. AmA, XVII–3: 258–260.

1955 The Cerro de las Mesas offering of jade and other materials. BAE-B, 157: 25–68.

1961 The La Venta Olmec support area. Kroeber Anthropological Society Papers, 25: 59–72.

Drucker, P., and Eduardo Contreras

1953 Site patterns in the eastern part of Olmec territory. Journal of the Washington Academy of Sciences, XLIII: 389–396.

Drucker, Philip, and Robert F. Heizer

1956 Gifts for the jaguar god. NGM, CX: 367–375.

1957 Radiocarbon dates from La Venta, Tabasco. Science, CXXVI: 72–73.

1960 A study of the milpa system of La Venta island and its archaeological implications. Southwestern Journal of Anthropology, XVI: 36–45.

1965 Commentary on W. R. Coe and Robert Stuckenrath's review of "Excavations at La Venta, Tabasco, 1955." Kroeber Anthropological Society Papers, XXXIII: 37–70.

Drucker, Philip, Robert Heizer, and Robert J. Squier

1959 Excavations at La Venta, Tabasco, 1955. BAE-B, 170.

Eisen, Gustav

1888 On some ancient sculptures from the Pacific slope of Guatemala. Memoirs of the California Academy of Sciences, II: 9–20. San Francisco.

Ekholm, Gordon

1944 Excavations at Tampico and Panuco in the Huasteca, Mexico. Anthropological Papers of the American Museum of Natural History, XXXVIII–5. New York.

Emmerich, André

1963 Art Before Columbus. New York.

Excavations in the Mixteca Alta.

1953 Mesoamerican Notes, 3. Mexico City College.

Ferdon, Edwin N., Jr.

1953 Tonalá, Mexico: an archaeological survey. School of American Research Monographs, no. 16. Santa Fe.

Flannery, Kent V.
1967   The Olmec and the Valley of Oaxaca: A model for interregional inter-action in formative times. MS.

Flannery, Kent V., Anne V. T. Kirkby, Michael J. Kirkby, and Aubrey Williams, Jr.
1967   Farming systems and political growth in ancient Oaxaca. Science, 159: 445–454.

Flores Guerrero, Raúl
1962   Historia general del arte mexicano (Epoca prehispánica). Mexico and Buenos Aires.

Foshag, W. E.
1957   Mineralogical attributions. *In* Robert Woods Bliss Collection of Pre-Columbian Art. New York.

Foster, George M.
1940   Notes on the Popoluca of Veracruz . . . Publicaciones del Instituto Pan-americano de Geografía e Historia, no. LI.
1942   A primitive Mexican economy. Monographs of the American Ethno-logical Society, V.
1945   Sierra Popoluca folklore and beliefs. University of California Publica-tions in American Archaeology and Ethnology, 42: 177–250.
1951   Some wider implications of soul-loss illness among the Sierra Popoluca. *In* Homenaje a Alfonso Caso, pp. 167–174. México.

Gamio, Manuel
1922   La población del Valle de Teotihuacan, 3 vols. México.

García Payón, José
1950   Restos de una cultura prehispánica encontrada en la region de Zem-poala, Ver. UNIVER, año II, no. 15, pp. 90–130. Jalapa.
1952   Totonacas y Olmecas. Universidad Veracruzana, año I, no. 4: 27–52. Jalapa.

Gonzalez, Pedro A.
1946   Los ríos de Tabasco. Contribución de Tabasco a la Cultura Nacional, no. 8.

Gullberg, Jonas E.
1959   Technical notes on concave mirrors. *In* Drucker, Reizer and Squier, pp. 280–283.

Guzmán, Eulalia
1934   Los relieves de las rocas del Cerro de la Cantera, Jonacatepec, Mor. AMNM, V–1: 237–251.

Habel, S.
1878   The sculptures of Santa Lucía Cosumalhuapa in Guatemala. Smith-sonian Contributions to Knowledge, 269: 1–90.

Handbook of the Robert Woods Bliss Collection of Pre-Columbian Art
1963   Dumbarton Oaks, Washington.

Hartt, Charles C.
1867   Remarks on Tabasco, México, occasioned by the reported discovery of remains of ancient cities being found in that locality. Proceedings of the Numismatic and Antiquarian Society of Philadelphia, 1865–1866: 81–82.

Hay, Clarence
1923   The buried past of Mexico. Natural History, XXIII: 259–271.

Heizer, Robert F.

1959   Specific and generic characteristics of Olmec culture. XXXIII Congreso de Americanistas, II: 178–182.

1960   Agriculture and the theocratic state in lowland southeastern Mexico. AmA, XXVI: 215–222.

1961   Inferences on the nature of Olmec society based upon data from La Venta site. Kroeber Anthropological Society Papers, 25: 43–57.

1962   The possible sociopolitical structure of the La Venta Olmecs. Akten des 34. Internationalen Amerikanistenkongresses, pp. 310–317. Wien.

1964   Some interim remarks on the Coe-Stuckenrath review. Kroeber Anthropological Society Papers, 31: 45–50.

1967   Analysis of two low-relief sculptures from La Venta. Contributions of the University of California Archaeological Research Facility, 3: 25–26. Berkeley.

Heizer, Robert F., and P. Drucker

1968   The fluted pyramid of the La Venta site. Antiquity, 42: 52–56.

Heizer, Robert F., Tillie Smith, and H. Williams

1965   Notes on colossal head no. 2 from Tres Zapotes, AmA, 31–1: 102–104.

Heizer, R. F., and H. Williams

1960   Olmec lithic sources. CIAM–B, VI: 16–17.

Historia Tolteca-Chichimeca.

1947   Anales de Quauhtinchan. Mexico.

Holmes, William H.

1907   On a nephrite statuette from San Andres Tuxtla, Veracruz, Mexico. AA, IX: 691–701.

1916   The oldest dated American monument, a nephrite figurine from Mexico. Art and Archaeology, III: 275–278.

Iglesia, Ramon

1944   El hombre Colón y otros ensayos, México.

Jiménez Moreno, Wigberto

1942   El enigma de los Olmecas. Cuadernos Americanos, I–5: 113–145.

1959   Síntesis de la historia pre-tolteca de Mesoamérica. *In* Esplendor del México Antiguo, pp. 1019–1096.

Johnson, Frederick

1951   Radiocarbon dating. AmA, Memoirs, 8.

Johnson, Jean Basset

1919   Some notes on the Mazatec. RMEA, III: 142–156.

Jones, Julie

1963   Bibliography for Olmec sculpture. Museum of Primitive Art, New York.

Joyce, T. A., and H. A. Knox

1931   Sculptured figure from Veracruz state. Man, XXXI: 17.

Kelemen, Pal

1943   Medieval American Art. 2 vols. New York.

Kelly, David H.

1962   Glyphic evidence for a dynastic sequence at Quiriguá, Guatemala. AmA, 27: 323–335.

Kerber, Edmund

1882   Eine Alte mexikanische Ruinenstätte bei S. Andres Tuxtla. Verhandlungen der Berliner Gesellschaft für Antropologie, Ethnologie, und Urgeschichte, XLV: 488–489.

Kidder, Alfred V.
  1942   Archaeological specimens from Yucatan and Guatemala. NMAAE, 9:
            35–40.
  1947   The artifacts of Uaxactun, Guatemala. CIW–P, no. 576.
Kidder, Alfred V., Jesse D. Jennings, and E. M. Shook
  1946   Excavations at Kaminaljuyu, Guatemala. CIW–P, no. 561.
Kidder, Alfred, II, and Carlos Samayoa Chinchilla
  1959   The art of the ancient Maya. Detroit.
Kirchoff, Paul
  1943   Mesoamerica. Acta Americana, 1: 92–107.
Krickeberg, Walter
  1933   Los Totonaca (Transl. from the German). México.
Krieger, Alex D.
  1961   On being critical. Kroeber Anthropological Society Papers, 25: 19–23.
Kroeber, A. L.
  1944   Peruvian archaeology in 1942. Viking Fund Publications, no. 4. New
            York.
Krynine, Paul D.
  1935   Arkose deposits in the humid tropics. American Journal of Science,
            series 5, vol. 29: 353–363.
Kubler, George
  1962   The Art and Architecture of Ancient America. Baltimore.
Kunz, George F.
  1889   Sur une hache votive gigantesque en jadéite, de l'Oaxaca et sur un
  (1891)   pectoral en jadéite du Guatémala. Congrès International d'Anthro-
            pologie et d'Archéologie Préhistoriques, Dixième Session, Paris, pp.
            517–523.
  1890   Gems and Precious Stones of North America. New York.
Lehmann, Walter
  1921   Altmexikanische Kunstgeschichte. Orbis Pictus. Berlin.
  1926   Reisebrief aus Puerto México. Zeitschrift für Ethnologie, pp. 171–177.
  1936–   La antigüedad histórica de las culturas gran-mexicanas. El México.
  1939   Antiguo, IV: 179–198.
Lines, Jorge
  1941   Dos nuevas gemas en la arqueología de Costa Rica. Eighth American
            Scientific Congress, I: 117–122.
  1942   Un baby face en Costa Rica. SMA–MO, p. 54.
López González, Valentín
  1953   Breve historia antigua del Estado de Morelos. Cuadernos de Cultura
            Morelense, I. Cuernavaca.
López González, Valentín, and Román Piña Chán
  1952   Excavaciones en Atlihuayán, Morelos. Tlatoani, I, no. 1: 12.
Lothrop, S. K.
  1926   Stone sculptures from the Finca Arévalo, Guatemala. Indian Notes,
            III–3.
  1936   Zacualpa: a study of ancient Quiché artifacts. CIW–P, no. 472.
  1957   Pre-Columbian Art. Robert Woods Bliss Collection. New York.
Lowe, Gareth W.
  1960   Mound 1, Chiapa de Corzo. NWAF–P, 12, no. 8.

1962 Algunos resultados de la temporada 1961 en Chiapa de Corzo. Estudios de Cultura Maya, II: 185–196.

MacNeish, Richard S.

1954 An early archaeological site near Panuco, Veracruz. Transactions of the American Philosophical Society 44: 537–641. Philadelphia.

1956 Prehistoric settlement patterns on the north-eastern periphery of Mesoamerica. *In* G. R. Willey, ed., Prehistoric Settlement Patterns in the New World. Viking Fund Publications in Anthropology, No. 23. New York.

1958 Preliminary archaeological investigations in the Sierra de Tamaulipas, Mexico. Transactions of the American Philosophical Society, 48–6. Philadelphia.

1962 Second annual report of the Tehuacan Archaeological-Botanical Project. R. S. Peabody Foundation for Archaeology. Andover, Mass.

1964 Ancient Mesoamerican civilization. Science, no. 3606: 531–537.

1964A The origins of New World civilization. Scientific American, 211–5: 29–37.

Mayas y Olmecas

1942 Segunda Reunión de Mesa Redonda sobre problemas antropológicos de México y Centro América. Tuxtla Gutiérrez, Chiapas.

Meade, Joaquín

1953 Historia prehispánica de la Huasteca. RMEA, XIII–2–3: 291–302.

Medellín Zenil, Alfonso

1960 Monolitos inéditos olmecas. La Palabra y el Hombre, Revista de la Universidad Veracruzana, XVI: 75–97.

1960A Cerámicas de Totonacapan Xalapa.

Medina, Juan de

1905 Relación de Tlacotalpan y su Partido. *In* Papeles de Nueva España, published by Francisco del Paso y Troncoso, vol. V. Madrid.

Melgar y Serrano, José María

1869 Antigüedades Mexicanas. SMGE–B, 2a, época I: 292–297.

1871 Estudios sobre las antigüedades y el origen de la cabeza colocal de tipo etiópico que existe en Hueyapan del cantón de los Tuxtlas. SMGE–B, 2a, época III: 104–109.

Morley, Sylvanus G.

1938 The inscriptions of Peten. CIW–P, no. 437. 5 vols.

Navarrete, Carlos

1959 Explorations at San Agustín, Chiapas. NWAF–P, 3, no. 3.

1959A A brief reconnaissance in the region of Tonalá, Chiapas. NWAF–P, 4, no. 3.

1960 Archaeological explorations in the region of the Frailesca, Chiapas. NWAF–P, 7, no. 6.

Neely, James A.

1967 Organización hidráulica y sistemas de irrigación prehistóricos en el Valle de Oaxaca. Boletín del INAH, No. 27: 15–17.

Noguera, Eduardo

1939 Exploraciones en el Opeño, Michoacán. XXVII Congreso de Americanistas, I: 574–586. México.

1940 Excavations at Tehuacan. *In* The Maya and their Neighbors, pp. 306–319.

1942   El problema olmeca y la cultura arcaica. SMA–MO, pp. 51–52.

1964   El sarcófago de Tlalancaleca. Cuadernos Americanos, XXIII–3: 139–148.

Orellana Tapia, Rafael
1955   Nueva lápida olmecoide de Izapa. México Antiguo, VIII: 157–166.

Palacios, Enrique J.
1928   En los confines de la selva Lacandona. México.

Parsons, Lee A.
1965   Archaeological research at Bilbao. Lore, 15–3: 89–96.

Parsons, Lee A., and Peter S. Jenson
1965   Boulder sculpture on the Pacific coast of Guatemala. Archaeology, 18–2: 132–144.

Paso y Troncoso, Francisco del
1892   Catálogo de los objetos que presenta la República de México en la Exposición Histórico-Americana de Madrid. 2 vols. Madrid.

Peterson, Frederick A.
1963   Some ceramics from Mirador. NWAF–P, 15, no. 11.

Piña Chán, Román
1953   Una figurilla de Tlatilco. Yan, 2: 148–149.

1955   Chalcatzingo, Morelos. INAH–DMP, 4. México.

1955A   Las culturas preclásicas de la Cuenca de México. México.

1958   Tlatilco. INAH–Serie Investigaciones, 1 and 2. México.

1960   Algunos sitios arqueológicos de Oaxaca y Guerrero. RMEA, XVI: 65–76.

1960A   Mesoamérica, ensayo crítico y cultural. INAH–Memorias, VI. México.

Piña Chán, R., and L. Covarrubias
1964   El Pueblo del Jaguar. Consejo para la planeación e instalación del Museo Nacional de Antropología. México.

Piña Chán, Román Arturo Romano, and Eduardo Pareyón
1952   Tlatilco, nuevo sitio preclásico de la Cuenca de México. Tlatoani, I, nos. 3–4: 9–14.

Porter, Muriel Noe
1953   Tlatilco and pre-classic cultures of the New World. Viking Fund Publications in Anthropology, no. 19.

Proskouriakoff, Tatiana
1950   A study of classic Maya sculpture. CIW–P, no. 593.

1960   Historical implications of patterns of dates at Piedras Negras, Guatemala. AmA, 25: 454–475.

1964   El Arte maya y el modelo genético de cultura. *In* Egon Z. Vogt and Alberto Ruz, eds., Desarrollo Cultural de los Mayas, pp. 179–193.

1967   Olmec and Maya art. MS.

Richardson, F. B.
1940   Non-Maya monumental sculpture of Central America. *In* The Maya and Their Neighbors, pp. 395–416.

Ricketson, O. G., Jr., and E. B. Ricketson
1937   Uaxactun, Guatemala, Group E. CIW–P, no. 477.

Romero, Javier
1958   Mutilaciones dentarias prehispánicas de México y América Central. INAH–Serie Investigaciones, 3. México.

Sanders, William T.

1953 The anthropogeography of central Veracruz. RMEA, XIII–2–2: 27–78.

1960 Prehistoric ceramics and settlement patterns in Quintana Roo, México. CIW–P, 606: 155–264.

1961 Ceramic stratigraphy at Santa Cruz, Chiapas. NWAF–P, 13, no. 9.

1962 Cultural ecology of nuclear Mesoamerica. AA, 64–1: 34–43.

1963 *Review of* Coe, México. AA, 65: 972–975.

Satterthwaite, Linton

1943 Notes on sculpture and architecture at Tonalá. NMAAE, 21: 127–136.

Saville, Marshall H.

1900 A votive adze of jadeite from Mexico. Monumental Records, 1: 138–140. New York.

1902 A votive adze of jadeite from Mexico. Records of the Past, I: 14–16.

1929 Votive axes from ancient Mexico. Museum of the American Indian. Indian Notes, VI: 266–299, 335–343.

Seler, Eduard

1904 Antiquities of Guatemala. BAE–B, 28: 75–121.

1908 Alterthümer aus Guatemala. *In* Gesammelte Abhandlungen zur Amerikanischen Sprach-und Altertumskunde. Vol. III: 578–640. Berlin. First published in 1895 in Veröffentlichungen aus dem Königlichen Museum für Völkerkunde, vol. IV, no. 1: 21–53. Berlin. English translation in 1904 in BAE–B, 28: 75–121.

Seler-Sachs, Caecilie

1900 Auf Alten Wegen in Mexiko und Guatemala. Berlin.

1922 Altertümer des kanton Tuxtla im Staate Veracruz. *In* Festricht Eduard Seler, pp. 543–556. Stuttgart.

Shepard, Anna O.

1948 Plumbate, a Mesoamerican trade ware. CIW–P, no. 573. Washington.

Shook, E. M.

1945 Archaeological discovery at Finca Arizona. NMAAE, no. 57.

1950 Tiquisate ufers scoop archaeological world, find ruined city on farm. Unifruitco. United Fruit Co. August.

1951 The present status of research on the Pre-classic horizons in Guatemala. XXIX Congreso de Americanistas, I: 93–100.

1956 An Olmec sculpture from Guatemala. Archaeology, IX–4: 260–262.

Shook, E. M., and A. V. Kidder

1952 Mound E III–3, Kaminaljuyu, Guatemala. CIW–CR, 55: 35–127.

Smith, A. L., and Karl Ruppert

1953 Excavations at house mounds at Mayapan: II CIW–CR, 10: 180–206.

Smith, Tillie

1963 The main themes of Olmec art tradition. Kroeber Anthropological Society Papers, 28: 121–213.

Sorenson, John L.

1956 An archaeological reconnaissance of west-central Chiapas. NWAF–P, 1: 7–19.

Spinden, Herbert J.

1915 Notes on the archaeology of Salvador. AA, 17–3: 446–487.

1927 Study dead city of "rubber people," New York Times, May 1.

Stern, Theodore
  1948   The rubber-ball game of the Americas. Monographs of the American Ethnological Society, no. 17. New York.

Stirling, M. W.
  1939   Discovering the New World's oldest dated work of man. NGM, LXXVI: 183–218.
  1940   An initial series from Tres Zapotes, Veracruz, México. National Geographic Society Contributed Technical Papers, Mexican Archaeology Series, 1–1.
  1941   Expedition unearths buried masterpieces of carved jade. NGM, LXXX: 277–302.
  1942   Recientes hallazgos en La Venta. SMA–MO, pp. 56–57.
  1943   Stone monuments of southern Mexico. BAE–B, 138.
  1943A   La Venta's green stone tigers. NGM, LXXXIV: 321–332.
  1947   On the trail of La Venta man. NGM, XCI: 137–172.
  1955   Stone monuments of the Río Chiquito, Veracruz, Mexico. BAE–B, 157: 1–23.
  1957   An archaeological reconnaissance in southeastern Mexico. BAE–B, 164: 213–240.
  1961   The Olmec artists in jade. *In* Essays in Pre-Columbian Art and Archaeology by S. M. Lothrop and Others, pp. 43–59. Cambridge, Mass.
  1967   Early history of the Olmec problem. MS.

Stirling, M. W., Froelich Rainey, and Matthew Stirling, Jr.
  1960   Electronics and archaeology. Expedition, II–4: 19–29, Philadelphia.

Stirling, M. W., and Marion Stirling
  1942   Finding jewels of jade in a Mexican swamp. NGM, LXXXII: 635–661.

Stone, Doris
  1957   The archaeology of central and southern Honduras. Papers of the Peabody Museum of Archaeology and Ethnology, XLIX–3.

Strebel, H.
  1901   The sculptures of Santa Lucia Cozumalhaupa. Annual Report of the Smithsonian Institution for 1899, pp. 549–561.

Stromsvik, Gustav
  1941   Substela caches and stela foundations at Copan and Quirigua. CIW–C, no. 37.

Swadesh, Morris
  1953   The language of the archaeological Haustecs. NMAAE, no. 114.

Thompson, J. Eric S.
  1941   Dating of certain inscriptions of non-Maya origin. CIW, Theoretical Approaches to Problems, no. 1.
  1943   Some sculptures from southeastern Quetzaltenango. NMAAE, no. 17: 100–112.
  1943A   A trial survey of the southern Maya area. AmA, IX–1: 106–134.
  1948   An archaeological reconnaissance in the Cotzumalhaupa region, Escuintla, Guatemala. CIW–C, no. 44.
  1950   Maya hieroglyphic writing: Introduction. CIW–P, no. 589.
  1951   Aquatic symbols common to various centers of the Classic period in Meso-America. XXIX Congress of Americanists, I: 31–36. Chicago.
  1954   The Rise and Fall of Maya Civilization. Norman, Oklahoma.
  1962   A Catalog of Maya Hieroglyphs. Norman, Oklahoma.

1965   A copper ornament and stone mask from Middle America. AmA, 30: 343–345.

Tolstoy, Paul, and André Guenette
1965   Le placement de Tlatilco dans le cadre du preclassique du Bassin de México. Université de Montreal. Jour. de la Soc. des Americanistes de Paris, LIV: 47–92.

Toynbee, Arnold
1948   A Study of History. London.

Tribes and Temples (Blom, Franz, and O. La Farge)
1926   A Record of the Expedition to Middle America Conducted by the Tulane University of Louisiana in 1925. New Orleans.

Vaillant, George C.
1930   Excavations at Zacatenco. Anthropological Papers of the American Museum of Natural History, XXXII–1.

1931   Excavations at Ticoman. Anthropological Papers of the American Museum of Natural History, XXXII–2.

1931A   A bearded mystery. Natural History, XXXI: 243–252.

1932   A Pre-Columbian jade. Natural History, XXXII: 512–520, 556–558.

1935   Excavations at El Arbolillo. Anthropological Papers of the American Museum of Natural History, XXXV–2.

1939   Tiger masks and platyrrhine and bearded figures from Middle America.

(1947)   XXVII Congreso Internacional de Americanistas, 2: 131–135.

Vaillant, S. B. and G. C. Vaillant
1934   Excavations at Gualupita. AMNH, XXXV–1.

Valenzuela, Juan
1938   Las exploraciones efectuadas en los Tuxtlas, Veracruz. AMNM, época V–III: 83–108.

1939   Informe preliminar de las exploraciones efectuadas en los Tuxtlas, Veracruz. XXVII Congreso Internacional de Americanistas, II: 113–130.

1945   La segunda temporada de exploraciones en la región de los Tuxtlas, Estado de Veracruz. INAH–Anales, I: 81–94.

Villacorta C., J. A., and C. A. Villacorta
1930   Arqueología Guatemalteca. Guatemala.

Vreeland, Charles E., and J. F. Bransford
1885   Antiquities of Pantaleon, Guatemala. Smithsonian Report for 1884, pp. 39–50.

Warren, Bruce B.
1961   Archaeological sequence at Chiapa de Corzo. *In* Los Mayas del sur y sus relaciones con los Nahuas meridionales. SMA, pp. 75–83. México.

Waterman, T. T.
1929   Is the Baul stela an Aztec imitation? Art and Archaeology, XXXVIII: 183–187.

Weiant, C. W.
1943   An introduction to the ceramics of Tres Zapotes, Veracruz. BAE–B, 139.

Westheim, Paul
1955   El jaguar que contempla los astros. Universidad de México, IX–12: 1–2, 4.

1962   La cerámica del México Antiguo. México.

Weyerstall, Albert
  1932   Some observations of Indian mounds, idols, and pottery in the Lower Papaloapan basin, state of Veracruz, Mexico. Middle American Research Institute Papers, 4: 22–69. New Orleans.
Wicke, Charles
  1965   Olmec: and early art style in Pre-Columbian Mexico. Doctoral dissertation, University of Arizona.
Willey, Gordon R.
  1948   A functional analysis of "horizon styles" in Peruvian archaeology. *In* A reappraisal of Peruvian archaeology, Society for American Archaeology, Memoirs, 4: 8–15.
  1962   The early great styles and rise of the Pre-Columbian civilizations. AA, 64–1: 1–14.
  1964   An archaeological frame of reference for Maya culture history. *In* Evon Z. Vogt and Alberto Ruz, eds., Desarrollo cultural de los mayas, pp. 137–178.
  1966   An introduction to American Archaeology. Englewood Cliffs, N. J.
Willey, G. R., W. R. Bullard, J. J. B. Glass, and J. C. Gifford
  1965   Prehistoric Maya settlements in the Belize Valley. PMAE–P, vol. LIV.
Williams, Howel, and Robert F. Heizer
  1965   Sources of rocks used in Olmec monuments. Contributions of the University of California Archaeological Research Facility, I: 1–39.
Wolf, Eric R.
  1959   Sons of the Shaking Earth. Chicago.

PLATES

Plate 1. The La Venta pryamid photographed from a helicopter in February 1968.

Plate 2. *Masculine figurine of black serpentine. Height 5¾ inches. Enciso Collection, National Museum of Anthropology.*

Plate 3. *Colossal head. Monument 5 from San Lorenzo. Height 6 feet, 4 inches. Museum of Anthropology, University of Veracruz, Jalapa.*

Plate 4. Stela 3, La Venta. Height 14 feet.

Plate 5. Monument A, Tres Zapotes. (a) First Olmec monolith published, 1869. (b) A recent photograph of this head.

Plate 6. *Tomb A, La Venta, as reconstructed in the La Venta Museum-Park, Villa-hermosa, Tabasco.*

Plate 7. *Mosaic floor representing a jaguar from La Venta. Total length about 6 feet. Restored in the La Venta Museum-Park, Villahermosa.*

Plate 8. Colossal head No. 1 from La Venta. Height 8 feet, 1 inch. Museum-Park of Villahermosa.

Plate 9. La Venta Head 2, profile view. Height 6 feet, 3 inches. Museum of Villahermosa.

Plate 10. Colossal head. Monument 1 from San Lorenzo. Height 9 feet, 4 inches.
Museum of Anthropology, University of Veracruz, Jalapa.

Plate 11. Colossal head from Tres Zapotes. Now at Santiago Tuxtla.

Plate 12. Monument 1 from Laguna de los Cerros. Height 2 feet, 5 inches.

(a)

Plate 13. Altar 5 from La Venta. Height 5 feet, 1 inch. Museum-Park of Villahermosa. (a) Front view. (b) North side. (c) South side. (d) Detail of Bonampak fresco, about ninth century A.D.

(b)

(c)

(d)

Plate 14. *Altar 4 from La Venta. Height 5 feet, 3 inches. Museum-Park at Villaher-mosa.*

Plate 15. *Altar from Potrero Nuevo.*

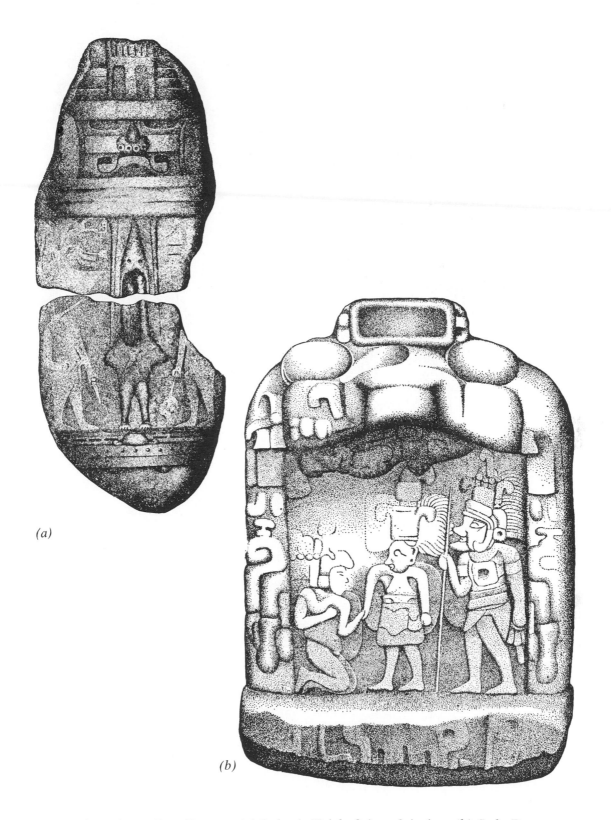

(a)

(b)

Plate 16. Stelae at Tres Zapotes. (a) Stela A. Height 8 feet, 3 inches. (b) Stela D. Height 58 inches.

Plate 17. Stela 2, La Venta. Height 11 feet, 5 inches.

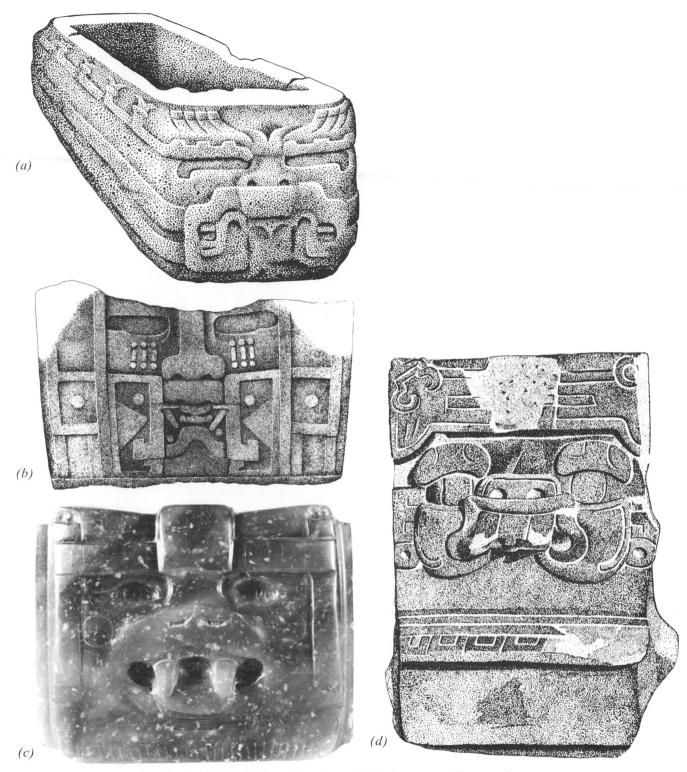

Plate 18. Jaguar masks. (a) Sarcophagus at La Venta. (b) Stela C, Tres Zapotes (reconstructed). (c) Jade plaque. National Museum of Anthropology. (d) Clay plaque from the fill of Mound IV, Monte Alban.

Plate 19. Sculpture from Cruz del Milagro, Veracruz. Height 54 inches.

Plate 20. Monolith from Misantla. Height 5 feet.

21

22

23

24

Plate 21. *Monument 11 from Laguna de los Cerros. Height 2 feet, 4 inches.*

Plate 22. *Sculpture from Las Limas, Veracruz. Height 22 inches.*

Plate 23. *Monument 5 from La Venta. Height 4 feet, 8 inches. La Venta Museum-Park, Villahermosa.*

Plate 24. *Monument 11 from San Lorenzo.*

(a)

(b)

(c)

Plate 25. *Monument from San Martin Pajapan. Height 57 inches. (a) As drawn by Covarrubias. (b) Schematic drawing of the same monument. (c) Same monument to-day. Museum of Anthropology, University of Veracruz.*

Plate 26. Monument 8 from Laguna de los Cerros. Height 6 feet, 5 inches.

Plate 27. The "Wrestler" from Santa María Uxpanapa. Height 49 inches. National Museum of Anthropology.

Plate 28. The "Scribe" of Cuilapan. Museum of Oaxaca.

29

30

31

Plate 29. Monument 13 from La Venta. Height 31½ inches. La Venta Museum-Park, Villahermosa.

Plate 30. Monument F from Tres Zapotes. Length 8 feet, 3 inches.

Plate 31. Monument 19 from Laguna de los Cerros. Height 5 feet.

Plate 32. *Mask from Medias Aguas. About 3 feet high.*

Plate 33. *Sculpture from La Venta (?). Museum of Villahermosa.*

Plate 34. *Monument 20 from Laguna de los Cerros. Height 32 inches.*

Plate 35. The La Venta sarcophagus at the time of its excavation, with its cover still in place.

Plate 36. Colossal Aztec jaguar with hole in back, probably meant to receive human hearts. National Museum of Anthropology.

Plate 37. Jade figurines from the La Venta tomb. All in the National Museum of Anthropology. (a) No. 1. Height 3⅛ inches. (b) No. 2. Height 2½ inches. (c) No. 3 Height 4 ⁵/₁₆ inches. (d) No. 4. Height 4 inches.

38

39

40

Plate 38. Celt from Tomb E, La Venta. National Museum of Anthropology.

Plate 39. Figurine from El Tejar, Veracruz. Height 5½ inches. National Museum of Anthropology.

Plate 40. Scene formed by stone figurines as they were found, La Venta.

Plate 41. Figurine from Offering 3, La Venta. Height 2 ⁵/₁₆ inches. National Museum of Anthropology.

Plate 42. *Jade ornaments and precious stones, La Venta. National Museum of Anthropology.*

Plate 43. *Magnetite mirror from La Venta. National Museum of Anthropology.*

Plate 44. *Olmec implements and ornaments in fine stone, La Venta. National Museum of Anthropology.*

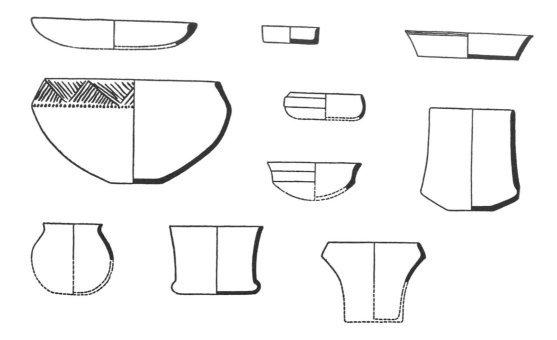

Plate 45. Ceramic pieces.

Plate 46. Inscription on Stela C from Tres Zapotes. National Museum of Anthropology.

Plate 47. The Tuxtla statuette. Height 3¾ inches. United States National Museum.

Plate 48. Monument 10 from San Lorenzo. Height 47 inches.

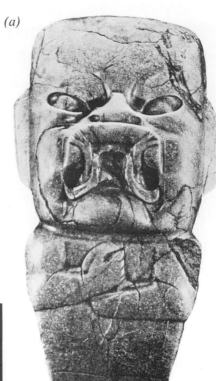

Plate 49. (a) The Kunz celt. Height 10 ³/₁₆ inches. American Museum of Natural History, New York. (b) Celt in the British Museum. 11 inches high.

Plate 50. Early Preclassic figurines. Middle left, F type. The others are C types. Museum of Anthropology, Mexico.

Plate 51. Figurines of the Middle Preclassic period. Top left, Type A. Top right, Type D2. Lower left to right, Types C, D1, and K. National Museum of Anthropology, Mexico.

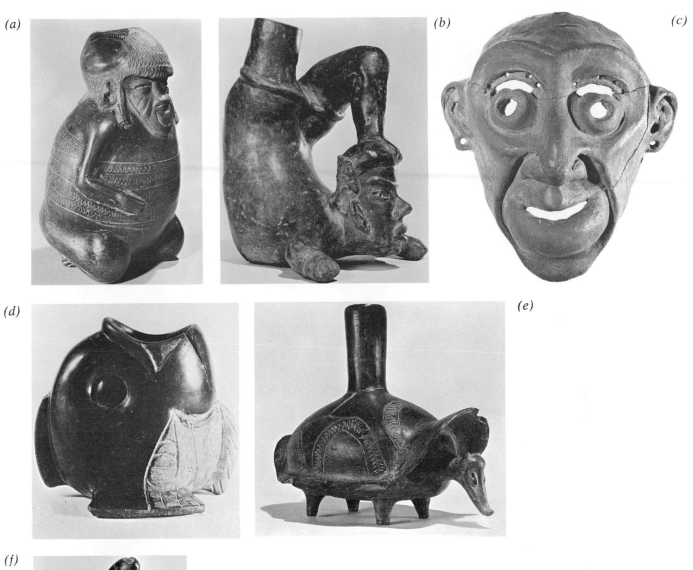

Plate 52. Ceramic pieces from Tlatilco. All in National Museum of Anthropology.
(a) Anthropomorphic vessel. (b) Acrobat. Height 10⅜ inches. (c) Mask. (d) Fish.
(e) Armadillo (Dasypus 1). (f) Dog.

Plate 53. Figurine from Tlatilco. National Museum of Anthropology.

Plate 54. Tlatilco figurines.

Plate 55. Left: jadeite figurine, Tlatilco. Right: serpentine figurine, No. 5, from the La Venta sarcophagus. Height 6 inches.

Plate 56. Small figurine ball player from Tlatilco. National Museum of Anthropology.

Plate 57. *Figure from Las Bocas, Puebla. 13 inches high.*

Plate 58. *Small yoke. 4 inches high. Collection Dumbarton Oaks.*

Plate 59. Man with jaguar skin from Atlihuayan, Morelos. National Museum of Anthropology.

Plate 60. Fragment from Gualupita, Morelos. National Museum of Anthropology.

61

62

Plate 61. Figurines from Guerrero. National Museum of Anthropology. (a) Deformed child. (b) Deaf child.

Plate 62. Stone figure from Mezcala, Guerrero. Height 8 $^7/_{16}$ inches. National Museum of Anthropology.

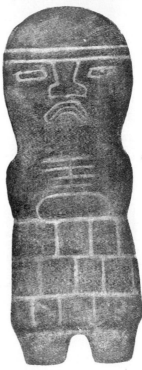

Plate 63. Wooden mask from Guerrero. American Museum of Natural History, New York.

Plate 64. Figurine from El Opeño.

Plate 65. Stela 4 from Cerro de las Mesas. Height 66 inches. Museum of Anthropology, University of Veracruz, Jalapa.

Plate 66. Monument 2, Cerro de las Mesas. Height 69 inches.

Plate 67. Monument 5 from Cerro de las Mesas. Museum of Anthropology, University of Veracruz, Jalapa.

Plate 68. Pieces from the offering at Cerro de las Mesas. National Museum of Anthropology. (a) Jade canoe. Length 8 $\frac{1}{16}$ inches. (b) Jade dwarf. Height 4 $\frac{11}{16}$ inches. (c) Hunchbacked figure. Height 2$\frac{1}{8}$ inches.

Plate 69. Brazier representing the old god of fire from Cerro de las Mesas. Height 33 inches. National Museum of Anthropology.

Plate 70. Stela I from Viejón. Height approximately 12 feet. Museum of Anthropology, University of Veracruz, Jalapa.

71

72

Plate 71. Braziers. (a) Brazier from Yagul depicting the young god of fire. (b) Brazier from Temple X, Monte Negro. National Museum of Anthropology. (c) Brazier from Mound TN at Monte Negro. National Museum of Anthropology.

Plate 72. Detail of the danzantes monument at Monte Alban, as seen by Batres in 1902.

(a)

(b)

(c)

Plate 73. Dancing figures, Monte Alban. (a) No. 55. (b) No. 48. (c) Height 65 inches. Now at National Museum of Anthropology.

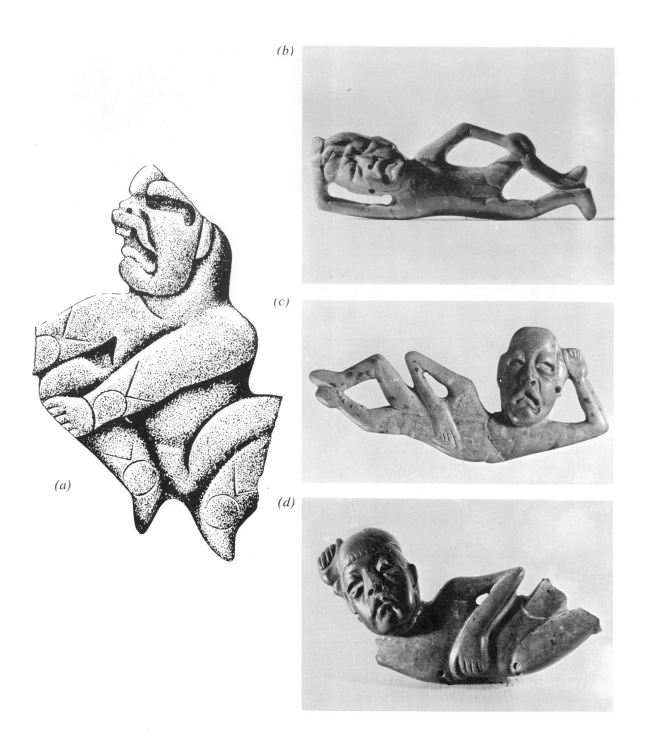

Plate 74. Small jade "dancing figures." (a) Guerrero (?). Height 5 5/16 inches. National Museum of Anthropology. (b) San Gerónimo, Guerrero. (c) Tepatlaxco, Puebla. Length 4 13/16 inches. (d) Tzintzuntzan, Michoacan. National Museum of Anthropology.

75

76

77

Plate 75. Vessel from Tomb 111, Monte Alban. National Museum of Anthropology. Height 7½ inches.

Plate 76. Stela 12, Monte Alban. Height 5 feet, 1 inch.

Plate 77. Vessels from Period I of Monte Alban. National Museum of Anthropology. (a) Object No. 23 from Tomb 111, Monte Alban. Height 7⁷/₁₆ inches. (b) Masked god from Zegache, Oaxaca. Height 7⁷/₁₆ inches.

78

79

80

81

Plate 78. Figurine from Tomb 33, Monte Alban. Height 2½ inches. National Museum of Anthropology.

Plate 79. Statue from Huamelulpan.

Plate 80. Tripod vessel with a xicalcoliuhqui design scratched on the outer surface. Period II of Monte Alban. National Museum of Anthropology, Mexico.

Plate 81. Stela 2, Chiapa de Corzo, Chiapas.

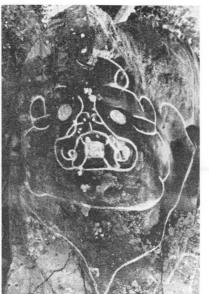

Plate 82. Monument 5, Tonalá.

Plate 83. Petroglyph 1, Tonalá.

Plate 84. Stela 9, Tonalá. (a) Front view. (b) Side view. (c) Back view.

Plate 85. *Stela 1 with altar from Izapa. National Museum of Anthropology.*

Plate 86. *Stela 50 from Izapa. National Museum of Anthropology.*

Plate 87. *Stela 21, Izapa. National Museum of Anthropology.*

Plate 88. Colossal heads, Monte Alto. (a) Monument 2. Height 4 feet, 7 inches.
(b) Monument 3, with jaguar mask. Height 5½ feet.

89

90

91

Plate 89. *Stylistic similarities. (a) Colossal head. Monument 3, El Baul. (b) Plumbate vessel from El Salvador. American Museum of Natural History.*

Plate 90. *Monument 47, Bilbao. Height 3 feet, 8 inches.*

Plate 91. *Stone statue from Tiquisate.*

92

93

94

95

Plate 92. *Figure from Finca Arévalo, Guatemala.*

Plate 93. *Monument 4, Monte Alto, Escuintla, Guatemala. Height 5 feet.*

Plate 94. *Stela 1, El Baul.*

Plate 95. *Bas relief carving, San Isidro Piedra Parada.*

96

97

98

Plate 96. Stela 1, San Isidro Piedra Parada.

Plate 97. Great tiger, El Baul.

Plate 98. Stela from Kaminaljuyu. La Aurora Museum, Guatemala.

Plate 99. Uaxactun. (a) Plan of Structure E-VII-Sub. (b) Northeast corner of the same building.

Plate 100. Head of green stone from Mayapan.

Plate 101. Brazier from Kaminaljuyu. Front and side views. Height 8½ inches.

Plate 102. Jade figure from Estado Cortés, Honduras.

Plate 103. Jade figurine from Guanacaste, Costa Rica.

INDEX